Implementing Universal Social-Emotional Programs

Implementing Universal Social-Emotional Programs is a step-by-step guide for educators and school-based mental health professionals seeking to effectively select, employ, and evaluate universal social-emotional programs using implementation science. With one out of five children having diagnosable mental health challenges and many more of our youth developing social-emotional concerns, today's schools must be able to effectively plan and implement evidence-based programs that promote social-emotional learning and positive academic outcomes. This book accompanies practitioners and graduate students in teaching, school psychology, counseling, social work, education, and administration through each stage of implementation science, common programs and screeners, the purpose and selection process of implementation teams, and schools' expectations for fidelity, timelines, and budgets. Throughout, the authors provide graphic organizers, diagrams, activities, exercises, vignettes, checklists, templates, charts, and other interactive features for active engagement.

Gary E. Schaffer is Graduate Professor of School Psychology and Counseling at Niagara University, USA, and was previously employed as a school psychologist across school, hospital, and state agency settings.

Stacy L. Bender is Associate Professor in the Department of Counseling and School Psychology at the University of Massachusetts Boston, USA, a licensed psychologist, a health service psychologist, and a nationally certified school psychologist.

Implementing Universal Social-Emotional Programs

A Step-by-Step Guide for Schools

GARY E. SCHAFFER AND STACY L. BENDER

Routledge
Taylor & Francis Group

NEW YORK AND LONDON

Cover image: Getty images

First published 2023
by Routledge
605 Third Avenue, New York, NY 10158

and by Routledge
4 Park Square, Milton Park, Abingdon, Oxon, OX14 4RN

Routledge is an imprint of the Taylor & Francis Group, an informa business

© 2023 Gary E. Schaffer and Stacy L. Bender

Library of Congress Cataloging-in-Publication Data
Names: Schaffer, Gary, author. | Bender, Stacy L., author.
Title: Implementing universal social-emotional programs : a step-by-step guide for schools / Gary E. Schaffer and Stacy L. Bender.
Identifiers: LCCN 2022026152 (print) | LCCN 2022026153 (ebook) | ISBN 9781032153117 (hardback) | ISBN 9781032380971 (paperback) | ISBN 9781003343479 (ebook)
Subjects: LCSH: Affective education. | Multiple tiered systems of support. | Response to intervention (Learning disabled children) | Educational planning.
Classification: LCC LB1072 .S34 2023 (print) | LCC LB1072 (ebook) | DDC 370.15/34—dc23/eng/20220810
LC record available at https://lccn.loc.gov/2022026152
LC ebook record available at https://lccn.loc.gov/2022026153

ISBN: 978-1-032-15311-7 (hbk)
ISBN: 978-1-032-38097-1 (pbk)
ISBN: 978-1-003-34347-9 (ebk)

DOI: 10.4324/9781003343479

Typeset in Avenir & Dante
by Apex CoVantage, LLC

Contents

About the Authors

Gary E. Schaffer Because he grew up as a struggling student with Attention-Deficit Hyperactivity Disorder and a learning disability, Gary E. Schaffer has dedicated his professional practices and life to helping all learners succeed. Gary received a bachelor's degree in special education and English and subsequently went on to become a school psychologist and clinical mental health counselor. As a school psychologist, Gary has practiced across school, hospital, and state agency settings, where he primarily worked with diverse learners and individuals with developmental disabilities. Currently, Gary is employed full time as Graduate Professor of School Psychology and Counseling at Niagara University (Lewiston, NY, USA), where he teaches graduate students in school psychology, school counseling, and clinical mental health counseling.

Outside of working for Niagara University, Gary continues to advocate for children and adults with disabilities and has met with both state and national legislators in regard to the Every Student Succeeds Act, Multi-Tiered Systems of Support, and increasing the availability of mental health services for children. Additionally, Gary has authored numerous scholarly articles, books, book chapters, and programs in the areas of MTSS, school psychology leadership, autism, and suicide prevention and intervention. He has presented on and offers consultation in Multi-Tiered Systems of Support and best preventative practices under three-tiered frameworks, such as Response to Intervention, Positive Behavior Supports, and Social-Emotional RTI. He can be reached through his email at geschaffer@gmail.com or followed on Twitter at GE_Schaffer.

Stacy L. Bender Stacy L. Bender, PhD, NCSP is Associate Professor of School Psychology at the University of Massachusetts (Boston, MA, USA). She received her PhD from Michigan State University and completed a competitive APA accredited internship at the Florida State University Multidisciplinary Evaluation and Consulting Center and a postdoctoral fellowship in child and adolescent clinical psychology at the University of Rochester Medical Center. As a licensed psychologist, registered health psychologist, and nationally certified school psychologist, she has provided treatment, consultation, and assessment for marginalized children and families with mental and behavioral health challenges in schools, hospitals, and other clinical settings.

Her research interests include improving the social-emotional/behavioral needs of students through behavior screening, intervention implementation, and supporting family engagement practices in schools. Stacy has conducted numerous research projects implementing intervention with students and families and supporting schools at the systems level to implement universal supports for students. She has authored/co-authored peer-reviewed publications, book chapters, and a book addressing these areas. She has also presented over 50 presentations at national conferences and has secured grant funding to support research projects.

Figures

Exercises

The Need for Children's Social-Emotional Supports $\quad$ 1

Learning Objectives

After reading this chapter, you should be able to:

- Explain the need for children's mental health supports.
- Define mental health concerns in children.
- Describe why children's mental health matters in relation to children's life and educational outcomes.
- Discuss why children turn to educators for mental health and wellness support.
- State the historical treatment of children's mental health concerns and legislative initiatives that lead to schools being viewed as ideal places to promote mental wellness in youth.

Why Are Children's Social-Emotional Supports Needed?

In recent years, schoolchildren have been exposed to many frightening, violent, and traumatic events such as school shootings, student suicide, threats to national security, natural disasters, ongoing racism, coups d'état of government leaders, and global pandemics, such as the coronavirus (COVID-19). Furthermore, the traditional vices affecting children's everyday mental health, well-being, and even safety have been augmented through technology and social media exposure. When factors that might negatively

DOI: 10.4324/9781003343479-1

influence a child's mental health are only a click, stream, or download away, it is easier for youth to be involved in or exposed to events that may significantly impact their social-emotional development. **Social-emotional development** can be defined as a child's ability to understand the feelings of others, control their own emotions and behaviors, and get along with peers (Eklund et al., 2018). With technology and social media exposure impacting how children feel about themselves and the world around them, educators of today's generation may be more challenged than ever to create and maintain a safe school environment that promotes mental wellness and prevents social-emotional concerns from arising. Therefore, it is not surprising that approximately one out of five children today have diagnosable mental health conditions (Centers for Disease Control and Prevention [CDC], 2020a).

Although one out of five children has a diagnosable mental health condition, this statistic does not take into account the number of youth who are placed "at risk" or who are starting to display mental health concerns. Even more alarming is that only 20% of children with diagnosable mental health conditions may receive mental health support for their diagnoses, and children who are placed at risk for mental health conditions often do not receive any treatment (CDC, 2020a). Youth that are marginalized are less likely to seek or stay in treatment for mental health needs, with lack of cultural responsiveness by providers and limited access being two of the biggest barriers to service utilization (González, 2005). Of the 20% of children who do receive treatment for social-emotional difficulties, approximately 70% to 80% receive mental health support in school settings (Farmer et al., 2003; Langer et al., 2015). In fact, children were found to be 21 times more likely to visit school-based centers for mental health concerns over community-based centers (Juszczak et al., 2003). This is important for all students, particularly marginalized youth who report lack of access as a barrier to receiving needed support. School-based practitioners have been found to be more effective at improving the social-emotional learning outcomes of students than non-school practitioners (Durlak et al., 2011; Maras et al., 2015). These statistics highlight the important role schools play and how they may serve as optimal settings for supporting students' social-emotional health.

Despite there being a growing need for school districts to promote mental wellness and prevent social-emotional concerns from arising in children, educators often struggle with formulating a cogent plan that effectively utilizes best practices. This book seeks to guide readers in employing universal social-emotional supports for all students using best evidence-based practices along with the stages of implementation science. **Evidence-based practice** is concerned with using empirically supported interventions and programs that have been proven effective at treating a presenting problem (McKevitt, 2012; Zyromski et al., 2018). For example, deep breathing is a quick evidence-based support that can be easily applied to reduce anxiety in children (Higa-McMillan et al., 2016; Khang, 2017). Whereas evidence-based practice is concerned with using empirically proven interventions, **implementation science** focuses on scientifically studying methods utilized to promote the uptake of these supports into everyday practice (McKevitt, 2012; Owens et al., 2014; Sanetti et al., 2019a). In other words, it is concerned with the ongoing process of integrating evidence-based interventions or research findings into the school day (Ownes et al., 2014). The term **implementation** itself refers to the process or set of activities needed to put a program or practice into place within an organization, such as a school. Therefore, implementation is a critical link between research and practice. Within this text, activities, discussions, and graphic organizers are used to take readers through using implementation science to best ensure the systematic uptake of universal evidence-based practices to prevent social-emotional concerns and improve social-emotional health for students in schools.

There are many factors that can affect children and adolescents' social-emotional functioning. Before proceeding into defining mental health concerns in children, Exercise 1.1 asks readers to consider factors that may positively and negatively impact a child's social-emotional health. Subsequently, readers will reflect on their own positive and negative circumstances and how these experiences may have impacted them in their lives.

Exercise 1.1 Factors Affecting Social-Emotional Health

Directions: Independently or with a partner list factors that may both positively and negatively impact a child's social-emotional health. After you have finished, reflect on one positive and one negative life event or circumstance that greatly affected you in childhood. If you are working with a partner and are comfortable sharing one or two of these life events or circumstances, briefly discuss how and why they impacted you.

Positive school, family, community, and healthcare factors	Negative school, family, community, and healthcare factors
• For example: Positive student-teacher relationship(s) in school	• For example: Racism-based trauma
List one positive and one negative life event or circumstance that greatly affected you in childhood by completing the sentences below. A positive life event or circumstance that affected me in childhood was: _____ A negative life event or circumstance that affected me in childhood was: _____	

Defining Social-Emotional Concerns in Children

Throughout their young lives, children may present with a number of social-emotional concerns from bouts of nervousness and episodes of sadness to irritability and mood swings. Luckily, many of these feelings and emerging social-emotional concerns tend to be episodic and not permanent (McGorry & Mei, 2018). Previous research suggests that between 25% and 50% of adult mental illnesses may be prevented through early intervention in childhood and adolescence alone (Kim-Cohen et al., 2003). Therefore, the timing of intervention is vital in preventing the entrenchment of maladaptive symptoms and behaviors before they become too severe and lead to major psychiatric diagnoses or educational classifications (McGorry & Mei, 2018). Overall, educators and school personnel can play critical roles in preventing social-emotional concerns from arising in children and assisting youth who are going through mood or behavior changes as a result of transitional changes (Slade & Longden, 2015.).

The focus of this text is to emphasize prevention of internalizing and externalizing concerns through universal supports. Universal supports are typically divided into interventions and programs, and both terms will be utilized throughout this text with a primary emphasis on implementing Tier 1 social-emotional programs. **Evidence-based interventions** consist of supports or treatments that have been peer-reviewed and demonstrate empirical support for effectiveness (King & Coughlin, 2016). Similarly, **evidence-based programs** have demonstrated empirical support but consist of many interventions, tend to be standardized, and are often sold commercially (King & Coughlin, 2016). An example of an evidence-based intervention would be using feeling cards to help students with recognizing emotions. An example of an evidence-based program would be using MindUP curriculum to teach students a variety of mindfulness skills and techniques (e.g., deep breathing, visualization, body scan).

Aside from utilizing the terms of interventions and programs throughout this text, the common terms "mental health concerns/difficulties," "social-emotional concerns/difficulties" and "mental/social-emotional distress" are utilized interchangeably to identify children who are at risk for, but not suffering from, full-blown mental illnesses. These children simply have mild to moderate internalizing and externalizing concerns that may or may not be noticeable to educators. **Internalizing concerns** can be defined as problem behaviors that are directed *inwardly toward the child* and include an inner-directed pattern of actions (Hunter et al., 2014). Therefore, children presenting with internalizing concerns attempt to overcontrol emotions or thoughts to an excessive and maladaptive extent (Hunter et al., 2014). Children experiencing internalizing concerns may experience difficulty developing fulfilling relationships, adapting to change, realizing their potential, and overcoming everyday challenges (Wlodarczyk et al., 2017). In other words, children with internalizing concerns may have difficulty with recovering quickly from challenges that they may experience (Gopalkrishnan, 2018). For instance, a child who gets a less-than-ideal test grade may ruminate on their personal "failures" by engaging in negative self-talk and thinking that they are "stupid" rather than thinking that they "can do better next time" (Vannest et al., 2019).s

Examples of internalizing concerns include poor self-esteem, social withdrawal, somatic complaints, negative thoughts, feelings of sadness, and periods of nervousness. Due to these behaviors being less likely to interfere with behavioral expectations set by teachers, administrators, parents, or law enforcement, both schools and mental health providers tend to overlook children presenting with internalizing concerns (Hunter et al., 2014; Tibbets, 2013). Consequently, if internalizing concerns are left untreated and children do not learn how to regulate their feelings and emotions accordingly, they could eventually lead to larger, more deep-rooted mental health conditions, such as Major Depressive Disorder or Generalized Anxiety Disorder

(McGorry & Mei, 2018). Throughout this text, the terms "internalizing" and "social-emotional concerns" will be utilized to describe mental health challenges faced children in lieu of more stigmatizing terms, such as "mental illness" or "mental health concerns." Due to early intervention playing a critical role in preventing social-emotional concerns and promoting mental wellness in children, readers need to be able to identify the warning signs along with the risk and protective factors of social-emotional concerns in children. Common warning signs of children experiencing internalizing distress include can be found in Figure 1.1.

Often children with internalizing concerns often display externalizing behaviors. **Externalizing behaviors** can be defined as negative conduct that is directed outwardly toward others and is considered undercontrolled (Hunter et al., 2014). In other words, externalizing behaviors occur when a child has difficulty self-regulating or inhibiting their actions to the point where such behaviors consistently disturb others around them (Hunter et al., 2014). Examples of externalizing behaviors include impulsivity, hyperactivity, defiance, speaking out of turn, and verbal and physical aggression. These behaviors are more likely to be identified as problematic by adults. Although the focus of this book is on addressing internalizing challenges, the universal

---

- Significant decline in school performance
- Poor grades despite trying very hard
- Considerable change in sleeping habits (i.e. sleeping too little or sleeping too much)
- Appearing more lethargic than usual (i.e. talking more slowly than usual or falling asleep in class)
- Withdrawal
- Loss of interest in formerly pleasurable activities
- Irritability (early childhood and school-age youth)
- Use of drugs and/or alcohol
- Frequent engagement in negative self-talk ((i.e. "I hate myself." or "I'm a failure.")
- Frequently talking about being scared or worried
- Frequent physical complaints despite there being no evidence of physical illness (i.e. the child may regularly complain of headaches or stomachaches or request to be sent down to the school nurse).

Figure 1.1 Warning Signs of Social-Emotional Concerns in Children
Source: (CDC, 2020a; National Institute of Mental Health [NIMH], 2019)

SEL programs discussed throughout this text have been found to be effective in addressing many externalizing problems (Kellam et al., 2011; Raffaele Mendez, 2017). Additionally, it is important to acknowledge that some behaviors (e.g., irritability, defiance) that may seem to be results of externalizing difficulties are actually due to internalizing problems.

Risk and Protective Factors for Social-Emotional Concerns

Aside from being aware of the early warning signs of social-emotional concerns, educators and school personnel should be aware of the common risk and protective factors with associated internalizing difficulties in children. **Risk factors** can be defined as conditions, events, behaviors, or life situations that increase a child's chances of developing a mental health concern or condition (O'Connell et al., 2009; Wlodarczyk et al., 2017; youth.gov, n.d.). For example, a child who was born very preterm (due to inequitable healthcare service provision to the child's mother) or who experiences housing insecurity (due to racial discrimination, ongoing racially targeted policies, and income inequities that oppress racially minoritized families) would likely have an increased risk for experiencing social-emotional difficulties (O'Connell et al., 2009; Yates et al., 2020). Conversely, **protective factors** can be described as conditions, events, or life situations that decrease the child's chances of developing a social-emotional concern or condition (O'Connell et al., 2009; Wlodarczyk et al., 2017; youth.gov, n.d.), such as a warm and consistent relationship with a trusted adult (e.g., caregiver, teacher). Exercise 1.2 will provide readers the opportunity to work individually or with a group to generate a list of risk and protective factors for childhood mental health concerns. To see a list of some of the risk and protective factors for childhood mental health concerns, see Figure 1.2.

Exercise 1.2 Risk and Protective Factors for Childhood Social-Emotional Concerns

Directions: Independently or with a partner generate as many risk and protective factors that may influence whether or not a child is likely to experience a social-emotional concern. After completing this exercise, compare your answers to those listed in Figure 1.2. In reviewing Figure 1.2, circle any risk or protective factors that you may not have thought of in completing Exercise 1.2.

Risk factors	Protective factors

Risk factors	Protective factors
Low birth weight	Positive physical development
Premature birth	High self-esteem
Little access to mental health supports/services	Access to mental health supports/services
Female gender	Good intellectual development
Low self-esteem	Reliable support, love, and discipline from caregivers
Head injury/Traumatic Brain Injury	Ability to solve problems and manage stress in healthy ways (sports, music, exercise).
Having a disability	
Parent(s) in prison	
Childhood exposure to lead or mercury	Predictable and stable home environment with clear expectations for behavior and values
Child abuse/maltreatment	
History of mental illness in family	Opportunities for positive engagement
Divorce	
Negative family environment (domestic abuse, drug or alcohol use in home)	Coming from a financially secure family
Marital conflict	Positive peer support group/friendships
Parental unemployment	
Poverty	Social, gender, and ethnic equality
Little to no friends	Access to positive role models in the school and community
Associating with deviant peers	
Loss of close relationship or friends	Parents engage in little to no marital conflict
Death of a loved one	
Negative, unsupportive, or unsafe school and community environments	Parents married or have separated amicably and still respect one another's role in the parenting process
Marginalized identity (e.g., BIPOC, LGBTQA+, low-income/economically marginalized)	Positive, supportive, and safe, school and community environments
Poor emotional self-regulation	Good emotional self-regulation

Figure 1.2 Risk and Protective Factors for Childhood Social-Emotional Concerns
Source: (O'Connell et al., 2009; Wlodarczyk et al., 2017; youth.gov, n.d.)

Trauma and Social-Emotional Concerns in Children

In reviewing Figure 1.2, readers may notice that several risk factors that increase children's chances of experiencing social-emotional concerns, such as domestic abuse or divorce, may be traumatizing for children to experience. **Trauma** is defined as a real or perceived experience that is significantly distressing and causes feelings of fear, terror, or helplessness (Felitti et al., 1998). Exposure to traumatic events in childhood is often linked to an array of social-emotional concerns, such as attention deficit hyperactivity disorder, depression, anxiety, personality disorders, and even suicide (Dye, 2018). Additionally, childhood trauma has been linked to physical ailments, including heart attacks, strokes, diabetes, and asthma (Dye, 2018; Felitti et al., 1998; K. Hughes et al., 2017; Kerker et al., 2015). If left unaddressed, the negative effects of trauma can persist into adulthood (Dye, 2018; K. Hughes et al., 2017). One of the greatest factors in determining how much a person may be impacted by previous traumatic events includes how often they have been exposed to adverse childhood experiences.

Adverse childhood experiences (ACEs) are potentially traumatic events that occur in childhood between 0 to 17 years of age (Felitti et al., 1998; Oral et al., 2016). Examples of ACEs include sexual abuse, emotional and physical neglect, divorce, parental alcohol or substance abuse, and exposure to a caregiver suffering from internalizing concerns (Felitti et al., 1998; Kerker et al., 2015; Mason & Cox, 2014). It is estimated that 46% of children under age 18 across the United States have at least one ACE, and approximately 20% have at least two (Bethell et al., 2017). As can be expected, having a higher number of adverse childhood experiences has been linked to a greater risk for mental and physical illness. For example, an ACE score of four or more increased the risk of a person experiencing depression by 460% and the possibility of committing suicide by 1,220% (Felitti et al., 1998; Ranjbar & Erb, 2019). Moreover, an ACE score of six or more increased the likelihood of heavy drinking by 280% and drug use by 370% (Ranjbar & Erb, 2019).

Part of the reason for higher ACE scores resulting in increased risk for developing mental and physical ailments may be due to toxic stress (Felitti et al., 1998). **Toxic stress** has been defined as stress that is the result of experiencing ongoing and frequent adverse events in the absence of protective behaviors, such as social support or physical safety (Mason & Cox, 2014). When children experience toxic stress, they have no opportunity to recover from elevated stress hormones, resulting in them being stuck in a flight, fright, or freeze response (Kerker et al., 2015; Mason & Cox, 2014). Subsequently, the impacts of these stress hormones may lead to neurobiological changes in the brain that are permanent (Mason & Cox, 2014). Therefore, studies have found that exposure to trauma in childhood is associated with lower academic achievement and test scores, depressed IQ scores, impaired working memory, poor attention span, increased impulsivity and hyperactivity, delayed language and vocabulary, and low self-esteem (Berger, 2019; Perfect et al., 2016).

Racial trauma, or trauma experienced by individuals due to the exposure and re-exposure of race-based adversity, discrimination, stress, and microaggressions, is another type of trauma that negatively affects the mental health and overall development of youth of color. Examples of racism-based trauma include threats of hate speech, threats of harm and injury, humiliating and shaming events, or any other forms of individual, historical, or institutional racism. Children also experience trauma after hearing about or witnessing another person's direct experiences, often referred to as secondary traumatic stress or vicarious trauma (Parris et al., 2020). **Acculturative stress** refers to the stressors associated with being an immigrant or ethnic minority and going through the acculturation process (Parris et al., 2020). A child learning a new language or modifying their dress or religious beliefs to fit into the dominant culture after leaving their home country are examples of acculturative stress.

Due to schools increasingly recognizing the negative academic and mental health effects various types of traumas may have on children, there has been a growth in the number of available interventions and programs in this area. Moreover, schools are increasingly seeking to become **trauma-informed**, or prepared and sensitive to respond to children impacted by trauma (Martin et al., 2017). Some of the Tier 1 programs and supports mentioned in this book may promote resiliency to help children to overcome short-term or indirect traumatic events that they may see on television or through social media, such as pandemics and coups d'état. For more information the treatment of trauma in schoolchildren, see Eric Rossen's (2020) book entitled *Supporting and Educating Traumatized Students (Second Edition)*.

Why Does Children's Mental Health Matter?

An extensive and growing body of research has demonstrated a significant relationship between academic performance and social-emotional health in children (Brännlund et al., 2017; Kang-Yi et al., 2018; Murphy et al., 2015; Teo et al., 1996). From all the research that has been conducted, findings suggest that youth who experience social-emotional concerns are more likely to repeat grades, drop out of school, have lower GPAs, commit suicide, be suspended or expelled from school, or end up in juvenile detention compared to their peers without mental health problems (Brännlund et al., 2017; Kang-Yi et al., 2018; Murphy et al., 2015; Teo et al., 1996). Previous studies have found that the rates of suspension and expulsion of children with mental health disorders are three times higher than those of their peers and that these children may miss as many as 18 to 22 days of school (Blackborby & Cameto, 2004; Gilliam, 2005; Zeng et al., 2019). This is higher even still for BIPOC youth, who continue to experience harsher and more exclusionary punishment than their White peers.

Moreover, without early intervention and supports, research has found that internalizing and externalizing problems are persistent over time (Mesman et al., 2001; Mian et al., 2011; Yates et al., 2020). For example, a study by Mesman et al. (2001) found that internalizing problems noted at ages 2 to 3 years predicted the same type of problems for children at ages 10 to 11 years of age. A more recent study by Yates et al. (2020) found that very preterm babies were at increased risk for mental health concerns compared to full-term infants. Moreover, the internalizing distress found in these very preterm babies remained stable when these children were checked up on at 7 and 13 years of age (Yates et al., 2020). On the other hand, when supports are provided, children demonstrate fewer behavior problems, more prosocial behavior, and improved social-emotional functioning (Bradshaw et al., 2012). Therefore, early intervention is a key in altering the social-emotional trajectory in children who are at risk for developing internalizing concerns. Such interventions may provide children the social-emotional services and strategies they need to lead lives in overcoming mental health concerns.

In considering school performance alone, Murphy et al. (2015) found that being at risk for social-emotional concerns in first grade leads to a 5% drop in academic performance in just two years. Another study involving 97,406 children in grades K–12 found that students who were exposed to social-emotional learning (SEL) programs in school scored an average of 13 percentile points higher in academic performance than peers who were not exposed to such programs (Taylor et al., 2017). Consequently, previous research highlights the importance of mental health in children concerning educational attainment, behavioral consequences, and social competence. As a result, there is a need for schools to best support the social-emotional development of children, and often educators are turned to first when children begin to show mental health concerns. Before a discussion can take place about why educators and school-based mental health professionals are turned to more than outside practitioners in the community for childhood social-emotional support, readers of this book are encouraged to take part in the game below (see Exercise 1.3). This game entails brainstorming why children may turn to educators or school-based mental health providers over outside mental health clinicians for social-emotional support.

Why Do Children Turn to Educators for Support?

Exercise 1.3 Reasons Why Children Turn to Educators for Support

Directions:

Group Format: If possible, in a group of three to four people, take out three index cards or pieces of paper and a stopwatch or smartphone. Subsequently, have one member of the group put 30 seconds on the stopwatch or smartphone and then distribute the index cards or pieces of paper to each group member that is not the timekeeper. With one person serving as the timekeeper, have the other members of the group write down as many reasons as they can as to why children and families may reach out to educators or school-based mental health professionals for support instead of mental health clinicians in the community. After the time has expired, the timekeeper can check who wrote down the most reasons, and group members can compare and contrast their responses. The person who writes down the most reasons for children seeking out social-emotional support from educators and school-based mental health professionals wins!

Independent Format: If you are playing in this activity independently, record on an index card or piece of paper reasons why you believe educators turn to educators for support in 30 seconds.

As can be seen from Exercise 1.3, there are many reasons why a family might seek out educators and school-based mental health providers for child's their social-emotional needs rather than outside practitioners. Research has consistently identified several reasons for families seeking out educators and school-based mental health providers as opposed to clinicians outside the schools.

First children and parents often seek out educators and school-based mental health providers due to their physical proximity to students (Maras et al., 2015). Since educators and school-based practitioners are located within the schools themselves, they likely can provide the child "in the moment" and "on the spot" care, counseling, or behavioral remediation when a youth is having difficulty (Maras et al., 2015).

Additionally, educators and school-based practitioners can monitor student progress over time, check in with them more frequently, and have the opportunity to observe their functioning within the school environment, a more natural context than the outside practitioner's office. Conversely, community-based clinicians do not have the same immediate access to children to provide counseling and support when they are experiencing difficulties. Often the child will see outside providers after an incident or significant feeling of distress or discomfort has passed. However, both educators and school-based mental health professionals are readily available when the child may be at their most vulnerable or when they are most in need of how to understand and appropriately respond to their feelings and discomforts.

Due to being in close physical proximity to educators and school-based mental health practitioners, one of the biggest reasons why families may seek these professionals instead of outside mental health clinicians may be due to their level of comfort and familiarity with them (National Association of School Psychologists [NASP], 2015; Swick & Powers, 2018). Relatedly, school-based personnel are more easily accessible compared to outside practitioners (Maras et al., 2015). Two of the reasons families often do not obtain health care services for their child are due to lack of time and inability to leave work (Guo et al., 2010). Therefore, it is not surprising to learn that 40–60% of families who begin community mental health services only attend only one to two sessions (Kern et al., 2017; McKay et al., 2001).

Within some communities, school-based practitioners may be the only providers of mental health services for youth. For example, Figure 1.3 shows that many states and counties across America have few to no licensed psychologists to support children outside the school setting (American Psychological Association, 2016). An additional analysis revealed that approximately 66.4 counties across the United States had no more than five psychologists, and 74.6 percent of counties had no more than ten psychologists (American Psychological Association, 2016). Even in states where there appears to be an adequate number of licensed psychologists to meet the mental health needs of children, like New York, a closer look at Figure 1.4 reveals that 35 out of 62 counties (56%) have fewer than 20 licensed psychologists (New York State Office of Professions, 2022). Due to there being a limited number of

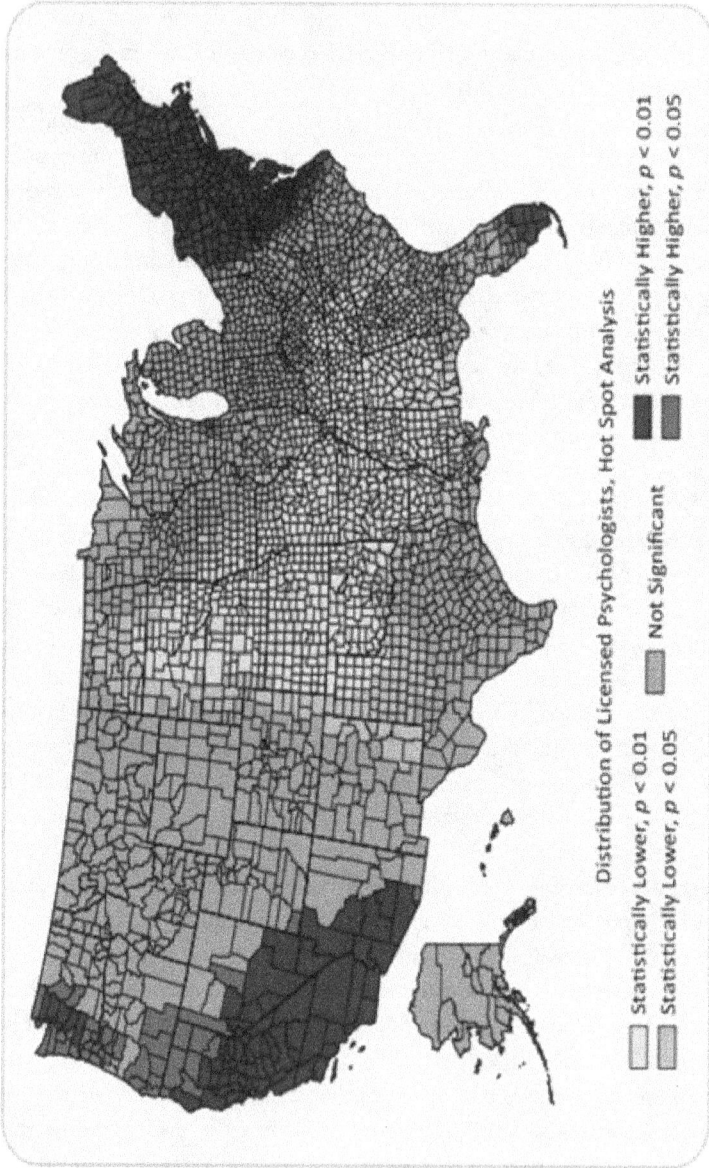

Figure 1.3 Hot Spot Analysis of Licensed Psychologists in the United States, 2012–2015 (American Psychological Association, 2016)

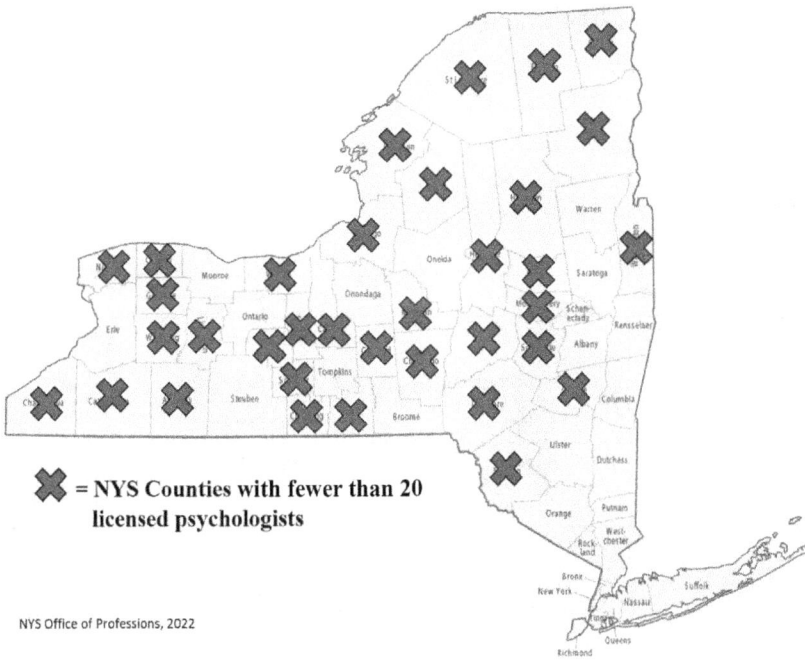

= NYS Counties with fewer than 20 licensed psychologists

NYS Office of Professions, 2022

Figure 1.3 Continued

mental health providers outside schools, there may be a delay for youth to receive timely social-emotional support (Children's Hospital Association, 2018; Jimenez et al., 2017; Steinman et al., 2015). Taken altogether, the ability for youth to receive timely mental health support outside the school system is severely hampered by wait times and a lack of professionals specifically trained to treat children.

Another reason why children and parents may seek out educators or school-based mental health practitioners over community-based professionals is that there appears to be less of a stigma involved in seeking out school-based practitioners (Swick & Powers, 2018). School-based practitioners have clearer understandings of how school systems function and how student behavior and mental health impact their ability to be successful in school (Kern et al., 2017; Swick & Powers, 2018). Moreover, schools are familiar environments for students and families, as opposed to community-based clinics and hospitals (Swick & Powers, 2018).

Parents and children may also seek out educators or school-based mental health practitioners for social-emotional guidance and support due to

NYS counties with fewer than 20 licensed psychologists

County		Number	County		Number	County		Number
Albany		237	Jefferson	✖	18	Saratoga		118
Allegany	✖	11	Kings		1,101	Schenectady		56
Bronx		213	Lewis	✖	3	Schoharie	✖	4
Broome		71	Livingston	✖	13	Schuyler	✖	5
Cattaraugus	✖	6	Madison	✖	16	Seneca	✖	3
Cayuga	✖	4	Monroe		383	Steuben		24
Chautauqua	✖	4	Montgomery	✖	5	St. Lawrence	✖	19
Chemung	✖	8	Nassau		1,283	Suffolk		902
Chenango	✖	6	New York		3,352	Sullivan	✖	19
Clinton	✖	11	Niagara	✖	18	Tioga	✖	9
Columbia	✖	28	Oneida		51	Tompkins		81
Cortland		10	Onondaga		211	Ulster		114
Delaware		6	Ontario		34	Warren		25
Dutchess		173	Orange		100	Washington	✖	5
Erie		326	Orleans	✖	3	Wayne		10
Essex	✖	13	Oswego	✖	8	Westchester		1,323
Franklin	✖	5	Otsego	✖	13	Wyoming	✖	2
Fulton	✖	10	Putnam		59	Yates	✖	3
Genesee	✖	4	Queens		615	**NYS TOTAL**		**11,533**
Greene	✖	16	Rensselaer		27	**OTHER US**		**3,574**
Hamilton	✖	1	Richmond		135	**NON-US**		**80**
Herkimer	✖	1	Rockland		199	**TOTAL**		**15,187**

✖ = Counties with less than 20 licensed psychologists

(NYS Office of Professions, 2022)

Figure 1.4 New York State Counties with Fewer Than 20 Licensed Psychologists (New York State Office of Professions, 2022)

there being few to no outside practitioners who speak the same language or are of the same race, ethnicity, religion, or culture as they. Parents and children may find comfort in educators and school-based practitioners who are culturally responsive to families' beliefs, views, and treatment regarding social-emotional concerns. For example, in some Asian cultures, having social-emotional difficulties may be considered a sign of weakness and may cause the child to "lose face" with their family due to causing them a loss of dignity (Gopalkrishnan, 2018). As opposed to seeking outside practitioners, a culturally responsive school environment may provide the opportunity to gain trust in educators and school-based mental health practitioners who may or may not have the same experiences, same backgrounds, or social identities but are willing to be culturally aware, humble, and responsive to the students and families they serve.

Even if children have access to clinicians outside the school setting, the cost of accessing such practitioners may be a considerable barrier to overcome (Cuellar, 2015; Swick & Powers, 2018). Often, insurance may not fully cover counseling sessions or limit children to only several sessions before parents have to take on the costs of counseling themselves (Cuellar, 2015; Swick & Powers, 2018). Not surprisingly, 25% of parents reported the reason they did not obtain social-emotional care for their children was due to services costing too much (DeRigne et al., 2009; Swick & Powers, 2018). In contrast to non-school-based mental health providers, school-based mental health services are provided to the child at no additional cost to parents. For all the aforementioned reasons, schools are ideal places to promote mental wellness, prevent social-emotional concerns, and provide ongoing support to students at critical times throughout their lives.

Although children are more likely to visit and receive help from school-based mental health practitioners, the average delay between a child's onset of mental health symptoms and intervention is approximately 8 to 10 years (National Institute of Mental Health, 2019). This is in light of over 50% of all lifetime cases of mental illness beginning by age 14 and 75% by age 24 (National Institute of Mental Health, 2019). Given the alarming statistics on the delay of social-emotional services for children, it is imperative for parents, educators, and policy-makers to advocate and ensure increased access to school-based mental health practitioners to provide children with adequate social-emotional support.

Conclusion

Children of today are more vulnerable than ever in being exposed to traumatic, frightening, and violent events due to an increasingly interconnected world as a result of the internet, social media, and the news. Consequently, it is not surprising that 20% of youth today have diagnosable mental health conditions, and many more may be at risk for developing them (CDC, 2020a; National Association of School Psychologists, 2015). Research has shown that children who develop mental health problems are more likely to drop out of school, repeat grades, have lower GPAs, or be suspended or expelled from school and possibly enter the juvenile justice system (Brännlund et al., 2017; Kang-Yi et al., 2018; Murphy et al., 2015; Teo et al., 1996).

Educators and school-based mental health practitioners can play critical roles in preventing social-emotional concerns in children and promoting mental wellness. Youth and families may seek out educators and school-based mental health professionals for social-emotional support and guidance due to physical proximity and convenience, levels of comfort, lower chances of being stigmatized, and accessible services (American Psychological Association, 2016; Jimenez et al., 2017; Maras et al., 2015; NASP, 2015; Swick & Powers, 2018).

One of the first steps educators and future educators can take in preventing mental health concerns from arising is children is by recognizing the warning signs of social-emotional deficits in youth. Some of the warning signs that mental health concerns may be present in children include withdrawal, declining academic performance, and a loss of interest in formerly pleasurable activities. Aside from warning signs, educators should be aware of the risks and protective factors associated with children who are more susceptible to experiencing mental health concerns. Common risk factors associated with a child developing social-emotional difficulties are poverty, having few to no friends or positive social-support group, and low self-esteem (O'Connell et al., 2009; Wlodarczyk et al., 2017; youth.gov, n.d.). One of the greatest risk factors that may impact a child's social-emotional well-being is their exposure to adverse childhood experiences. Factors that may assist a child in overcoming mental health concerns or adverse childhood experiences in their life include coming from a financially secure family, having friends or a positive social-support group, and high self-esteem (O'Connell et al., 2009; Wlodarczyk et al., 2017; youth.gov, n.d.).

Multi-Tiered Systems of Support and Social-Emotional RTI

2

Learning Objectives

After reading this chapter, you should be able to:

- Explain Multi-Tiered Systems of Support
- Identify commonalities across intervention service delivery models that comprise MTSS
- Compare and contrast MTSS and intervention service delivery models
- Summarize key components of social-emotional RTI
- Discuss each tier of social-emotional RTI

Multi-Tiered Systems of Support

Although the main focus of this text is on how to employ universal social-emotional supports and programs using implementation science, it would be remiss not to briefly review MTSS for three major reasons. First, although this book will teach readers how to implement universal social-emotional programs using implementation science, much of the same process can be applied to employing secondary and tertiary supports. Secondly, readers will learn about what supports within social-emotional RTI look like at Tier 1, Tier 2, and Tier 3. Finally, readers may be wondering about how implementation science relates to or assists in the employment of programs within social-emotional RTI and MTSS as a whole. Therefore, in this chapter, readers will

DOI: 10.4324/9781003343479-2

learn how to systemically dissect MTSS as well as the intervention service delivery model of social-emotional RTI. It is hoped that through this chapter, readers will have a better understanding of MTSS and social-emotional RTI before they learn about implementation science in the next chapter.

Since the passage of ESSA, educators and school personnel have increasingly heard of Multi-Tiered Systems of Support. One of the earliest known uses of "Multi-Tiered Systems of Support" came from the state of Kansas in 2008 to reduce confusion over initiatives to shift from standard RTI to school-wide RTI (Kansas Technical Assistance Network, 2012; Pullen et al., 2018). Since then, **MTSS** has evolved to encompass a framework that "houses" two or more intervention service delivery models or "multi-tiered systems," such as Response to Intervention (RTI) and School-Wide Positive Behavior Support (SWPBS) (Averill & Rinaldi, 2011; Eagle et al., 2015). Overall, MTSS can be viewed as a problem-solving framework that is used to improve learning, behavior, and social-emotional outcomes in children (Wexler, 2018).

Intervention service delivery models can be defined as triangular three-tiered systems that increase in intensity and duration and are utilized to provide evidence-based supports to children in general education (Schaffer, 2023). Through intervention service delivery models, districts organize their supports across a continuum that is based on the public health model and consists of three tiers (Schaffer, 2023; Wexler, 2018):

- At Tier 1, interventions are delivered to all students and are known as universal supports
- At Tier 2, interventions are delivered to some students and are referred to as targeted supports
- Lastly, Tier 3 interventions are provided to a few students who require significant remedial efforts and are referred to as intensive supports

MTSS is built on six foundational principles. First, MTSS asserts that *all* children possess the capability of meeting grade-level expectations, regardless of individual factors such as socioeconomic or disability status. Second, MTSS is a preventative model in nature and proactively determines which children need increasing supports based on their academic, behavioral, or social-emotional needs (Wexler, 2018). Third, MTSS emphasizes the utilization of empirically validated instruction and interventions to best support students (Wexler, 2018; Sugai & Horner, 2008). Fourth, MTSS utilizes data to make decisions about instruction, intervention planning, the allocation of resources, and the overall effectiveness of school practices (Wexler, 2018; Shapiro, 2013). Fifth, through MTSS, instruction should meet the students' unique needs (Wexler, 2018).

Finally, MTSS provides a unique opportunity for districts to adopt reform efforts to their school cultures (Wexler, 2018; Sugai & Horner, 2008).

MTSS largely emerged from the growing recognition that critical components of Response to Intervention and School-Wide Positive Behavior Support (SWPBS) often mirrored and complemented one another (Freeman et al., 2015). Such mirroring provided an outlet for initial efforts to merge common elements of intervention service delivery models under the framework of MTSS (Eagle et al., 2015). Additionally, a growing body of research suggests that integrated approaches under MTSS are associated with greater improvements in both academic and behavioral outcomes (Eagle et al., 2015; Stewert et al., 2007). Although RTI and SWPBS are the most common intervention service delivery models that fall under the Multi-Tiered Systems of Support framework, deviations of these models have started to be developed by districts in the area of social-emotional support (Gresham, 2005; Miller, 2014).

As can be inferred, each intervention service delivery model housed under an MTSS has a specific area of focus (see Figure 2.1). For example, Response to Intervention is a three-tiered intervention service delivery model, the focus of which is on promoting academic proficiency and remediating learning challenges before they lead to disability placement. Similarly, School-Wide Positive Behavior Support is a three-tiered intervention service delivery model focused on teaching appropriate conduct and helping students to overcome behavioral deficits. Finally, social-emotional RTI is a three-tiered intervention service delivery model designed to promote mental wellness and prevent social-emotional concerns from developing in children.

In examining the relationship between MTSS and the intervention service delivery models that comprise it, readers can easily think of Multi-Tiered Systems of Support as a whole chocolate cake. This chocolate cake is comprised

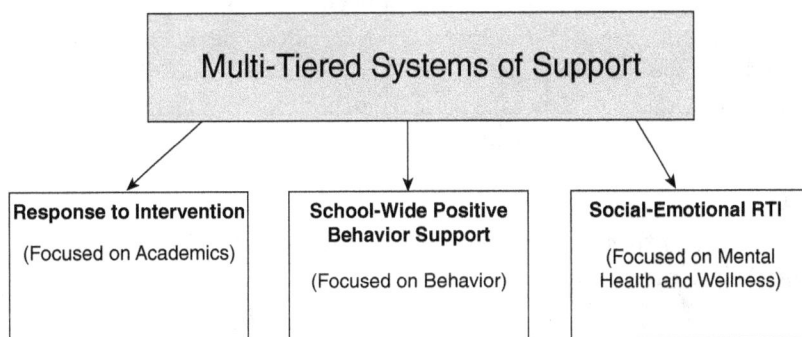

Figure 2.1 MTSS and Three of the Most Common Intervention Service Delivery Models Under an MTSS Framework

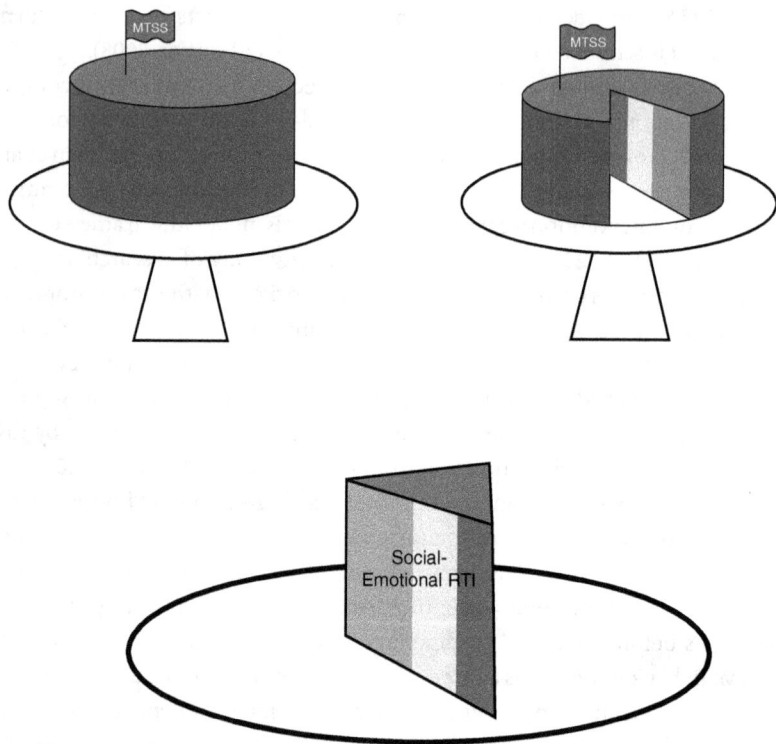

Figure 2.2 MTSS Chocolate Cake Analogy

of slices, with each slice representing a singular multi-tiered system of intervention service delivery. Therefore, if readers were to cut a slice out of the cake, they would be able to observe that the cake itself is comprised of a set of component parts or intervention service delivery models, such as School-Wide Positive Behavior Supports or social-emotional RTI. As mentioned, each of these intervention service delivery models is specifically designed to prevent or remediate a specific area of deficit, like social-emotional concerns. Therefore, each slice of this chocolate cake has a different flavor. Figure 2.2 displays the relationship between MTSS and intervention service delivery models.

Commonalities Across Intervention Service Delivery Models Comprising MTSS

Intervention service delivery models that are housed within the MTSS framework share four common components. These four critical elements that link interventions service delivery models together and help build an effective MTSS framework include: a) varying levels of preventative evidence-based supports and instructional practices; b) universal screening; c) progress monitoring; and d) data-based decision-making (Freeman et al., 2015; Harn et al., 2015; NASP, 2016). Descriptions of each of these critical elements can be found below.

A) Varying Levels of Preventative Evidence-Based Supports

Like the three-tiered pyramid found in public health, the first critical element that links all intervention service delivery models under MTSS is that of varying levels of preventative evidence-based supports and instructional practices. Through varying levels of preventative evidence-based supports and instructional practices, students are assigned to tiers (e.g. Tier 1, Tier 2, and Tier 3) that increase in intensity and duration based on their lack of responsiveness to interventions at a prior level (Gresham et al., 2010; Schaffer, 2017). Tier 1, or universal supports, refers to interventions and services that are available to all students (Gresham et al., 2010; Harn et al., 2015; NASP, 2016). Therefore, Tier 1 refers to the core curriculum delivered to all students and has a high likelihood of bringing most students to acceptable levels of proficiency (Averill & Rinaldi, 2011). Examples of Tier 1 supports include implementation of a core mathematics curriculum, coming up with a school motto to promote positive behavior, or employing a classroom-wide mental wellness program. It is expected that 80% to 85% of students will respond to interventions at the Tier 1 level (Gresham et al., 2010; Harn et al., 2015; Wexler, 2018).

Tier 2, or targeted supports, are provided to some students who may need additional interventions to assist them in overcoming their academic, behavioral, or social-emotional deficits. Tier 2 services are supplementary to core instruction and provide students with more time and opportunities to practice the skills with which they are having difficulty (Wexler, 2018). At the Tier 2 level, typically three to six children are placed in a group and receive services three to five times a week. Interventions and supports at this tier may include small-group reading intervention, small-group counseling, or behavior skills training (Harn et al., 2015; NASP, 2016). Approximately 10% to 15% of students receive Tier 2 interventions or services (Gresham et al., 2010; Wexler, 2018).

Finally, Tier 3, or targeted interventions, are designed for individual students with severe or long-standing deficits that are beyond the capacity of Tier 1 or Tier 2 intervention efforts (Shinn & Walker, 2010). Like Tier 2, Tier 3 is designed to supplement Tier 1 instruction and supports. However, unlike

Tier 2, Tier 3 interventions and supports are only delivered through pull-out services and tend to be delivered on a one-to-one basis. An example of a Tier 3 service might be one-on-one counseling with a school psychologist. When compared to Tier 1 or Tier 2, Tier 3 interventions and supports are more intense and rigorous (Shinn & Walker, 2010; Wexler, 2018). Approximately 1% to 5% percent of students receive Tier 3 interventions and services (Shinn & Walker, 2010; Wexler, 2018). Examples of Tier 3 interventions and services may include individualized instruction, FBA/BIP development, or one-to-one intensive counseling.

In referring to the chocolate cake example from earlier, if readers were to cut a slice of the cake and observe it, they would see that it is comprised of three layers or tiers of varying levels of support. Each of these varying levels of support increases in intensity and duration as a child does not respond to the supports put into place. Through utilizing varying levels of support, educators can differentiate their instruction and interventions to best assist all learners in the educational environment. **Differentiated instruction** refers to teachers tailoring the classroom environment, instructional practices, and teaching environments to create appropriately different learning experiences for students with different interests, needs, readiness, and learning profiles (Heward et al., 2017). Figure 2.3 provides a better look at the three tiers of an intervention service delivery model using the cake analogy from earlier.

B) Universal Screening

A second critical component common to all models of intervention service delivery under MTSS is that of universal screening. **Universal screening**

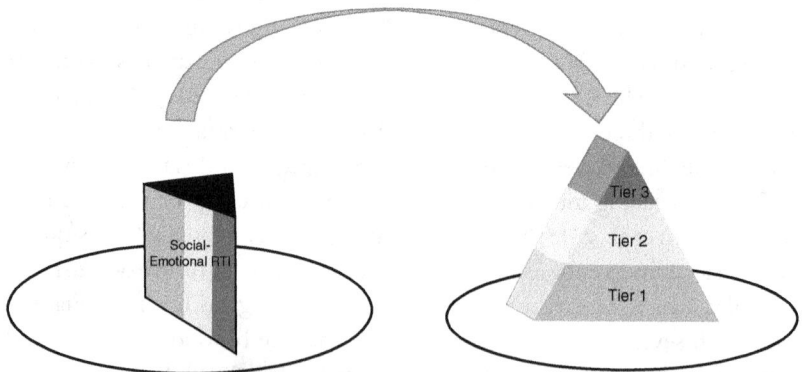

Figure 2.3 Closer Look at Social-Emotional RTI Tiers

involves the systemic brief assessment of the school population to identify children at risk for academic, behavioral, or social-emotional deficits
(Gresham et al., 2010; NASP, 2016). Universal screening typically takes
place in the fall, winter, and spring of each school year and is viewed as
the first step in identifying children who may be at risk for not responding to core instruction at the Tier 1 level (J. R. Jenkins et al., 2007; Jenkins
et al., 2014; Kilapatrick et al., 2018). The goal of universal screening is to
detect deficits early on to provide children timely and effective evidence-
based interventions to overcome their academic, behavioral, or social-
emotional difficulties. There are several examples of universal screeners
(Schaffer, 2017), including Aimsweb's Reading CBM, BASC-3 Behavior and
Emotional Screening System (BASC-3 BESS; Kamphaus & Reynolds, 2015),
and *Systemic Screening for Behavior Disorders*, 2nd edition (SSBD-2; Walker
et al., 2014). Readers will find detailed descriptions of some of the most
highly regarded universal social-emotional screeners in Chapter 6. Before
discussing progress monitoring, Exercise 2.1 asks readers to reflect on why
they believe universal screening is important and whether they have seen it
used to prevent diseases in the medical field.

Exercise 2.1 Why Is Universal Screening Important?

Directions: Independently or with a partner, answer the questions below.

1) Can you list some occurrences in which universal screening is used in
   schools? An example has been provided to get you started!

   _____Hearing screening_____   _____

   _____   _____

   _____   _____

2) Why do you think it is important for schools to universally screen students for social-emotional concerns?

   _____

   _____

   _____

C) Progress Monitoring

A third feature common to intervention service delivery models under MTSS is that each utilizes progress monitoring. **Progress monitoring** involves the repeated assessment of skills and strategies learned to determine whether a child is responding to the interventions and services being provided (Shapiro, 2013). Progress monitoring takes place at Tier 2 and Tier 3 of MTSS. At Tier 2, progress monitoring tends to occur on a weekly or bi-weekly basis (Christ et al., 2013; Shapiro, 2013). At Tier 3, progress monitoring occurs one or more times per week (Christ et al., 2013; Shapiro, 2013). Recently, there has been a call by scholars to collect 12 to 14 data points to determine whether a child is responding to remediation efforts as opposed to the former recommendation of 6 to 8 data points (Christ et al., 2013; Shapiro, 2013). Examples of progress monitoring measures include Aimsweb's Reading CBM or the Devereux Student Strengths Assessment-Mini (DESSA-Mini).

D) Data-Based Decision-Making

Finally, proper implementation of intervention service delivery models within MTSS entails making effective data-based and data-driven decisions. **Data-based decision-making** is defined as the ongoing process of gathering and examining data to alter and improve practices to best benefit learners (Prenger & Schildkamp, 2018). Through analysis of universal screening and progress monitoring data, data-based decisions should be made to determine whether a child needs a more intense level of intervention, whether a child is responding to the instruction or interventions being offered, or whether a change in intervention approach may be needed (Christ et al., 2013; Shapiro, 2013). In addition to universal screeners and progress monitoring measures, educators need to consider other types of formal and informal data to evaluate the student's area(s) of deficit, such as computer-adaptive assessments, state tests, and behavioral data. In regard to social-emotional concerns, educators may want to consider data such as parent, teacher, and student interviews, observations, or how many times to student has gone to the nurse's office with somatic complaints, such as stomachaches.

Throughout this section, readers have been provided information on the four critical components that link intervention service delivery models together under MTSS. In the next section, readers will be taken through social-emotional RTI and provided examples of varying levels of preventative evidence-based supports, universal screening, progress monitoring, and data-based decision-making as they pertain to social-emotional RTI. For a more comprehensive book on MTSS and how to implement the intervention service delivery models that comprise it, see the text by Schaffer (2023) entitled *Multi-Tiered Systems of Support: A Practical Guide to Preventative Practice.*

Introduction to Social-Emotional RTI

While RTI has been used to support students academically and SWPBS is utilized to teach and encourage appropriate behavior, social-emotional RTI is an intervention service delivery model focused on promoting social-emotional wellness and preventing social-emotional difficulties in youth. One of the central tenets of social-emotional RTI is prevention, in which promoting and teaching social-emotional health skills early and consistently to improve wellness and reduce the number of youth that need more intensive supports and services (Greenberg et al., 2017). Like every intervention service delivery model, social-emotional RTI comprises three tiers, with a specific focus on teaching students social-emotional strategies and providing support to children with social-emotional concerns (Gresham, 2005; Greenberg et al., 2017). A key goal of social-emotional RTI is to foster the development of social-emotional learning (Greenberg et al., 2017). **Social-emotional learning** has been defined as:

> the presence through which children and adults acquire and effectively apply the knowledge, attitudes, and skills necessary to understand and manage emotions, set and achieve positive goals, feel and show empathy for others, establish and maintain positive relationships, and make responsible decisions
> (Collaborative for Academic, Social, and Emotional Learning [CASEL], 2019, para 1).

Social-emotional learning consists of five skill areas(Eklund et al., 2018; Moy & Hazen, 2018):

- **Self-awareness**: Ability to recognize one's own emotions, thoughts, and values and how each of these factors may influence behavior
- **Social awareness**: Whether one can take on the perspective of others and empathize with them
- **Self-management** consists of the ability to successfully regulate emotions, thoughts, and behaviors across different situations and contexts (Eklund et al., 2018)

- **Relationship skills** are defined as an individual's ability to establish and maintain healthy and rewarding relationships with diverse groups and individuals
- **Responsible decision-making** is the ability to make constructive choices about personal behavior and social interactions based on social norms, safety concerns, and ethical standards

Social-emotional RTI views each of these five areas of SEL competency as interrelated and critical to children developing positive coping strategies (Eklund et al., 2018; Greenberg et al., 2017). Therefore, social-emotional RTI seeks to develop the five SEL competency areas in children by systematically delivering interventions and supports that promote mental wellness and remediating internalizing concerns through three levels of support (Greenberg et al., 2017). Studies have shown that the benefits of incorporating SEL into schools include improved academic outcomes, increases in graduation rates, and lower rates of school dropouts (Eklund et al., 2018; Moy & Hazen, 2018). Before delving into the three tiers of social-emotional RTI, Exercise 2.2 will ask readers to think of real-life examples in which they demonstrated the five areas of SEL competency.

Exercise 2.2 Personal Examples of SEL

Directions: In the template below, write down a personal example in which you or someone you know demonstrated each of the five SEL competency areas. If possible, share some of your examples with a partner or group of four people.

---

1) Self-Awareness
- The ability to recognize one's own emotions, values, and thoughts and how each may influence behavior (Eklund et al., 2018)
  Personal Example

_____

2) Social Awareness
- The ability to take on the perspective of others and empathize with them (Eklund et al., 2018)
  Personal Example

_____

---

3) Self-Management
- The ability to successfully regulate emotions, thoughts, and behaviors in different situations and across different contexts (Eklund et al., 2018)

  Personal Example

---

4) Relationship Skills
- The ability to establish and maintain healthy and rewarding relationships with diverse groups and individuals (Eklund et al., 2018)

  Personal Example

---

5) Responsible Decision-Making
- The ability to make constructive choices about social interactions and personal behavior based on social norms, ethical standards, and safety concerns (Eklund et al., 2018)

  Personal Example

Social-Emotional RTI Tiers

In considering the tiers of social-emotional RTI, recall that Tier 1 interventions apply to all students and are known as universal supports. Tier 2 interventions apply to some students and are also known as targeted supports. Lastly, Tier 3 interventions apply to few students and are known as tertiary supports. Within social-emotional RTI, each of these tiers attempts to provide a continuum of social-emotional interventions and programs to students from those with no to little mental health concerns to those displaying a significant deal of mental distress. The overall hope of social-emotional RTI is that, through a continuum of supports and services, children will learn how to successfully and appropriately recognize and regulate their emotions, empathize with others, establish and maintain healthy positive relationships, and make constructive choices (CASEL, 2019; Eklund et al., 2018; Moy Hazen, 2018). As can be seen, the goals of utilizing social-emotional RTI align with the five core-competency areas of SEL. Below is a description of the three tiers of social-emotional RTI.

Tier 1

Tier 1 supports and interventions within social-emotional RTI focus on the promotion of mental wellness for all students, with approximately 80% to 85% of children expected to respond to such interventions (Ziomek-Daigle & Heckman, 2019). The ultimate goal of Tier 1 interventions within social-emotional RTI is to prevent mental health concerns from arising that might act as a barrier to a child reaching their true academic potential. Educators and future educators might be relieved to learn that some of the simplest interventions and supports from social-emotional RTI are the same or very similar to those of SWPBS. Therefore, an effective way schools can promote social-emotional wellness for students is through the creation of a safe, warm, welcoming, and culturally responsive educational environment. One example is when schools universally implement a positive school motto that encourages social-emotional wellness and discusses behavioral expectations (see Figure 2.4). Such a motto could be placed in the classrooms or in the hallways of schools to remind students of behavior that promotes a welcoming and caring school environment.

Tier 1 of social-emotional RTI also teaches students how to appropriately label and express their feelings, adapt and cope with stressful situations, enter new groups and establish relationships, and develop awareness and respect for others' feelings and perspectives (Greenberg et al., 2017; Moy & Hazen, 2018). Fortunately, many of the areas addressed by Tier 1 can be easily taught or incorporated into everyday lessons. One way students may be able to gain a deeper understanding of their feelings is through art class (Richerme, 2020). Naturally, the art room provides a great place for students to tap into their feelings and emotions when they might not be able to verbally express themselves (Richerme, 2020). For example, an art activity might have younger children draw or paint their emotions on a blank face and subsequently describe to the teacher or their classmates the faces they make when they are angry, sad, scared, or even nervous. Subsequently, students can describe methods they use to manage their emotions or techniques that they have been taught to regulate their feelings. It is especially powerful when all educators and school personnel are reinforcing these skills exhibited by students throughout the school day and across the school-related areas (e.g., across the building, playground, bus drop-off area). Exercise 2.3 asks readers to partake in this activity to obtain a better understanding of their emotions and to better regulate such feelings.

Be Safe	✓ Keep hands, feet, objects to self
	✓ Use materials appropriately
	✓ Keep two feet on the floor while seated
	✓ Use walking feet down hallways and in the classroom
Be Respectful	✓ Use polite and kind words like thank you, please, and excuse me
	✓ Raise your hand and wait your turn
	✓ Use an indoor voice
	✓ Consider the feelings of others
Be Responsible	✓ Return classroom materials back to where you found them
	✓ Turn in homework at the appropriate time
	✓ Keep your desk clean
	✓ Say I'm sorry if you upset a friend or classmate
Be a Good Friend	✓ Take turns when playing games or in group work
	✓ Share materials and toys if you are not using them
	✓ Use listening ears when others are talking
	✓ Offer to help others in need

Figure 2.4 School Motto and Explanation of Expectations

Exercise 2.3 Understanding Emotions

Directions: On the blank face below, draw the expression you make when you are angry or facial features that would tell others that you are mad. For example, you might draw that your cheeks become red when you are angry and your forehead furrows. After completing the drawing, provide some coping strategies you use to manage your emotions.

What are some positive things you do to cope when you feel angry?

_____

_____

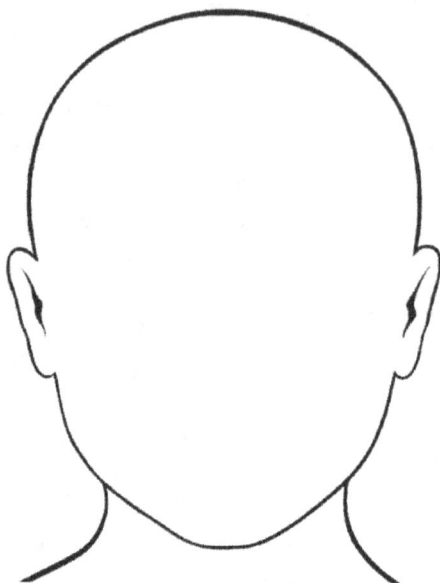

What are some negative things you do to cope when you feel angry?

_____

_____

Another activity may involve students working together on problem-solving activities or games that involve cooperation, perspective-taking, and respectfully expressing one's thoughts and feelings. For example, a math lesson may involve students working in pairs to see which pair can solve an algebra problem the fastest. The algebra problem the students are presented with may have multiple solutions. After the students have completed solving the problem, the teacher may conclude the lesson by having students review difficulties they may have encountered during the activity and explore whether there were differences in opinion over how to complete the task. The teacher may then have students explain how they overcame differences in perspective and tie it into how mathematicians have to work in teams to advance the field.

Other than classroom lessons and activities that incorporate SEL, teachers may include familiar games in their classroom with some minor alterations to the rules of playing the game. For example, the teacher may create social-emotional Jenga by simply writing different emotions on blocks (Gotay,

2013; Hasbro, 2017). Emotions may include feelings such as happiness, sadness, fear, jealousy, and nervousness. When playing the game, upon students pulling out a block with an emotion on it, the student will have to explain to the other players what that emotion means and how they show that emotion through behavior and facial expressions. Aside from games, the teacher may have books available during downtime or silent reading that promote mental wellness and coping with social-emotional concerns, such as the *Fix-It Friends: Have No Fear!*, by Nicole C. Kear (2017).

In addition to incorporating lessons and games that promote SEL at Tier 1, teachers may model for students how to complete brief mindfulness activities. Mindfulness is defined as a therapeutic technique that assists children in becoming aware of the present moment through acknowledging one's feelings, thoughts, and bodily sensations (Sapthiang et al., 2019). Studies have shown that the incorporation of mindfulness activities decreases children's levels of anxiety, depression, stress, hostility, and intrusive thoughts (Sapthiang et al., 2019). Teachers may easily integrate mindfulness and trauma-informed activities into students' daily routines by modeling and having students participate in meditation, deep breathing, or yoga. Moreover, teachers may incorporate self-soothing activities into their students' days through having them listen to ambient music while working on tasks or utilizing calming smells, such as oatmeal. Teachers may even have blocks of times set aside during the day in which students can practice mindfulness activities. For instance, a teacher may have her students practice deep breathing when they enter the classroom at the start of the day and do yoga at the end of the day before going home.

In addition to these activities that promote mental wellness, teachers may want to create "cool-down corners" in their classrooms. A cool-down corner is a designated place in the classroom where children who are upset can go to calm down and de-stress. Cool-down corners typically involve several objects and activities to assist children in calming down, including pillows, squishy balls, books, noise-canceling headphones, fidget toys, crayons, and paper. Cool-down corners provide safe spaces for students who are having difficult times. Through the use of cool-down corners, students have opportunities to temporarily escape what is bothering them and cope with their emotions more appropriately.

Aside from these more informal strategies of building social-emotional learning and mental wellness at Tier 1, a number of programs have been developed to foster prosocial behaviors in students and develop healthy coping strategies. SEL programs tend to share three common features: (a) increasing students' knowledge of socially and emotionally competent behavior,

(b) utilizing social and emotional competence in daily interactions with others, and (c) relying on social and emotional competence to prevent disruptive, antisocial, or harmful behaviors (Moy & Hazen, 2018). Two well-known programs that can be used at Tier 1 to develop SEL are the MindUP curriculum, an SEL program for children in grades Pre-K through eight that is designed to promote mindful awareness and promote the five SEL competencies (Crooks et al., 2020), and Second Step, a Tier 1 Pre-K through eighth-grade SEL program designed to promote interpersonal and intrapersonal competencies and reduce the development of social-emotional problems (Moy & Hazen, 2018).

Finally, at Tier 1 of social-emotional RTI, children are typically universally screened three times per year using measures like the BASC **Behavior and Emotional Screening System (BESS;** Kamphaus & Reynolds, 2015). The BESS is a brief norm-referenced universal screener that evaluates whether students are at risk for developing concerns in the following areas: externalizing problems, internalizing problems, school problems, and adaptive skills (Kilgus et al., 2018). In Chapter 6, readers will find detailed descriptions on common universal social-emotional screeners and programs utilized within social-emotional RTI.

Tier 2

Tier 2 supports are designed for the 10% to 15% of students who have not responded favorably to Tier 1 services (Ziomek-Daigle & Heckman, 2019). These supports at Tier 2 are provided in addition to Tier 1 services. Therefore, interventions and programs at Tier 2 provide children additional opportunities to practice and receive feedback on new skills and include parent/guardian communication (Drevon et al., 2018). Due to available interventions and supports for internalizing concerns lagging behind those of academic and behavioral interventions, time frames for the delivery of such services may vary over six to 12 weeks (Joyce-Beaulieu & Sulkowski, 2020). Similarly, time frames for progress monitoring may vary, but it is generally recommended at Tier 2 that children's progress is monitored at least every two weeks (Bruhn et al., 2018; Dart et al., 2019).

Although many of the services offered at Tier 2 rely on programs consisting of cognitive-behavioral interventions, there are some easy-to-implement supports that teachers can provide students. One of the easiest supports that teachers can provide students struggling socially and emotionally is that of coping cards. Coping cards are index-sized cards that children can carry with them in their pocket or binder to remind them of triggers that may cause them to feel distressed (Wenzel, 2018). Subsequently, coping cards provide children strategies that they learned for overcoming internalizing distress, such as using squeezing a stress ball or engaging in deep breathing (Wenzel, 2018). Additionally, coping cards may provide children a list of two to three people to talk to when they are experiencing difficulties dealing with their emotions (Wenzel, 2018). Due to each child experiencing different emotions in different situations, coping cards are versatile interventions that can be tailored to each student's needs. Children who utilize coping cards effectively may obtain a sense of accomplishment that they are in control of their emotions and possess strategies to help them cope with their feelings in a healthy and independent manner (Wenzel, 2018). Figure 2.5 provides an example of a coping card.

Aside from using easy Tier 2 interventions like coping cards, Tier 2 services for students with internalizing concerns consist of group counseling. Group counseling at Tier 2 typically involves three to 10 students and consists of standardized programs that are run by either a school psychologist or school counselor (Joyce-Beaulieu & Sulkowski, 2020). For example, at Tier 2, a group may meet using the program of Skillstreaming to teach children about social-emotional learning and character development (Raffaele Mendez, 2017). For students who have experienced mild to moderate trauma, programs such as Students Exposed to Trauma (SSET) are available to help children overcome feelings of nervousness and distress (Schultz et al., 2012; Support Students

---

Coping Card

Some activities, events, and settings that may make me upset include:
1) Reading aloud
2) Speaking in public

My body may be telling me I am upset when:
1) I feel lightheaded
2) I have a slight headache
3) My face feels sweaty

When I begin to feel upset, I can:
1) Talk to my teacher
2) Squeeze my stress ball
3) Take four deep breaths

Figure 2.5 Coping Card

Exposed to Trauma, n.d.). Through utilizing Tier 2 interventions and programs, it is hoped that children will learn and develop skills to positively cope with their social-emotional concerns.

Lastly, at Tier 2, children's progress is monitored at least once every two weeks using measures such as the **Behavior Intervention Monitoring Assessment System** (**BIMAS-2**; McDougal et al., 2016). The BIMAS-2 is both a universal screener and progress monitoring measure for behavioral, social, and emotional functioning in children and adolescents from ages 5 to 18 years (Jenkins et al., 2014). As mentioned earlier, readers can find a chart that details critical information on common universal screening and progress monitoring measures utilized within social-emotional RTI.

Tier 3

Tier 3 of social-emotional RTI is designed for the 1% to 5% of students who have shown limited response to Tier 1 and Tier 2 supports (Ziomek-Daigle & Heckman, 2019). These students have significant social-emotional concerns and may require intensive and sustained small-group or individualized counseling to address their long-standing difficulties (Ziomek-Daigle & Heckman, 2019). Consequently, these children are at considerable risk for developing a mental health disorder that may significantly impact their educational and daily life functioning. Unlike children at Tier 2, whose needs can be addressed by relatively simple and manualized programs, students at Tier 3 require intensive supports that are tailored to their specific area(s) of concern (Joyce-Beaulieu & Sulkowski, 2020; Ziomek-Daigle & Heckman, 2019). Consequently, Tier 3 services are designed to treat children who present with the highest mental health care needs outside of special education (Ziomek-Daigle & Heckman, 2019). Moreover, children at this tier tend to be progress monitored every week.

Although many interventions and supports at Tier 3 are designed to be delivered individually to students, other manualized Tier 3 counseling programs are developed to address specific areas of deficit that are relevant to several children through group therapy. For example, one program that utilizes an individualized or group counseling format to address the specific social-emotional needs of children is the Coping Cat program. The **Coping Cat program** is a 16-session manualized counseling curriculum designed for children ages 7 to 13 who are exhibiting signs and symptoms of anxiety disorders (Lenz, 2015; Norris & Philip, 2020). Coping Cat can be delivered individually or with a group of up to five students, with each session lasting approximately 50 to 60 minutes. As children progress throughout each counseling session, they learn to recognize thoughts, feelings, and bodily actions associated with anxiety through psychoeducation, exposure tasks, cognitive restructuring, and problem-solving (Lenz, 2015; Norris & Philip, 2020). An extension of the Coping Cat program has been released for children ranging in age from 14 to 17 known as the **CAT Project** (Kendall et al., 2018).

Since programs such as Coping Cat are not specifically geared toward addressing trauma in childhood, other programs have been developed to support children that have experienced adverse childhood experiences, such as the Cognitive-Behavioral Intervention for Trauma in Schools (CBITS). In brief, the CBITS is a Tier 3 program that utilizes psychoeducation, cognitive restructuring, relaxation, and exposure to help children overcome trauma (Cognitive-Behavioral Intervention for Trauma in Schools, n.d.; Franco, 2018). Exercise 2.4 asks readers to review components of social-emotional RTI that they are aware of being implemented within their school or that they have viewed in other schools.

Exercise 2.4 What Supports Are Available in Your School/ District?

Directions: For each of the three tiers listed below, write down interventions, supports, or services that you are aware of being implemented in your school or that you have viewed in other schools in regard to social-emotional RTI.

Tier 1

_____

_____

_____

_____

Tier 2

_____

_____

_____

_____

Tier 3

_____

_____

_____

_____

_____

Case Example:
Social-Emotional RTI

Child Background

Leon Johnson is a fifth grader at Thompson Elementary School in Niagara Falls, NY. Currently, he resides with his grandparents, Jim and Joanna Smith, in downtown Niagara Falls. His mother, Vanessa Smith, visits him on the weekends, and he currently does not maintain contact with his father. Leon has been residing with his grandparents for the past six months as a result of his mother and father going through a turbulent separation after years of dating. Leon has lost contact with his father after witnessing him become physically aggressive toward his mother. Consequently, the police were called, and his father was arrested and charged with battery. Leon's grandparents suspect that he witnessed more than one physical altercation between his mother and father.

Per Leon's mother, he was the product of a 39-week pregnancy, and at birth he weighed 7 pounds, 5 ounces. No complications were noted throughout pregnancy and delivery. Developmental milestones, such as walking, talking, and talking, were met on time. Leon's teacher, Mrs. Jones, and mother both report that they noticed a change in his demeanor and frustration tolerance after he witnessed his father physically assault his mother. More specifically, she noted that Leon appears to be "lost in his own world" and appears easily distracted by his internal thoughts rather than what is going on in the environment around him. Moreover, Leon's mother and grandparents have noticed that he appears to give up on homework easily, appears moody and irritable, is withdrawn, and often complains of stomachaches. When his grandparents took Leon to the doctor regarding his stomachaches, there were no signs or symptoms of physical illness.

Tier 1

To promote social-emotional wellness and prevent further development social-emotional concerns, Leon's school is implementing social-emotional RTI with embedded trauma-informed practices. Tier 1 of social-emotional RTI is designed to teach social-emotional wellness and appropriate coping strategies to all children in school. At Leon's school, several interventions and supports have been put into place, one of which involves three in-service trainings per year to help educate school personnel in the areas of social-emotional wellness and social-emotional learning, signs of concerns, and trauma-informed practices. Each of these in-service trainings focuses on how to implement strategies and techniques highlighted by the Collaborative for Academic, Social, and Emotional Learning (CASEL) in the five SEL areas of: self-management, self-awareness, social awareness, responsible decision-making, and relationship skills (Collaborative for Academic, Social, and Emotional Learning [CASEL], 2019).

In addition to conducting in-service trainings, Leon's school has employed a number of techniques to promote a caring, safe, and culturally responsive environment. The first of these techniques involves the school placing posters in hallways reminding students of coping strategies to use when they are upset, such as deep breathing and muscle tension and relaxation. Some of these posters incorporate quotes or pictures of racially, ethnically, and linguistically diverse famous and influential public figures. In addition to these posters, Leon's school has "mindfulness Mondays," in which students practice mindfulness exercises in their classrooms.

In addition to these strategies, teachers have the expectations posted in the classrooms that reflect the five SEL areas outlined by CASEL. For instance, a classroom expectation may indicate that the child "will make good choices," and a teacher led discussion could reinforce the components of "responsible decision-making," as outlined by CASEL. Moreover, Leon's teacher has incorporated a "cool-down corner" into her room for students to use when they are feeling scared, angry, or sad. In the cool-down corner, Leon's has placed bean bag chairs, pillows, noise-canceling headphones, coloring supplies, books, and squishy balls. Finally, Leon's school uses the MindUP curriculum to assist students in improving their self-regulation, building resilience to stress, and developing positive mindsets.

Tier 2

Although Leon fully participates in the Tier 1 supports in his classroom and throughout the school, his universal screening score was in the range for experiencing social-emotional concerns. Consequently, the child study team met, and Leon was placed into Tier 2. At Tier 2, Leon began participating in a weekly small-group counseling program consisting of five students whose scores were similar to Leon's on the universal screener. The group was led by the school counselor, who began implementing the Support for Students Exposed to Trauma program. Aside from participating in the Support for Students Exposed to Trauma curriculum, Leon and his school counselor worked together in developing a coping card for him. Throughout the 12 weeks that Leon attended the Support for Students Exposed to Trauma program, his progress was monitored on a bi-weekly basis.

Tier 3

Leon's progress monitoring data suggested that he would benefit from more intensive social-emotional support. Subsequently, the CST team met and recommended that Leon receive Tier 3 interventions. At Tier 3, Leon received one-on-one counseling with the school psychologist using the Cognitive-Behavioral Intervention for Trauma in Schools program. While taking part in the CBITS curriculum two times per week, Leon received training in relaxation techniques and education about his reaction to trauma. In addition to CBITS, the school psychologist and school counselor worked together to locate an outside mental health counselor to provide Leon with additional counseling. Over the ten weeks that Leon attended CBITS, his progress was monitored on a weekly basis. Results showed that Leon was making adequate progress. Therefore, the CST team met to outline how Leon's Tier 3 supports would be faded over time.

Conclusion

Multi-Tiered Systems of Support is a framework that houses two or more intervention service delivery models or "multi-tiered systems," such as Response to Intervention or School-Wide Positive Behavior Support (Averill & Rinaldi, 2011; Eagle et al., 2015). The intervention service delivery models housed within MTSS are best viewed as triangular three-tiered systems that increase in intensity and duration and are used to systemically deliver evidence-based supports to children in general education. There are four critical elements that link intervention service delivery models together under MTSS. These four critical elements include: a) varying levels of preventative evidence-based supports and instructional practices; b) universal screening; c) progress monitoring; and d) data-based decision-making (Freeman et al., 2015; Harn et al., 2015).

Although RTI and SWPBS are two of the most common intervention service delivery models, social-emotional RTI is growing in its use. This three-tiered intervention service delivery model focuses on promoting social-emotional wellness and preventing social-emotional concerns in youth (Schaffer, 2023). A key goal of social-emotional RTI is to foster the development of social-emotional learning (Greenberg et al., 2017). Social-emotional learning teaches children to effectively apply the knowledge and skills necessary to understand and manage emotions, set and achieve positive goals, feel empathy for others, establish and maintain positive relationships, and make responsible decisions (CASEL, 2019). Social-emotional RTI views each of the aforementioned areas of competency as interrelated and critical to developing positive coping strategies (Eklund et al., 2018). Ultimately, through using social-emotional RTI, educators can improve social-emotional wellness skills to best prepare children to cope with social-emotional setbacks and promote mental wellness.

A Primer on Implementation Science

3

Learning Objectives

After reading this chapter, you should be able to:

- Define implementation science
- Identify the aims of implementation science
- Describe the stages of implementation science
- Explain why implementation stages are important
- Discuss the relationship between MTSS, social-emotional RTI, and implementation science

Implementation Science

The remainder of this book will focus on the implementation of universal programs to prevent social-emotional difficulties for children. Readers should recall that implementation of universal programs within social-emotional RTI falls into Tier 1. Therefore, in reference to the chocolate cake analogy from earlier, if readers were to remove Tier 2 and Tier 3 from the cake, they would be left with Tier 1 (see Figure 3.1). Although this book is focused on how to best employ Tier 1 programs using the stages of implementation science, many of the strategies, steps, tips, and exercises provided in this text can also be used for selecting and implementing Tier 2 and Tier 3 supports.

The practice of implementation science began in the 1960s and was first used by the medical, business, and community professions (Forman et al., 2013; Moir, 2018). However, it did not begin to gain momentum until the

DOI: 10.4324/9781003343479-3

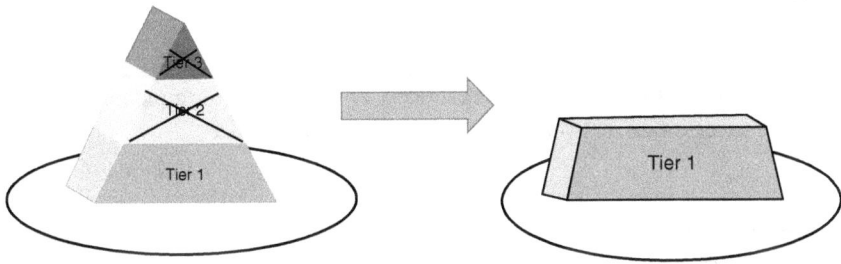

Figure 3.1 Elimination of Tier 2 and Tier 3

1980s, when many empirical studies noted how important quality implementation was to reaching intended outcomes (Meyers et al., 2012). The study of how programs and supports were implemented was further advanced when it was linked to the evidence-based practice movement, which first began to take hold in medicine and subsequently social welfare and education (Forman et al., 2013; Meyers et al., 2012; Moir, 2018).

Arguably one of the greatest reasons implementation science has grown in importance over the past 30 years is that there has been increasing pressure on schools to make the most of their funds (Bauer et al., 2015). Due to schools increasingly being required to maximize positive student outcomes in the most cost-efficient ways, implementation science has become more prevalent in the field of education (Moir, 2018). Consequently, one of the aims of implementation science is to ensure that organizations, such as schools, are getting the greatest return on investment on the programs and supports they purchase by becoming attentive to problems that may arise in employing these supports (Moir, 2018). For example, if a costly social-emotional program is implemented incorrectly or poorly by educators and subsequently shows little effectiveness in promoting mental wellness in children, it becomes a wasted resource and a financial burden on schools.

Implementation science is the scientific study of methods to promote the systemic adoption and integration of evidence-based supports into routine practice (Bauer et al., 2015; Bauer & Kirchner, 2020; Sanetti et al., 2019b). In other words, implementation science is a technical term concerned with the process of effectively moving research-based supports and programs into everyday use (Douglas & Burshnic, 2018). This provides educators a structure to successfully manage the use of new evidence-based interventions and programs (Duda & Wilson, 2015). By providing such a structure, implementation science provides a platform that can help schools apply and sustain programs with fidelity (Duda & Wilson, 2015). **Fidelity,** also known as integrity, refers to

Using implementation science	Without using implementation science
2–4 years to implement a new practice 80% success rate in 3 years	17 to 20 years to implement a new practice 14% success rate in 17 years

Figure 3.2 Success in Implementing New Practices
Source: (Balas & Boren, 2000; Fixsen et al., 2001, 2005)

the degree to which a support, such as a social-emotional learning program, is implemented as intended (Carroll et al., 2007; McKenna & Parenti, 2017).

Part of the focus of implementation science is on studying why evidence-based supports and programs may be slow to be adopted in real-world settings (Douglas & Burchnic, 2018). For instance, it has commonly been reported that evidence-based interventions and programs take an average of 17 to 20 years to ever make it into everyday practice (Balas & Boren, 2000; Chalmers & Glasziou, 2009; Morris et al., 2011). Moreover, only about half of evidence-based practices ever reach widespread clinical use, and only 14% of implementations result in substantive changes in practice (Balas & Boren, 2000; Bauer et al., 2015).

The good news is that the education fields may be able to significantly reduce the time it takes for evidence-based practices to be used in everyday practice through implementation science. By using implementation science, evidence-based supports and programs can be adopted and fully implemented with an average 80% success rate in as little as three years (Fixsen et al., 2001). Research has shown that implementation science is possible in school settings, with several tools and strategies empirically validated to support successful and effective implementation (Sanetti & Collier-Meek, 2019a, 2019b). Figure 3.2 highlights the success rate and time frame for employing a support or program with and without using implementation science.

Aims of Implementation Science

The aims of implementation science may vary, depending on the context and organization in which they operate. In regard to education, and more specifically universal social-emotional supports, the aims of implementation science are to:

1) Generate reliable strategies and techniques for improving social-emotional wellness-related processes and outcomes at Tier 1

2) Facilitate the school-wide adoption of strategies and programs that promote mental health and wellness
3) Produce insights and generalizable knowledge regarding the process to implementing social-emotional programs
4) Recognize the barriers and develop strategies to overcome obstacles to implementing social-emotional programs
5) Understand how evidence-based social-emotional programs can be successfully integrated and sustained

(Douglas & Burshnic, 2018; Eccles & Mittman, 2006;
Forman et al., 2013)

Through these aims, implementation science aspires to improve student outcomes by enhancing their overall mental health and well-being (Goldstein & Olswang, 2017). Implementation science seeks to close the research to practice gap by studying the success and failure of intervention and program adoption (Bauer et al., 2015; Bauer & Kirchner, 2020; Moir, 2018) and evaluating whether a school effectively adopts, employs, and sustains the use of a program (Sanetti et al., 2019a). Moreover, implementation science helps to determine whether such a program has the desired effect on students (Fixsen et al., 2009). For instance, if a school district utilizes an evidence-based Tier 1 social-emotional program, such as the MindUP curriculum, and it does not produce desired effects, the less likely teachers are to continue to employ the program and sustain its use (Owens et al., 2014). Therefore, it could be the case that it is not the program but rather the process of implementation that contributes to desired or undesired outcomes.

By using implementation science, schools can build their capacity to support all learners by not only using a program or intervention but rather consider carefully how the program or intervention will be implemented. Common elements of stages of implementation science include (a) a practice or program that is new or perceived as new, such as a school adopting a Tier 1 social-emotional program; (b) a communication process or information sharing between those who know about the new practice or program and those who do not know about it; (c) an organization in which the implementation process occurs, such as a school; and (d) an individual or group actively working to bring the new practice or program into the school (Forman et al., 2013). The stages of implementation science will be discussed next, but first readers are encouraged to take part in Exercise 3.1.

Exercise 3.1 Implementing a New Plan or Procedure

Directions: Throughout any school history, new plans, procedures, or evidence-based supports will need to be put into place. Think of a time when a school you worked for implemented a new plan or process, whether it be procedures for student arrival and dismissal, a referral submission process for special education, or a new social-emotional or reading program. Subsequently, answer the following questions.

Why was the new plan or procedure put into place?

_____

_____

_____

Did the plan or procedure put into place address a need that the organization, school, or staff were experiencing? If so, what was that need?

_____

_____

_____

Who initiated the implementation of the new plan or procedure? A principal, school personnel, a grade-level team?

_____

_____

Was there any training on the new plan or procedure offered? If so, can you describe it?

_____

_____

Was there a process for putting the new plan or procedure into place? If so, can you describe the plan?

_____

_____

Was there ongoing training on the process for putting the new plan or procedure into place?
___Yes   ___No

Circle how well-trained were you in the process of putting the new plan or procedure into place:

| Not trained | Somewhat well-trained | Well-trained | Very well-trained |

Was the process of putting the new plan or procedure into place successful or unsuccessful? Why or why not?

_____

_____

Were any modifications or alterations made to the original process for putting the new plan or procedure into place? What were they?

_____

_____

How was the new plan or procedure monitored to ensure compliance?

_____

_____

How did you and your co-workers know whether the plan being implemented was successful or unsuccessful?

_____

_____

Stages of Implementation Science

Exercise 3.1 asked specific questions to help readers reflect on whether or not they have experienced a new plan or procedure being put into place for a school or organization they have worked for in the past. These questions were modeled after some of the stages of implementation science and show that a lot more goes into employing a new intervention, program, or procedure than simply having access to it. As can be inferred from the exercise, implementation science views the practice of implementation as an ongoing process with the following unique stages: exploration, installation, initial implementation, and full implementation (Fixsen et al., 2005). Although each of these stages proposes a set direction with specific tasks related to implementation science, they are not linear, nor do they have a clear beginning and ending (Aarons et al., 2011; Fixsen et al., 2005). Therefore, it is best to view the stages of implementation science as overlapping one another (see Figure 3.3). In the next section of the chapter, a brief review of implementation sciences stages will be discussed. In the following chapters of this book, further detail and exercises will help prepare readers for employing a Tier 1 social-emotional program using the stages.

The first stage of implementation science is known as **exploration**. The exploration stage takes place when a school has not started training in a given area and is still in the assessment phase of determining the readiness of schools to move forward with an implementation effort (Aarons et al., 2011; Freeman et al., 2015). **Implementation readiness** can be defined as the capacity to employ an evidence-based intervention or program effectively (Aarons et al., 2011). For instance, during the exploration stage, the school district may evaluate the social-emotional needs of students, barriers to meeting such needs, and identifying Tier 1 programs that best address their students' mental health and wellness concerns (Freeman et al., 2015). Therefore, during the exploration stage, the school is building its capacity and understanding of available Tier 1 social-emotional programs (Bauer et al., 2015; Bertram et al., 2015)

Implementation Stages

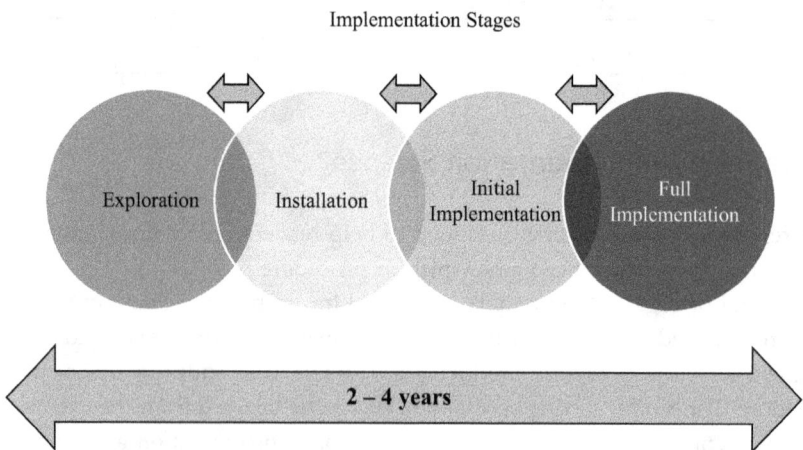

Figure 3.3 Implementation Stages

The **installation stage** involves the adoption of a new program and the development of performance assessment processes, initial training efforts, and the securing of resources (Aarons et al., 2011; Bertram et al., 2015). During the installation stage, district teams help secure needed resources to complete the work ahead and prepare staff for new practices. Therefore, the installation stage may involve the selection of appropriate staff to implement a Tier 1 social-emotional program, identifying resources to provide training in a social-emotional program, and ensuring access to equipment and materials (Fixsen et al., 2005).

The **initial implementation stage** entails staff attempting to utilize newly learned skills and is highlighted by the learning curve professionals experience as the school adjusts and integrates new changes into daily work (Aarons et al., 2011; Freeman et al., 2015). For example, a first-grade teacher may be learning how to incorporate a Tier 1 social-emotional program into her school day. This teacher may have been familiar with adjusting her day to incorporate different academic lessons but may be new to incorporating a mental wellness curriculum into her everyday routine.

Finally, the **full implementation stage** is reached when over half of school personnel are delivering a new universal social-emotional program with fidelity (Aarons et al., 2011; Bertram et al., 2015). During the full implementation stage, the "new" ways of providing social-emotional supports have become accepted and standard and are considered routine practices by over 50% of district staff (National Implementation Research Network, n.d.). Moreover, in the full implementation stage, the Tier 1 social-emotional learning program continues to be improved upon by the school and staff using it. Consequently, the program becomes an accepted practice that is incorporated into the everyday routine of the school and staff implementing it (Fixsen et al., 2005; Freeman et al., 2015).

One of the often overlooked components of the full implementation stage involves de-implementation. While implementation involves the increase in frequency and use of appropriate evidence-based interventions, **de-implementation** involves the decrease and discontinuation non-evidence-based practices and beliefs, such as grade retention, whole word reading, or the belief that schools cannot contribute to the social-emotional well-being of children (Shaw, 2021). Figure 3.4 provides a concise review of the implementation stages. More detailed descriptions of each stage are provided in the following chapters. Finally, readers can obtain a further visual overview of each of the stages of implementation science and components within each stage in Appendices A—E found at the end of this book.

Implementation Stages

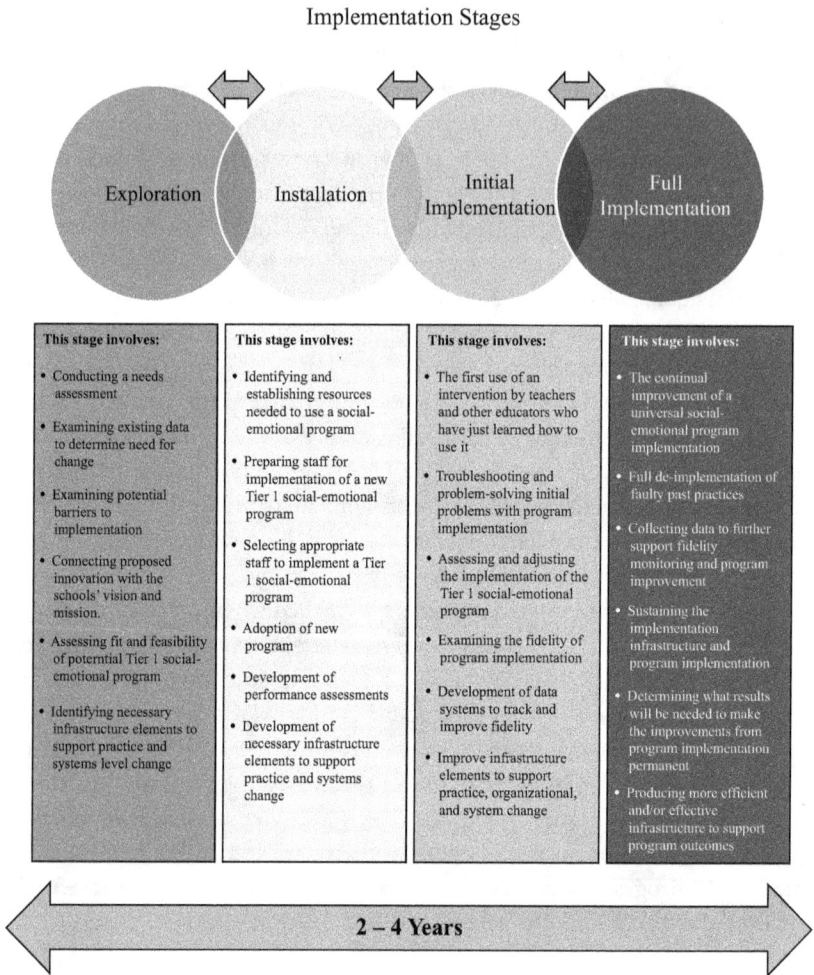

This stage involves:	This stage involves:	This stage involves:	This stage involves:
• Conducting a needs assessment	• Identifying and establishing resources needed to use a social-emotional program	• The first use of an intervention by teachers and other educators who have just learned how to use it	• The continual improvement of a universal social-emotional program implementation
• Examining existing data to determine need for change	• Preparing staff for implementation of a new Tier 1 social-emotional program	• Troubleshooting and problem-solving initial problems with program implementation	• Full de-implementation of faulty past practices
• Examining potential barriers to implementation	• Selecting appropriate staff to implement a Tier 1 social-emotional program	• Assessing and adjusting the implementation of the Tier 1 social-emotional program	• Collecting data to further support fidelity monitoring and program improvement
• Connecting proposed innovation with the schools' vision and mission.	• Adoption of new program	• Examining the fidelity of program implementation	• Sustaining the implementation infrastructure and program implementation
• Assessing fit and feasibility of potential Tier 1 social-emotional program	• Development of performance assessments	• Development of data systems to track and improve fidelity	• Determining what results will be needed to make the improvements from program implementation permanent
• Identifying necessary infrastructure elements to support practice and systems level change	• Development of necessary infrastructure elements to support practice and systems change	• Improve infrastructure elements to support practice, organizational, and system change	• Producing more efficient and/or effective infrastructure to support program outcomes

2 – 4 Years

Figure 3.4 Brief Overview of Implementation Stages
Source: (Bertram et al., 2015; Eagle et al., 2015; Halle et al., 2015)

Why Are Implementation Stages Important?

Educators may wonder why implementing a program or intervention in stages is important. Recall that implementation is a process and not a one-time event (Sanetti et al., 2019a). By becoming familiar and utilizing each of these stages of implementation science, educators can best ensure that universal social-emotional programs are being delivered successfully and with fidelity (Eagle et al., 2015; Forman et al., 2013). Moreover, by using stages, the large task of employing an intervention or program might be seen as more manageable (Forman et al., 2013; Moir, 2018). Aside from being viewed as more manageable, stages allow educators and other school personnel involved in implementation to understand that different stages require different actions from them (Forman et al., 2013). For example, how an educator responds to an area of difficulty at the exploration stage of implementation will largely differ from that of the full implementation stage.

Furthermore, by identifying the stage of implementation where the intervention is currently, team members are provided the opportunity to provide targeted support to staff within that particular stage (Duda & Wilson, 2015). For example, rather than focusing on the whole process of implementation science to address a concern, leadership can address the problem within the stage that intervention or program is being implemented in. Therefore, if the team is in the initial implementation stage, it would make no sense for a school principal to address the problems encountered within the context of full implementation. By doing so, school personnel may become frustrated, and resources could be wasted (National Implementation Research Network, n.d.). Overall, through paying attention to the stages of implementation, educators can:

1) Match their activities to that stage and increase the likelihood of successfully moving through the stage and onto the next one
2) Prepare for challenges and activities that they may face at the next stage
3) Reduce wasted resources and time
4) Increase the likelihood of the sustained use of educational practices
(National Implementation Research Network, n.d.).

Relationship Between MTSS, Social-Emotional RTI, and Implementation Science

In Exercise 3.2, readers are asked to work individually or in pairs to describe how they view MTSS, social-emotional RTI, and implementation science as being related to one another. An explanation as to how the three concepts are linked follows the exercise.

Exercise 3.2 How Are MTSS, Social-Emotional RTI, and Implementation Science Linked to One Another?

Directions: In your own words, describe how MTSS, intervention service delivery models, and implementation science are linked to one another.

_____

_____

_____

_____

_____

How do MTSS, social-emotional RTI, and implementation science relate to one another? As readers may recall, MTSS is a framework that houses models of intervention service delivery, such as social-emotional RTI and school-wide positive behavior support (Eagle et al., 2015; Wexler, 2018). In relationship to MTSS, intervention service delivery models are a singular three-tiered triangular system, the purpose of which is to systemically deliver increasing levels of evidence-based supports to children (Greenberg et al., 2017; Gresham, 2005; Harn et al., 2015). Finally, implementation science is concerned with the adoption of evidence-based supports and programs found within an intervention service delivery model (Eagle et al., 2015; Freeman et al., 2013).

Therefore, implementation science indicates that simply having access to evidence-based interventions or programs does not automatically mean that they will be widely adopted or properly employed or produce desired outcomes. As a result, implementation science suggests that schools study and evaluate the common factors and barriers that may be interfering with the proper adoption and execution of evidence-based supports (Eagle et al., 2015; Freeman et al., 2013). After all, if evidence-based supports are not being employed properly within an intervention service delivery model, the model itself is likely to fail students in the areas it is supposed to be assisting them in.

For example, a school district may have properly designed and implemented MTSS and the intervention service delivery models comprising of MTSS. However, if the evidence-based supports within those models are not employed properly or adopted widely by school staff, the intervention service delivery model, and more broadly MTSS, will ultimately fail the students it is supposed to be helping. Therefore, the underpinning of MTSS and the intervention service delivery models that comprise it is the proper and widespread execution of evidence-based supports (Forman et al., 2013). In other words, evidence-based supports themselves do not produce effective results on their own; the educators that implement these interventions and programs do. Implementation science is concerned with maximizing the potential of these evidence-based interventions and programs by placing educators in the best place to succeed. Through using and referencing the stages of implementation science, educators can better build and sustain Tier 1 social-emotional programs.

Conclusion

Implementation science involves the study of methods to promote the adoption and integration of evidence-based supports and programs into everyday practice (Bauer et al., 2015). The study of how programs and supports were implemented was first used by the medical, business, and community professions in the 1960s but did not begin to gain momentum until the 1980s, when many empirical studies noted how important implementation was to reaching intended outcomes (Forman et al., 2013; Meyers et al., 2012). One of the main reasons implementation science has grown in importance over the past 30 years in education is due to schools increasingly being required to maximize positive student outcomes by making the most of their available funds (Moir, 2018). Therefore, the aims of implementation science, as related to mental wellness, include generating reliable strategies to improve mental health, facilitating school-wide adoption of social-emotional programs, producing generalizable knowledge regarding the process to implementing these programs, and overcoming barriers of employing social-emotional supports.

   Generally, implementation science is broken up into four stages of implementation, which include exploration, installation, initial implementation, and full implementation (Aarons et al., 2011; Freeman et al., 2015). Common elements of these four stages include the adoption of a new practice or program, a communication process between those who know about the new program and those who do not know about it, an organization in which the implementation process occurs, such as the school, and an individual or group working to bring the new program into the school (Forman et al., 2013). Through utilizing the stages of implementation science, educators are better able to increase the likelihood of adopting a new program, utilize resources (e.g., time, cost) more effectively, and improve sustainability (National Implementation Research Network, n.d.).

Implementation Teams and Selection of Implementation Team Members

4

Learning Objectives

After reading this chapter, you should be able to:

- Define what an implementation team is
- Discuss considerations in selecting implementation team members
- Identify potential members of the implementation team
- Describe interdisciplinary teamwork and how to work on an interdisciplinary team
- Summarize the roles and responsibilities of implementation team members

Implementation Teams

Prior to formally engaging in the stages of implementation, a group of professionals needs to be assembled to initially lead the process of employing a new universal social-emotional intervention or program. This group of professionals, known as an **implementation team**, are charged with selecting and leading the employment of an intervention, program, or organization-wide procedure (Higgins et al., 2011). The term **team** itself can be defined as a group of people who share a common goal and are jointly responsible for

DOI: 10.4324/9781003343479-4

the completion of a task (Nielsen et al., 2017). The formation of a team is a means of organizing work so that professionals can accomplish more than they can on their own (Bell et al., 2018). To best meet their goals, implementation teams may include key personnel, such as school administrators or teachers, or key stakeholders, such as program developers or parents (Metz et al., 2015). Research shows that working in teams is associated with increased task planning, task completion, and social interaction (Nielsen et al., 2017). The overall purpose of the implementation team is to:

1) Increase "buy-in" and readiness for program employment
2) Install and sustain the implementation infrastructure
3) Assess fidelity and outcomes
4) Communicate with team members, such as families, educators, students, etc.
5) Engage in problem-solving and sustainability

(Tout et al., 2013)

Although professionals working in teams is common practice in many occupations, implementation teams differ in several notable ways. First, members of implementation teams both select and assist in the implementation of a new intervention or program (Higgins et al., 2011). Therefore, implementation teams do not simply choose a program or vision and instruct educators to use it (Higgins et al., 2011). Instead, members of implementation teams are actively involved in the employment of the support (Higgins et al., 2011). Second, implementation teams are concerned with broad and large-scale change within an organization or school rather than being charged with decision-making, consultation, or information gathering (Higgins et al., 2011). Third, professionals who are part of the implementation team serve both as team members (e.g., on the school team) and as stakeholders, representing educators and students who are most affected by the team's reform efforts (Higgins et al., 2011). Therefore, unlike other teams, implementation team members do not have just one identity (e.g., school principal) but enter the work of employing a program with multiple identities in tow (e.g., school principal, implementation team member, and parent-teacher-student liaison). Fourth, compared with those in conventional workgroups, implementation team members may show increased initiative and be more innovative in decision-making because they can facilitate ongoing improvements in school-wide or organizational practices (Grant & Parker, 2017; Nielsen et al., 2017). Understanding the differences in how implementation team members function compared to more traditional group work will assist in determining professionals who may best help in employing universal social-emotional programs. Exercise 4.1 asks readers to consider the top five characteristics that are most important to them in choosing team members to work with.

Exercise 4.1 Identifying Important Characteristics for Team Members

Directions: Rank the top five characteristics that are most important to you in choosing a team member to work on a project with you. If possible, compare your answers with a partner or group of four people.

1. _____   4. _____

2. _____   5. _____

3. _____

Considerations in Selecting Implementation Team Members

In considering members for the implementation team to employ a universal social-emotional program, several factors should be taken into account. First, the implementation team should be kept as small as possible, given the work to be accomplished (Bell et al., 2018). To be sustainable, the National Implementation Research Network (n.d.) recommends that teams should consist of a minimum of three to five individuals. Although other individuals may be invited to participate in the implementation team at times due to their expertise, these individuals may not have the same amount of time to participate in ongoing work (National Implementation Research Network, n.d.). Therefore, another consideration in selecting members for an implementation team is their availability. To ensure the successful implementation of a universal social-emotional intervention, team members need to be able to communicate, meet, and assist in the process of implementation regularly. Moreover, each team should contain one or more members who are knowledgeable about the program, understand how to support the facilitation of the program, and are committed to using data and feedback for continuous improvement (Bell et al., 2018; Metz et al., 2015).

These areas of expertise are important because implementation teams need to be fluent in the components of the program and the ability to make informed decisions regarding program adaptation to support fidelity (Metz et al., 2015). Additionally, implementation team members need to be able to use strategies to efficiently solve problems and improve program usage through data-based decision-making and user feedback (Metz et al., 2015). Furthermore, implementation team members need to be able to be aware of how to support and sustain program implantation through the implementation science stage-based approach (Metz et al., 2015). Moreover, team members need to be open to communication and willing to collaborate to improve access and reach of the program being implemented (Metz et al., 2015). **Collaboration** refers to the process of two or more people working together to achieve a common goal (Aarons et al., 2014). Collaboration is important to implementation teams because it often leads to important, influential, and motivational states that assist in the process of employing a program (Bell et al., 2018). For implementation to be successful, educators need to be ready to collaborate on the individual, group, and school level (Puga et al., 2013). For example, educators should be ready to collaborate in implementing a Tier 1 social-emotional program with another colleague, group of colleagues, or as a whole school.

Central to collaborating as a team is the ability to have a shared mental model of the task that is to be performed and of the teamwork involved. A **shared mental model** is defined as the perception, understanding, or knowledge about a situation or process that is shared among team members through communication (Puga et al., 2013). Research shows that teams who engage in collaboration coordinate efforts better under such a model because they have an accurate understanding of the tasks at hand and anticipate others' actions and needs (Puga et al., 2013). Some activities that may promote a shared mental model may include in-service trainings, meetings, videos, and reading common books or articles on implementing Tier 1 social-emotional programs. Additionally, some questions to create a shared vision over implementing Tier 1 social-emotional program include:

1) What is mental health and mental wellness?
2) What does positive mental health and mental wellness look like for children?
3) What social-emotional concerns is our team trying to address?
4) Why is it important that our school or a certain grade level to have a Tier 1 social-emotional program?

5) What is the cultural composition of our school?
6) Are any Tier 1 social-emotional programs currently available that are culturally responsive and for our students and our school? How so?

Aside from being collaborative and adhering to a shared mental model, implementation teams should be composed of a diverse group of educators. Regarding team composition, there are two categories of group member attributes: surface-level and deep-level. **Surface-level attributes** are social identity categories (e. g., age, sex, race) or contain easily accessible information (e.g., reputation, role, tenure in position) that shape how team members feel, think, and behave toward other team members (Bell et al., 2018). As educators or team members work together over time, they begin to uncover deep-level attributes. **Deep-level attributes** are characteristics that group members tend to learn about one another over time, such as personality traits, values, attitudes, and abilities (Bell et al., 2018). Both surface-level and deep-level attributes can influence the relationships team members form and how they collaborate with one another. Additionally, culture, privilege, and power also influence relationships and teams should consider how the interactions and team dynamics are affected by this. An attribute that may prove of great assistance to implementation teams is that of members with high levels of positional diversity. **Positional diversity** refers to those individuals who have represented a greater variety of positions within an organization or who have worked across various schools (Higgins et al., 2011).

Finally, in selecting implementation team members, it should be noted that team members' moods, receptiveness toward teamwork, and conscientiousness may influence the overall productivity of the group, as well as others' perceptions of these traits. For example, a team member's mood toward the work they are engaged in can quickly spread to others in the group (Bell et al., 2018). Therefore, if a person is positive or negative toward the project of implementing a Tier 1 social-emotional program, it can greatly affect how other members of the team interpret and engage in the project. Aside from receptiveness toward a project, team members who value teamwork and who are social have been found to be more confident in cooperative in engaging with others (Bell et al., 2018). These personality traits help the team in becoming a cohesive unit working toward the same goal (Bell et al., 2018). Lastly, teams with conscientious members tend to be better off at self-regulating teamwork. For example, a conscientious team member may not evade work and, as a result, is more likely to step in and assist others with their work (Bell et al., 2018).

Overview of Potential Implementation Team Members

To best consider team members appropriate for the oversight and implementation of universal Tier 1 social-emotional programs, it is important to highlight the roles and responsibilities that educators play at this level. **Roles** can be described as the positions that team members are assigned, while **responsibilities** involve the specific tasks or duties that team members are expected to complete according to their roles (Aarons et al., 2014; Lessard et al., 2016; Puga et al., 2013). An overview follows of the roles and responsibilities key educational collaborators play in implementing Tier 1 social-emotional programs.

General Education Teacher Roles and Responsibilities

The roles and responsibilities of today's general education teachers go far beyond instructing students in learning academic content. Instead, teachers of this generation arguably play a larger role in the development of children's behavioral and social-emotional well-being than they ever have before. When it comes to assisting students in developing social-emotional competence and fostering positive relationships with others, quality general education teachers are likely the engine that drives learning in these areas (Schonert-Reichl, 2017). In fact, a national survey of more than 600 preschool through high school teachers believes that social-emotional skills are teachable and that promoting SEL skills will benefit children in school and life (Bridgeland et al., 2013). Therefore, it is not surprising that teachers may take on significant roles in the delivery of Tier 1 mental health interventions (Franklin et al., 2012). Interestingly, a systemic review found that out of 49 school mental health studies analyzed, teachers were actively involved approximately 41% of the time in the delivery of social-emotional interventions and are often involved in the delivery of social-emotional supports at Tier 1 (Franklin et al., 2012). Clearly, this highlights the crucial and invaluable role general educators play in this process!

Given this, general educators are often regarded as being on the "front lines" or as "first responders" to assisting children (Sink, 2016; Wixson & Valencia, 2011). Consequently, they are often responsible for the delivery of the core social-emotional curriculum and implementation of classroom-level social-emotional interventions and supports (Björn et al., 2015; Franklin et al., 2012; Shanklin, 2008). One of the universal ways that general education teachers can promote mental wellness and social-emotional learning within the classroom is to create supportive and caring classroom environments for all students. To create such environments, the general education teacher may positively outline behavioral expectations, model prosocial behaviors, allow students opportunities to practice establishing relationships, rehearse how to enter in with new groups of people, facilitate opportunities and feedback for students to explore and express their feelings appropriately, and promote perspective-taking (Greenberg et al., 2017; Moy & Hazen, 2018). Another universal way general educators may promote mental wellness in their classrooms is to implement a Tier 1 social-emotional curriculum, such as Second Step.

Taking all the roles and responsibilities of the general education teacher into account, readers can see just how vital they are to promoting mental health and social-emotional learning in children. Moreover, through revisiting Chapter 2's example of a math teacher having students solve an algebra problem, one can understand how promoting mental health and wellness in children can be easily incorporated into an activity. To remind readers how the teacher promotes mental wellness, prosocial behaviors, and social-emotional learning in the classroom, a breakdown of the example can be seen below. Moreover, suggestions are provided as to how the teacher can even further advance the promotion of mental wellness and prosocial behaviors. Afterward, Exercise 4.2 follows, in which educators and future educators can think of times in which they have viewed these components being put into place.

Example from Chapter 2

During a lesson, a math teacher decides to have students work in pairs to see which pair can solve a problem the fastest. After the math students are in pairs, the math teacher presents the students with a problem that has multiple solutions. Once the students have completed solving the problem, the teacher concludes the lesson by having students review difficulties they may have encountered during the activity and explore whether there were differences in opinion over how to complete the task. The teacher then has the students reflect and explain how they overcame differences in perspective and ties it into how mathematicians have to work in teams to advance the field.

Lesson components dissected	How these components promote mental wellness and prosocial behaviors
• The math teacher has students work in pairs to see which pair can solve a problem the fastest	• Allowing students opportunities to practice establishing relationships
• Review of difficulties students may have encountered during the activity and explore whether there were differences in opinion	• Facilitation of opportunities for students to explore and express their feelings appropriately
• The teacher may have students explain how they overcame differences in perspective	• Promotion of perspective-taking
Additional components the teacher could have included	**Why are these additional components important?**
• Positively outline and remind students of behavioral expectations before having students start the activity	• Reinforces behavioral expectations when working with others
• Have students work with other children that they normally wouldn't work with	• Provides children opportunities to enter new groups and work with others who may not share the same opinion as them
• Model for students how to handle disagreements and provide an example of how two mathematicians have disagreed over solutions to problems in the past	• Allows children to see that even professionals have disagreements but still express themselves professionally

Exercise 4.2 Promoting Social-Emotional Wellness, Prosocial Behaviors, and Social-Emotional Learning

Directions: Using your experience in education, complete the chart below by thinking of a time in which you or a colleague used each of the components to promote mental wellness, prosocial behaviors, and social-emotional learning.

Components to promoting mental wellness, prosocial behaviors, and social-emotional learning	Examples in which you or your colleague used these components
• Allow students opportunities to practice establishing relationships	
• Facilitate opportunities for students to explore and express their feelings appropriately	
• Promote perspective-taking	
• Reinforce behavioral expectations when working with other students	
• Provide students opportunities to enter new groups and work with others who may not share the same opinion as they	
• Allow students to see that even professionals have disagreements but still express themselves professionally	

Aside from promoting mental wellness, general education teachers are expected to ensure that the instruction being provided in social-emotional learning is appropriate for the developmental and maturity levels of the students being taught (Werts & Carpenter, 2013). As a result, the general education teacher works collaboratively with special education teachers, school administrators, school counselors, or even school psychologists to assess and determine what programs and materials are needed (Werts & Carpenter, 2013). An additional responsibility of the general education teacher is to provide vital feedback as to whether a core social-emotional program is effective and whether there are any barriers to implementation (Franklin et al., 2012; Werts & Carpenter, 2013) within their classrooms. If a student is struggling in the social-emotional domain, general education teachers may seek out assistance from the school psychologist, school counselor, or special education teacher. Overall, general education teachers wear many hats in ensuring that students develop social-emotional competence.

Special Education Teacher Roles and Responsibilities

Due to classrooms being increasingly diverse and inclusive of all learners, it is important that students, as well as their general education teachers, develop the skills to better understand one another and work together effectively. Special education teachers can play a big role in supporting general education teachers to advance common understanding and differentiate instruction in regard to social-emotional learning and prosocial behavior (Björn et al., 2015). Over the past 100 years, special education teacher roles have evolved from solely working in residential facilities to providing supports in self-contained classrooms (Simonsen et al., 2010). Today, special education teachers have escaped their rather restrictive historical roles and are now increasingly teaching alongside general education instructors (Brownell et al., 2008; Hoover & Patton, 2008).

Special educators' expansion in their roles may be due to them having knowledge and specific training in (a) content and how to teach it, (b) specific problems that students with social-emotional concerns may experience, (c) the role of technology in supporting social-emotional learning, and (d) explicit and intensive instruction within a social-emotional curriculum (Brownell et al., 2008; Hoover & Patton, 2008). Consequently, given their training, special educators are well positioned to assist general educators in differentiating instruction and supporting students who are showing minor signs of developing social-emotional deficits (Björn et al., 2016). They can also work toward ensuring that children do not develop more severe or chronic social-emotional challenges (Björn et al., 2016; Simonsen et al., 2010).

To assist general education teachers in adapting their instruction to support all learners, special educators may utilize a variety of strategies. One strategy is **explicit instruction,** which is a way to teach skills or concepts to students using direct, structured instruction (C. A. Hughes et al., 2017). This entails explicit instruction, the teacher modeling the skill to be taught with clear expectations, verbalizing the thinking process behind skill acquisition, providing students opportunities to practice the skill, and providing feedback (C. A. Hughes et al., 2017). For example, the special education teacher may assist the general education instructor in demonstrating the concept of sharing to students and describing what is being done as it is being modeled. A second strategy is for special educators to provide peer coaching and performance feedback (Simonsen et al., 2010). Through providing peer coaching and performance feedback, special education teachers can help general educators increase the fidelity with which social-emotional programs and interventions are implemented (Simonsen et al., 2010). A third strategy is assisting in universal screening and progress monitoring of student academic, behavioral, and social-emotional progress (Björn et al., 2015; Simonsen et al., 2010). Ultimately, special education teachers tend to become increasingly involved in supporting students as they appear to have increasing difficulty in mastering social-emotional learning and prosocial behaviors (Björn et al., 2015; Simonsen et al., 2010).

School Counselor Roles and Responsibilities

Like special education teachers, the roles of school counselors have evolved greatly over the past 30 years. No longer are school counselors relegated to working mostly at the high school level with a few students or focused mainly on vocational guidance (Sink, 2016). Today, school counselors work across the K–12 grade levels and focus on academic, career, and social-emotional development (Sink, 2016). According to the American School Counselor Association (2019), school counselors collaborate with teachers, administrators, school psychologists, families, and community providers to maximize student success.

In regard to promoting mental wellness and preventing social-emotional concerns from arising in children, school counselors may work with school psychologists and administrators to identify a standards-based Tier 1 social-emotional program (American School Counselors Association [ASCA] 2019). To assist in the selection of a Tier 1 social-emotional program, school counselors may assess the school system and take into account the socio-economic status and cultural composition of the students being served (Bowers et al., 2018). After a Tier 1 social-emotional program has been selected, the school counselor may assist the teacher in delivering it (Sink, 2016). In delivering the program, school counselors can assist the general education teacher in infusing and reinforcing social-emotional learning opportunities with students, such as relationship building (Bowers et al., 2018). Other roles that school counselors may engage in outside of helping to deliver a Tier 1 social-emotional program include advocating for the most hospitable and equitable conditions in a school, assessing a student's learning environment and informing administrators of potential hindrances, creating realistic and achievable goals for their school systems, and reevaluating their supports and services and making adjustments based on student and teacher outcomes (Belser et al., 2016; Bower et al., 2018; Sink, 2016).

School Psychologist Roles and Responsibilities

The profession of school psychology is one that is often underutilized by school districts. However, these professionals possess a wealth of knowledge beyond that of completing evaluations for special education eligibility. According to the American Psychological Association (n.d.), school psychology is a specialty of professional psychology that is concerned with providing services to children, families, and learners of all ages with a special emphasis on schools and other systems. Some of the tasks that school psychologists engage and are trained in include data collection and analysis, counseling, consultation, instructional support, crisis preparedness and response, and development of academic, behavioral, and social-emotional interventions (Bahr et al., 2017; National Association of School Psychologists [NASP], 2020; Nickerson & Sulkowski, 2021; Splett et al., 2013).

In regard to assisting teachers and administrators in promoting mental wellness, school psychologists have extensive training in curricular and instructional methodology and behavioral health supports (Eagle et al., 2015; Splett et al., 2013). Therefore, they are uniquely qualified to provide leadership in the adoption and execution of implementing a Tier 1 program and in sustaining its use. One way in which school psychologists may assist in the adoption of a Tier 1 program is through evaluating whether it has empirical support (McKevitt, 2012; Shernoff et al., 2017). For example, the school psychologist may research whether the MindUp program has demonstrated an evidence base for managing stress and regulating emotions.

Another way in which school psychologists may assist educators in implementing a Tier 1 social-emotional support is through completing a program evaluation. A **program evaluation** involves the systematic assessment of whether a program or intervention that has been introduced directly led to a significant improvement in the performance of students, whether it be academically, behaviorally, or socially-emotionally (CDC, 2012). For instance, even though the MindUp curriculum is considered an evidence-based Tier 1 program, winter universal screening in the social-emotional domains may reveal that over 50% of a class is at risk for experiencing mental health concerns. Therefore, the school psychologist may conduct interviews or complete observations of the program being executed by teachers to determine what or if any areas are interfering with executing the program effectively.

Through these interviews and observations, school psychologists can determine whether a program is being implemented with fidelity. **Fidelity** or integrity refers to the degree to which an intervention or program is implemented as intended (McKenna & Parenti, 2017). When a program is delivered as it is intended, it has the best chance of succeeding. However, if a program is not delivered with integrity, it will not produce the desired results for students and educators. Some factors that may interfere with a Tier 1 social-emotional program being implemented with fidelity include the complexity of the support being delivered, the teacher's receptiveness toward implementing the program, familiarity with the program, and whether the teacher was effectively trained in the program.

Finally, school psychologists' knowledge in data-based decision-making may greatly assist in determining the effectiveness of a Tier 1 social-emotional program or in deciding which students need additional support (Eagle et al., 2015). As mentioned earlier in this text, data-based decision-making is the ongoing process of collecting and interpreting data to alter and improve practices to best benefit learners (Prenger & Schildkamp, 2018). The term "decision" in data-based decision-making delineates a variety of actions that can be undertaken in reviewing information that has been collected in regard to program evaluation (van Geel et al., 2016). Some of the actions that can be undertaken when engaging in data-based decision-making include those of setting program goals, adapting instruction and curriculum, evaluating the effectiveness of programs and interventions, improving policy, and reallocating time, funds, and resources (van Geel et al., 2016).

In making data-based decisions, school psychologists may work with school administrators in determining whether a Tier 1 social-emotional program is having desired results in assisting students. For example, similar to the example used earlier, a school psychologist may evaluate grade-level universal screening data and determine that over 30% of the grade is at risk for experiencing social-emotional concerns. Consequently, the school psychologist may work with the school administrator to determine whether the Tier 1 social-emotional program is being delivered with fidelity or is a good fit for students (Eagle et al., 2015). On a more individual level, school psychologists may analyze universal screening data to determine whether a student is placed at risk for social-emotional concerns (Eagle et al., 2015; Skalski et al., 2015). If the student's universal screening data suggest that the student is at risk for social-emotional concerns, the school psychologist may meet with the child study team and refer the child to Tier 2. Outside of universal screening data, additional data sources for educators to consider in determining whether a student might be at risk for social-emotional concerns may involve teacher interview, student observation, parent report, and frequent visits to the nurse since social-emotional may manifest in the form of somatic complaints (e.g., a student complains frequently of having a stomach or headache with no known medical cause). Overall, school psychologists can help to make data collection and analysis a less daunting experience for educators (Schildkamp et al., 2017).

School Administrator Roles and Responsibilities

When it comes to implementing new programs or interventions, effective school leadership is essential. Schools that are poorly led and overly managed by school administrators tend to lack a sense of direction and struggle to obtain educator buy-in (Little et al., 2017; Vekaria, 2017). **Buy-in** can be defined as an educator's acceptance and willingness to actively support and participate in a new plan or policy, such as the implementation of a Tier 1 social-emotional program (Yoon, 2016). When implementing a Tier 1 social-emotional program, school administrators can establish educator buy-in through (1) forming a shared vision over the promotion of mental wellness, (2) developing a collaborative and caring school environment, (3) seeking input from school psychologists, counselors, and teachers over Tier 1 social-emotional programs, (4) obtaining professional development on mental wellness, (5) using data to make decisions, and (6) utilizing staff effectively to reinforce the implementation of social-emotional supports (Choi et al., 2019; Kennedy, 2019). By engaging in these responsibilities, school administrators can help to empower educators in promoting mental wellness within the school and adopting a Tier 1 social-emotional program (Choi et al., 2019).

Aside from the aforementioned responsibilities, one of the major ways in which school administrators can support the employment of a Tier 1 social-emotional program is through establishing organizational support (Eagle et al., 2015; Kennedy, 2019). Consequently, school administrators are responsible for the allocation and dedication of staff, time, resources, and finances to implementing a universal social-emotional program. To best assist in streamlining and allocating time and resources for the implementation of a Tier 1 social-emotional program, school administrators may want to promote distributed leadership practices. **Distributed leadership** is an approach to management that purports that the designation and completion of tasks should not be left to a single person in charge or authority figure but should be shared among professionals within a workplace based on their area(s) of expertise (Augustyniak et al., 2016). Therefore, distributed leadership utilizes a "shared power" approach to capitalize on the diverse expertise of varied educational professionals and to foster cooperative practices to meet the more complex demands of school accountability (Augustyniak et al., 2016).

Distributed leadership sharply contrasts with the historical views held by school systems in which leadership is a centralized and specialized role designated for school administrators, such as school principals (Augustyniak et al., 2016). Therefore, in utilizing a shared leadership approach, school administrators may utilize school psychologist's knowledge and training in research and program evaluation to generate a list of evidence-based Tier 1 social-emotional learning programs. Subsequently, the school administrator may ask school counselors and teachers to review the list of Tier 1 programs and takes into account which ones might be of best fit for the school based on the cultural composition of the students being served and ease of implementation. In summary, distributed leadership is "leadership by expertise," as opposed to leadership by role, title, or years of experience (Augustyniak et al., 2016). Consequently, distributed leadership requires high levels of trust, transparency, and mutual respect.

After promoting distributed leadership practices among school staff, school administrators may allocate blocks of time within the school day for staff to work together in selecting and implementing a Tier 1 social-emotional program (Eagle et al., 2015). Moreover, school administrators may locate in-service trainings for the Tier 1 program and provide opportunities for educational professionals to embrace and work outside of their traditional roles in implementing such a program (Eagle et al., 2015). For example, a school administrator may provide an opportunity for school counselors to work with teachers on implementing a Tier 1 social-emotional program as opposed to engaging in their traditional role of scheduling classes.

Lastly, school administrators should seek to hire teachers who are receptive and have experience in teaching social-emotional programs at Tier 1 (Kennedy, 2019). School administrators should work with other school staff members on the hiring committee to best ensure that the professionals they may be hiring to implement a Tier 1 social-emotional program are knowledgeable about such programs (Kennedy, 2019). Moreover, administrators and hiring committees should consider whether potential job candidates are culturally diverse, have experience with culturally diverse students and families and can explain how a program might be adapted to best meet the needs of students from various cultural backgrounds (Kennedy, 2019).

Parent/Caregiver Roles and Responsibilities

Previous research suggests children whose parents or caregivers are involved in their schooling tend to have higher grades, improved attendance, lower school suspension rates, reduced risk for school dropout, and greater social-emotional adjustment (McCormick et al., 2016; Reinke et al., 2019; Wang et al., 2014). Therefore, children who have warm and supportive parents have relatively easy access to at least one individual in their lives to help them address and overcome their social-emotional concerns (Wang et al., 2014). In an educational context, **family-school engagement** is a term that includes both parent involvement (interactions and behaviors caregivers engage in with the school to benefit and enhance their children's educational outcomes and future success; McCormick et al., 2013; Wang et al., 2014) and family-school partnerships, where families and schools work collaboratively to enhance success for students (Smith et al., 2020).

Family-school engagement can assist in promoting the strategies and skills learned through a universal social-emotional program through reinforcing such concepts in the home environment (McCormick et al., 2013). For example, on the school website, a school counselor may create a video summarizing points learned through a Tier 1 social-emotional program and how parents can assist in further solidifying these concepts for students. Subsequently, a parent may model for their child how to engage in conflict resolution or provide relevant examples of when they viewed their child engage perspective-taking. In addition to reinforcing concepts learned through Tier 1 social-emotional programs, parents can assist in being involved in the promotion of mental wellness in their child's life through maintaining a healthy and supportive home environment, promoting positive values that mirror those promoted by the school, maintaining household routines, attending parent-teacher conferences, and volunteering at school events (McCormick et al., 2013). Overall, caregivers play a large role in the social-emotional development of their children.

Community Partners Roles and Responsibilities

Although many schools involve community agencies and partners for additional support for struggling students at Tier 2 and Tier 3, such organizations may prove extremely useful at further reinforcing social-emotional learning at Tier 1. Moreover, school and community partnerships can further promote family engagement, improve student attendance, increase on-time graduation rates, and improve student behavior and social-emotional well-being (Bryan et al., 2018). Furthermore, relationships with the community allow for the school to better understand their students' community context and therefore improve cultural responsiveness within the schools. For these reasons, schools, families, and community agencies need to form partnerships with mutual goals of increasing resources for children in the academic, behavioral, and social-emotional domains (Bryan et al., 2018). **School-family-community partnerships** are collaborative initiatives and relationships between school professionals, families, and community members to implement programs and resources that address children's needs, increase their educational resilience and strengths, and foster their social-emotional development (Bryan et al., 2018). Schools that form partnerships within the community may have powerful allies in promoting social-emotional well-being since many local community organizations may operate outside of school hours and on weekends.

Community partners do not simply encompass local mental health organizations but can include youth centers, religious and civic group programs, libraries, health-related services, and businesses that may further the school's mission to promote mental wellness. For example, a school may partner with a town's parks and recreation department to assist them in incorporating social-emotional learning strategies into some of their events, activities, and recreational sporting leagues. By doing so, the local parks and recreation department can further reinforce concepts learned from a school-based Tier 1 social-emotional program. Consequently, some of the responsibilities of community partners have include identifying areas in which the school and local organization can assist one another, combining and maximizing available resources to benefit children's social-emotional learning, setting short- and long-term goals for partnering with the schools, and formulating a means for data collection and analysis to see whether goals are being accomplished (Bryan et al., 2018; Shapiro et al., 2010; Vaillancourt & Amador, 2014). Figure 4.1 summarizes the roles and responsibilities of educators within an MTSS framework. Additionally, Exercise 4.3 has readers complete a similar chart to that of Figure 4.1 based on their schools.

Position	Responsibilities
General Education Teacher	✓ Create a supportive and caring classroom environment to promote social-emotional learning ✓ Facilitate opportunities for students to explore and express their feelings appropriately ✓ Promote perspective-taking ✓ Utilize evidence-based Tier 1 social-emotional program to promote mental wellness in students ✓ Deliver core Tier 1 social-emotional instruction with fidelity. ✓ Differentiate and scaffold Tier 1 social-emotional instruction to accelerate student learning ✓ Collaborate with special education teachers, school counselors, school administrators, and school psychologists to assess and determine Tier 1 social-emotional programs and supports ✓ Assist in the universal screening of students' social-emotional well-being ✓ Provide insight into the barriers to implementing a universal social-emotional curriculum or program ✓ Attend grade-level and child study team meetings to collaborate and monitor students who are struggling socially-emotionally
Special Education Teacher	✓ Assist general education teachers in further differentiating and scaffolding core social-emotional instruction and curricula to meet the needs of all learners ✓ Support general educators in utilizing explicit instruction to help make Tier 1 social-emotional lessons or concepts clear to students ✓ Provide peer coaching and performance feedback to general education teachers ✓ Monitor the fidelity of universal social-emotional program implementation ✓ Participate in child study team meetings. ✓ Become increasingly involved in supporting the needs of students struggling socially-emotionally at Tier 2 and Tier 3

Figure 4.1 Responsibilities in Implementing a Tier 1 Social-Emotional Program
Sources: (ASCA, 2019; Björn et al., 2016; Brownell et al., 2010; Bryan et al., 2018; Choi et al., 2019; McKevitt, 2012; McCormick et al., 2013; Sink, 2016; Wixson & Valencia, 2011)

Position	Responsibilities
School Counselor	✓ Partner with administrators, school psychologists, and teachers to assist in the selection of evidence-based Tier 1 social-emotional program ✓ Assess the cultural composition and socioeconomic status of the school to help determine the goodness of fit of a Tier 1 social-emotional program ✓ Assist the general education teacher in delivering a Tier 1 social-emotional program. ✓ Advocate for hospitable and equitable school conditions that best promote mental wellness and social-emotional learning. ✓ Refer and consult with in-school and out-of-school clinicians for students who display significant social-emotional concerns (i.e. consulting with the school psychologist or a mental health counselor) ✓ Maximize access to school-based and community-based resources and link children and families to these supports.
School Psychologist	✓ Assist in the selection of Tier 1 social-emotional programs through the completion of a program evaluation. ✓ Determine whether a Tier 1 social-emotional program is being delivered with fidelity through conducting interviews and observations ✓ Lead teams in selecting and implementing school-wide universal screening systems in the social-emotional domain ✓ Facilitate ongoing monitoring of Tier 1 social-emotional program effectiveness using universal screening data. ✓ Set up regular meetings to analyze data and make data-based decisions in regards to school progress in social-emotional program implementation ✓ Consult with teachers, administrators, and other school staff to determine whether a Tier 1 social-emotional program is effective

School Administrator	✓ Provide support for a Tier 1 social-emotional program to ensure educator empowerment and "buy-in" ✓ Create a shared vision regarding promoting mental wellness and preventing social-emotional concerns by working with educational staff ✓ Secure financing for Tier 1 social-emotional program initiatives ✓ Establish continuous educator supports and resources for a Tier 1 social-emotional program in regards to in-service trainings, books, or videos. ✓ Promote distributed leadership practices in implementing a Tier 1 social-emotional program ✓ Review and participate in policy changes regarding Tier 1 social-emotional programs with local education agencies ✓ Provide opportunities for school psychologists, school counselors, and special education teachers to work outside of their traditional roles in implementing a Tier 1 social-emotional program ✓ Hire culturally diverse and responsive teachers who have experience or are receptive to teaching Tier 1 social-emotional programs
Parent(s)/ Guardian(s)	✓ Reinforce the social-emotional strategies and skills learned in the school environment at home ✓ Maintain a healthy and supportive home environment ✓ Promoting positive values promoted by the school ✓ Maintain a household routine ✓ Attend parent-teacher conferences ✓ Communicate regularly with school staff ✓ Volunteer at school events

Figure 4.1 Continued

Position	Responsibilities
Community Partners	✓ Reinforce social-emotional learning strategies used in the school through activities and events ✓ Identify areas in which the school can partner with the community organization to best benefit children's social-emotional well-being ✓ Combine and maximize available resources to benefit children's social-emotional learning ✓ Set short- and long-term goals for partnering with the schools ✓ Formulate a means for data collection and analysis to if whether goals are being met

Figure 4.1 Continued

Exercise 4.3 Identifying Members of Your Implementation Team

Directions: Please complete the chart below to reflect the title, names, responsibilities, and areas of expertise of potential members on your implementation team. Recall that it is recommended to keep implementation teams between three and five members.

Title	Name	Responsibilities	Areas of Expertise
General Education Teacher			
Special Education Teacher			
School Counselor			
School Psychologist			
School Administrator			
Parent(s)/Caregiver(s)			
Community Partners			

Interdisciplinary Teamwork

After an implementation team is created, members need to meet regularly to become familiar with one another's roles and responsibilities. Previous research has shown that interdisciplinary teaming has a multitude of benefits for educators including personal and professional growth, increased job satisfaction rates, and communal support (Crow & Pounder, 2000; Fairman & Mackenzie, 2015; Nancarrow et al., 2013). **Interdisciplinary teamwork** is a complex process in which different types of staff work together to share expertise, skills, and knowledge to impact student and school outcomes (Crow & Pounder, 2000; Nancarrow et al., 2013). The need for interdisciplinary teamwork may be increasing in education due to:

1) The growing complexity of skills and knowledge required to provide services and supports to children
2) The increasing specializations and skillsets of educators
3) The need for educators to understand their roles and responsibilities when implementing universal social-emotional supports
4) The pursuit of continuity of care within the school system to best meet the social-emotional needs of children
5) The utilization of implementation science to best employ evidence-based supports and programs
   (Crow & Pounder, 2000; Eagle et al., 2015; Nancarrow et al., 2013)

In working with an interdisciplinary team, meetings should occur regularly and consistently (Metz, 2015). Moreover, creating an agenda and distributing it before meetings can help with organization, clarity, and an understanding of the purpose of the meeting. Upon meeting with fellow team members, while it is useful to share concerns about what is not working in meeting the social-emotional needs of students, the entire meeting should not be taken up by venting frustration. Therefore, one way to enhance the effectiveness and efficiency of meetings is to assign meeting members with particular roles as a way to be clear in expectations and accountability.

Some of the most common responsibilities of team members when running an effective meeting include that of a facilitator, timekeeper, note taker, data analyst, and active team member. The **meeting facilitator** acts as the leader of the implementation team and helps to clarify the aims of the group and ensures that all group members understand the topics to be discussed by the group (Reinke et al., 2019). Moreover, the facilitator helps to determine how to group is to meet the goal of implementing a Tier 1 social-emotional (Reinke et al., 2019). The role of the **timekeeper** involves assisting the facilitator in maintaining the meeting agenda's order by tracking how much time is allotted for each section of the agenda (Reinke et al., 2019). Therefore, the timekeeper ensures that excessive time is not spent on one topic during the

Roles	Before the Meeting	During the Meeting	After the Meeting	Skills Required
Facilitator	• Collect agenda items from team • Create meeting agenda • Distribute agenda to team 24 hours before meeting	• Start meeting on time • Manage meeting flow • Prompt team members • Actively participate • Determine date, time, and location of next meeting	• Complete action items	• Leadership • Communication • Organization • Time management
Timekeeper	• Bring equipment needed to take notes and to project notes/data (optional)	• Record decisions/notes • Asks clarification of decisions as necessary • Actively participate	• Edit and send minutes to team within 36 hours • Maintain records of previous meetings • Complete action items	• Word processing skills • Technology skills • Listen and take notes simultaneously • Fluency with meeting minutes form

Figure 4.2 Interdisciplinary Team Meeting Roles and Responsibilities

Roles	Before the Meeting	During the Meeting	After the Meeting	Skills Required
Note Taker	• Gather a note pad, writing material, or preferably a laptop	• Record what has transpired in the meeting in terms of key decisions made, future tasks, and dates of future meetings for implementation team members	• Summarize notes taken during meeting • Disseminate notes to implementation team members • Note future roles and responsibilities for upcoming implementation team meetings	• Good short-term memory • Able to process and record information quickly • Quick at taking or typing meeting notes • Word processing skills • Familiar with email to send notes to team members
Data Analyst	• Review data • Gather information on defined problems • Define new problems using data • Prepare visuals to display data at meeting	• Present and interpret data for the team • Actively participate	• Complete action items	• Like and feel comfortable with data • Fluency in using data management system (e.g., SWIS) • Able to interpret data

Active Team Member	• Recommend agenda items to Facilitator, as needed	• Interpret data • Ensure that new problems are defined using data • Discuss solutions • Determine how implementation and effectiveness will be evaluated • Actively participate	• Complete action items	• Able to define new problems with precision • Investment and active participation in the team • Commitment to completing action items • Consistent attendance at meetings • Commitment to inform problems and solutions • Evaluate outcomes

Figure 4.2 Continued

Meeting Agenda

Date: _____   Time of Meeting: _____

Facilitator: _____   Timekeeper: _____

Note Taker: _____   Data Analyst: _____

Team Member: _____

<u>Agenda Item</u>	<u>Check if Item Complete</u>
# 1 (Time: From _____To _____)	
_____	☐
# 2 (Time: From _____To _____)	
_____	☐
# 3 (Time: From _____To _____)	
_____	☐
# 4 (Time: From _____To _____)	
_____	☐
# 5 (Time: From _____To _____)	
_____	☐

Next Meeting Date: _____

Next Meeting Time: _____

Figure 4.3 Blank Sample Meeting Agenda

meeting and points out to meeting members when time is almost up so that matters can be wrapped up and addressed accordingly. The **note taker's** job is to keep a running record of what has occurred during the meeting and summarize discussions and decisions made by the rest of the group (Reinke et al., 2019). After taking the meeting notes, the note taker should distribute a summary of what has been transpired at each meeting to all group members (Reinke et al., 2019). Aside from the note taker, it would benefit implementation teams to have a designated role for a **data analyst.** The responsibility of the data analyst is to collect and analyze data before team meetings and to present such data to the implementation team in an easily understandable manner, such as through charts or graphs (Reinke et al., 2019). Finally, the role of an **active team member** is to respect and listen to the opinions of others and responding to questions (Reinke et al., 2019). Figure 4.2 presents the roles and responsibilities of interdisciplinary team members during team meetings, while Figure 4.3 presents a blank sample meeting agenda.

Conclusion

Before starting to engage in the stages of implementation science, educators should establish a formal implementation team. The implementation team is charged with the task of selecting and leading the employment of a new program or organization-wide procedures (Higgins et al., 2011). Implementation teams differ from other teams of professionals who might work together because they both select and assist in the implementation of a new intervention or program (Higgins et al., 2011). Additionally, implementation teams are concerned with making large-scale changes within a school and team members also happen to be educators who are most affected by the large-scale change (Higgins et al., 2011).

In general, implementation teams are kept small and consist of only three to five professionals within a school. Consequently, educators need to be aware of the roles and responsibilities of potential implementation team members. Some of the potential members that can comprise an implementation team employing a Tier 1 social-emotional program include the general education teacher, special education teacher, school counselor, school psychologist, and school administrator. It is important for educators who work together on an implementation team to utilize a distributed leadership approach to managing tasks and responsibilities (Augustyniak et al., 2016). Distributed leadership is a management approach that purports that the designation and completion of tasks should not be left to a single person, or authority figure but should be shared among professionals based on their area(s) of expertise. After establishing an implementation team, meetings between members should take place regularly and particular roles should be assigned. Some of the responsibilities that should be assigned to implementation team members include that of a meeting facilitator, timekeeper, note taker, data analysist, and active team member (Reinke et al., 2019). Finally, when possible, schools should form partnerships with families and community agencies and businesses to further reinforce social-emotional learning.

Exploration Stage

5

Learning Objectives

After reading this chapter, you should be able to:

- Discuss the exploration stage
- Summarize the key components of the exploration stage in regard to completing a needs assessment and engaging in resource mapping
- Describe the steps to selecting a universal social-emotional program
- Identify key resources for selecting universal social-emotional programs
- Describe to formulate a comprehensive program description when engaged in final program selection

Exploration Stage

The first stage of implementation involves that of exploration (Aarons et al., 2011; Bohanon et al., 2016). The exploration stage occurs when a school is determining its readiness to move forward with an implementation effort, such as implementing a Tier 1 social-emotional program (Aarons et al., 2011; Freeman et al., 2015). Consequently, the exploration stage takes place well before a new program or practice is put into place and involves assessing the need for change and creating a sense of urgency for such change (Bohanon et al., 2016; Metz, 2015). A common misconception about implementing a universal SEL program is that the physical employment of the program is the most important aspect of the implementation process. However, each stage

DOI: 10.4324/9781003343479-5

within implementation science is equally important in properly employing a universal SEL program.

To assist the implementation team in developing a common understanding for implementing a Tier 1 social-emotional program, it is important for them to create a shared vision (Bohanon et al., 2016). By creating a shared vision, an undivided focus on the promotion of mental wellness and prevention of social-emotional concerns can be established by the implementation team (Teague & Anfara, 2012). Moreover, a shared vision provides team members courage by encouraging them to think in new ways that shape their collective values in working toward common goals (Teague & Anfara, 2012). These collective values can then be spearheaded across the school to impact the ways in which educators advance social-emotional learning. Therefore, the exploration stage includes connecting the proposed innovation with that the implementation teams' vision and mission (Bohanon et al., 2016). Eventually, it is hoped that the implementation teams' vision and mission are shared by the whole school to best address mental wellness and social-emotional concerns in children.

To maintain open communication during the exploration stage, it is recommended that implementation team meetings take place on a weekly basis (Metz, 2015), although this may not always be feasible. However, by meeting weekly during the exploration stage, core implementation team members can plan for the infrastructure needed to appropriately support the new Tier 1 social-emotional program (Metz, 2015). In addition to weekly meetings, it is important for implementation teams to develop a communication process to best support the work they are undertaking, decide on a plan of action for meeting short and long-term goals, and judge the feasibility of different Tier 1 social-emotional programs fitting into the school.

Needs Assessment

One of the best ways in which implementation teams can judge the feasibility of different Tier 1 programs fitting into a school is through a needs assessment. A **needs assessment** is a systematic process for identifying and prioritizing needs or "gaps" between current and desired conditions (Altschuld & Watkins, 2014; Morrison & Harms, 2018). A needs assessment allows for the implementation team to understand what is desired and needed to achieve a goal (Pinkelman et al., 2015). Additionally, a needs assessment helps educators to understand current conditions and what staff want to accomplish to make such conditions better (Pinkelman et al., 2015). There are generally five steps to completing a needs assessment: 1) identifying key collaborators, 2) outlining goals and parameters, 3) noting strengths and weaknesses, 4) collecting and analyzing data, and 5) developing a timeline for additional data collection. Each of the steps to completing a needs assessment is discussed in greater detail in the following sections.

Step 1: Identification of Key Collaborators

The first step to developing a needs assessment is to identify key collaborators with specialized areas of expertise that align with the school's priorities and goals relating to social-emotional/behavioral health (Skalski et al., 2015). During this step, team members such as school administrators and mental health providers may review the school or district improvement plan and subsequently work together in forming a team comprised of teachers, paraprofessionals, and counselors to assist in developing a comprehensive needs assessment. This team can be the same as the implementation team that was referred to in the previous chapter or can consist of a different mental health or MTSS team. Exercise 5.1 asks readers to identify who is on their implementation team.

Exercise 5.1 Who Is on Your Implementation Team?

Directions: Looking at the previous chapter, who is on your implementation team? If you haven't completed this table in Chapter 4, take a moment to complete it now.

Title	Name	Responsibilities	Areas of Expertise
General Education Teacher			
Special Education Teacher			

Title	Name	Responsibilities	Areas of Expertise
School Counselor			
School Psychologist			
School Administrator			
Parent(s)/ Caregiver(s)			
Community Partners			

Step 2: Outlining Goals and Parameters

The second step in developing a needs assessment entails outlining the goals, objectives, and parameters of the needs assessment (McGoldrick & Tobey, 2016; Skalski et al., 2015). During this step, common goals need to be identified that align with the shared vision by the implementation team to prevent competing initiatives from emerging. For example, a shared vision by team members might entail promoting mental wellness and preventing social-emotional concerns from arising in children to the best of the school's ability. A common goal by team members might be to expand the school's inventory of Tier 1 social-emotional programs beyond that of grade one to that of grades two through four. A second goal by the team might entail identifying key populations placed at risk for social-emotional concerns within the school and basing universal program selection on these key populations.

Consequently, it can be helpful for the team to discuss and prioritize two or three overarching goals as to why a needs assessment is being developed and what is to be accomplished by completing a needs assessment (McGoldrick & Tobey, 2016). By prioritizing two or three overarching goals that fit into the shared vision, the likelihood of team members being on the same page will be improved. To help generate two to three overarching goals that can be incorporated into the overall shared vision of the team, the following questions in Exercise 5.2 may be helpful.

Exercise 5.2 Identifying Overarching Goals

Directions: Answer the questions below.

1. What do stakeholders (e.g., administrators, teachers, families, community) think the three most prevalent needs are in regard to mental wellness and social-emotional learning? Are these needs similar or different to what the implementation team thinks?

    _____

    _____

2. Who is the target population for the Tier 1 social-emotion program (e.g., students in particular grade levels, students placed at risk, certain buildings in the district, entire district)?

    _____

    _____

3. What is the cultural and ethnic groups make up our student population?

    _____

    _____

4. Is there an evidence-based program available to meet the cultural and social-emotional needs of our student population? If not, how will we adapt it to be culturally meaningful and responsive for our students?

    _____

    _____

5. How can the team and implementers of the social-emotional program enhance the well-being of students (e.g., reduce behavior problems, improve social skills, improve strengths, reduce bullying)?

_____

_____

6. How will the program (if selected) address the need, fill the gap, or enhance the well-being of students?

_____

_____

Step 3: Identification of Strengths and Weaknesses

The third step of a needs assessment involves the development of questions about areas of perceived strength, areas of perceived weakness, and the availability of time and resources to implement universal SEL programming with integrity (McGoldrick & Tobey, 2016; Skalski et al., 2015). For example, a question may ask teachers and school staff to indicate their knowledge of social-emotional/behavioral functioning or intervention implementation on a scale of one to five, with a one reflecting little knowledge and five reflecting great knowledge of MTSS. Another question could ask staff to identify the greatest obstacle they see to implementing universal SEL programming and list common barriers to implementation. Getting stuck on the barriers and not being able to see how the barriers could be resolved, in addition to educators thinking that their concerns about the very real barriers they face as it relates to implementation are not being heard, could be problematic in buy-in and moving forward in the implementation process. Therefore, hearing from those who are being asked to implement programming is essential. Exercise 5.3 has readers identify common barriers encountered in implementing a program.

Exercise 5.3 Identifying Barriers to Implementation

Directions: In the chart below, describe in detail the barriers YOU see in each of these areas (if applicable) and barriers that you predict implementers (e.g., teachers) may report. After completing each of these two areas, reflect with a partner or group any common themes that were noted in barriers among theme members and suggestions for overcoming the barriers.

Common barriers to implementation	Barriers YOU see	Barriers IMPLEMEN-TORS might see	Any common themes noted in barriers among team members?	Notes about over-coming barriers
Funding				
Staff/personnel to implement or support implementation				
Training				
Time to implement				
Technology needs				
Resources for implementation (e.g., materials, copying, books)				
Other:				

When developing needs assessment questions, whether it be to assess barriers, knowledge, or desires of implementation, questions should be developed in a clear, concise, and easily understandable manner to ensure that information is collected accurately (McGoldrick & Tobey, 2016). One of the most common mistakes in creating a needs assessment is presenting respondents with confusing, loaded, or double-barreled questions. For example, a double-barreled question is a question that is comprised of more than two separate issues or topics but that can only have one answer (Menold, 2020), such as "How would you rate your knowledge of social-emotional/behavioral interventions and progress monitoring?" To correct this, the needs assessment should ask two separate questions: "How would you rate your knowledge of social-emotional/behavioral interventions?" and "How would you rate your understanding of progress monitoring?" The data collected from a needs assessment can be helpful and accurate, especially when questions are clear and concise. Excellent needs assessment resources can be used and/or adapted for schools to use from the National Center of School Mental Health (2020).

Step 4: Data Collection and Analysis

The fourth step of a needs assessment entails the collection and analysis of existing data (McGoldrick & Tobey, 2016; Skalski et al., 2015). Data can assist in informing the team as to whether the district or school is ready for universal SEL program implementation and can help guide what type of program that could be considered. An important question for the team to ask themselves is "What does the data tell us about the target population (e.g., screening data, office disciplinary referrals)?" Analyzing data will help point the team in a direction to move forward and can then also be used to illustrate data trends over time (e.g., Are students improving? How much are they improving?), and identify students placed at risk (e.g., Are there particular students who are not responding? If not, why?). Some questions to consider include the following:

- What do we hope for our students? (e.g., improved social-emotional functioning)
- What do we hope for our staff? (e.g., improved classroom support and management practices)
- What do we hope for our administration? (e.g., decreased time spent on reactionary and/or harsh discipline)
- What do we hope for our families? (e.g., understanding of social-emotional skills students are learning in school)

Step 5: Development of a Timeline for Additional Data Collection

The final step to developing a needs assessment involves outlining a timeline and means for collecting additional data (McGoldrick & Tobey, 2016; Skalski et al., 2015). To complete this task, developers of the needs assessment should consider how data will be collected, when it will be collected by, and which professionals will be involved in data analysis. In data collection and analysis, tools like Google Forms, SurveyMonkey, or QuestionPro may greatly ease data collection and interpretation by allowing the needs assessment to be posted and easily accessed online. To ensure data is collected in a timely and organized manner, a professional should be allocated to lead efforts. For example, perhaps a school psychologist and math teacher proficient in statistics might partner in leading data collection efforts since their strengths and skills may lend itself well on how to best organize, tabulate, and interpret the information gathered.

Resource Mapping

Upon analyzing the results from the needs assessment, the implementation team can begin the process of resource mapping. In brief, **resource mapping**, otherwise known as asset mapping, is an ongoing process to identify, visually represent, and share information about internal and external supports and services to the school (Lightfoot et al., 2014; Skalski et al., 2015). Consequently, resource mapping consists of evaluating programs, personnel, and services that are available to students and identifying how such resources are currently being used (Skalski et al., 2015). Exercise 5.4 asks readers to summarize available resources. In the context of putting a universal social-emotional program into place, resource mapping entails that the implementation team addresses four areas by:

1. Identifying the school's resources and programs that facilitate social-emotional development and learning
2. Identifying existing limitations in resources, coordination of resources, and gaps in access to existing resources
3. Strategizing optimal use of resources to address identified potential barriers to implementation
4. Exploring community resources that can address barriers that school resources alone cannot address (e.g., how to support social-emotional learning after school hours)

(Sanetti et al., 2011)

Exercise 5.4 Summarizing Available Resources

Directions: In reviewing the key areas that resource mapping addresses, review your answers to previous exercises in this book and summarize such answers in the chart below. For areas that cannot be answered from the previous exercises, please fill these answers into the chart.

Questions	Answers
What resources and programs are currently available in the school to facilitate social-emotional development and learning?	
What are the limitations to available social-emotional resources and programs?	
What social-emotional areas do the available resources and programs address?	
Are the available social-emotional resources and programs up to date, or are there more recent editions that have come out?	
What are the potential barriers to accessing and implementing social-emotional resources and programs?	
Rank the greatest to least significant barriers in implementing social-emotional resources and programs in your school.	
How do you and your school plan to overcome these barriers?	
What resources in your community are available to further support the social-emotional efforts that your school is promoting? (e.g., Can your school connect with the local youth center or YMCA to coordinate and promote social-emotional learning?)	

Through completing Exercise 5.4, readers have obtained an understanding of one of the key goals of resource mapping, which is to ensure that implementation team members have a clearer understanding of available resources inside and outside of the school (Lightfoot et al., 2014; Skalski et al., 2015). Another important feature of resource mapping entails the optimization and enhancement of available interventions and programs made available to students. Finally, one of the most significant areas of resource mapping includes improving the overall infrastructure of service delivery to children through identifying areas of service overlap and discrepancies in service delivery (Skalski et al., 2015). Therefore, a resource map assists educators in identifying a school's available inventory of social-emotional programs and staff to assist in the implementation of such programs. Completing a resource map consists of three stages, including pre-mapping, mapping, and maintaining, sustaining, and evaluating mapping (Lever et al., 2014; Sanetti et al., 2011). Often these stages may have been partially addressed through completing a needs assessment. A detailed look at each stage of completing a resource map follows.

Stage 1: Pre-Mapping

The first stage involves **pre-mapping** and entails the implementation team establishing a clear vision, defining goals, and coming to a consensus on what will be mapped and what will be the process for mapping (Lever et al., 2014). For example, at this stage, the implementation team may establish a clear vision that they want to promote mental wellness throughout their school. The implementation team, through evaluating staff input and previous data, may note that many staff report difficulty locating universal Tier 1 supports and programs within the school. Therefore, the implementation team might come up with the goal that over 80% of school staff will be able to express knowledge of where to locate available social-emotional programs by citing the school's resource map.

At the pre-mapping stage, implementation teams need to identify the audience for which the resource map is being created for and any pre-existing lists of social-emotional programs that the school may already possess (Lever et al., 2014; Sanetti et al., 2011). If members of the implementation team are not fully aware of the Tier 1 social-emotional programs and other resources that the school has, key members of the team may want to inquire from other school staff members if they are aware of any such resources (Lever et al., 2014). Additionally, members of the implementation team may want to identify any lists that currently exist on Tier 1 social-emotional programs and find out the date it was created or if it has been updated since its inception (Lever et al., 2014). Exercise 5.5 asks readers to identify the audience that the resource map is intended for in accessing and utilizing Tier 1 social-emotional programs and resources.

Exercise 5.5 Access to the Resource Map

Directions: Using the checklist below, please identify who may reference the resource map to access and use universal social-emotional programs. After completing the checklist, answer the question.

☐ School administrators	☐ Special education teachers	☐ Families
☐ School psychologists	☐ School nurse	☐ Community partners
☐ School counselors	☐ School maintenance staff	☐ Outside clinicians
☐ General education teachers	☐ Students	☐ Other: _____

(Adapted from Lever et al., 2014)

Why do you think it is important for your team to engage in resource mapping?

_____

_____

_____

Stage 2: Mapping

The **mapping stage** involves convening the implementation team to begin brainstorming about available programs and staff needed to implement such programs (Lever et al., 2014; Sanetti, 2011). At this stage, implementation team members may notice some overlap or similarities in activities to that of completing needs assessment. However, it is at this stage or resource mapping in which implementation team members will truly solidify programs, resources, staff, and times that staff are available to implement a Tier 1 social-emotional program. Additionally, it is at this stage that implementation team members may want to identify funding sources for obtaining universal social-emotional resources and programs that they need (Lever et al., 2014; Sanetti, 2011). Some questions to consider or re-consider during the mapping stage include:

1) What staff are available to assist in implementing and consulting in implementing a Tier 1 social-emotional program?
2) What universal social-emotional resources programs do we have?
3) Are these social-emotional programs addressing our current areas of need for students?

4) Do any of the universal social-emotional programs and resources that the school has serve a similar purpose? If so, how are they the same or different?

5) What funding streams are available to assist us in purchasing additional universal social-emotional resources and programs?

6) How do we know if a program that we possess will be helpful for our students?

7) How often will the list of available social-emotional resources and programs be updated?

8) Who will oversee updating the list of the available Tier 1 social-emotional resources and programs?

9) How will school staff be able to view the list of available Tier 1 social-emotional resources and programs?

10) How will the school follow-up to determine which social-emotional Tier 1 resources and programs were ineffective?

11) Are there any Tier 1 social-emotional resources that are or can be shared with community partners?

(Lever et al., 2014; Sanetti, 2011)

Stage 3: Maintaining, Sustaining, and Evaluating Mapping

The **maintaining, sustaining, and evaluating mapping** stage is utilized to assess the effectiveness of resource mapping through monitoring various data sources (Lever et al., 2014; Sanetti, 2011). Given that available school programs, resources, and even student populations change over time, it is important to note the effectiveness of such universal supports in providing for the social-emotional needs of children. Consequently, at this stage, the implementation team must consider what data will be utilized to determine the effectiveness of available programs and the resource map itself (Lever et al., 2014; Sanetti, 2011). Additionally, at this stage, the implementation team should consider how data and feedback from staff will be distributed and utilized to inform future decision-making regarding available Tier 1 social-emotional programs and the ease of accessing and utilizing the resource map as a whole (Lever et al., 2014). Through data and staff feedback, the implementation team can better understand whether their social-emotional program and resource mapping goals were achieved.

For example, if the universal screening data indicates that 60% of children within a grade continue to be placed at risk for social-emotional concerns, the implementation team may evaluate whether the program was implemented correctly (or with fidelity), if proper supports were put into place, or if the program, in itself, was not a good fit for the student population (Lever et al., 2014). Additionally, through data and staff feedback, the team may find out that there were not enough materials to implement the Tier 1 social-emotional program or that the school counselor was unavailable to assist in implementing the program at certain times in the day. Therefore, data and feedback on social-emotional programs and the resource map itself assists in understanding the following:

1) The effectiveness of the universal social-emotional program(s) in place
2) Potential gaps in implementing the universal social-emotional program(s) that are listed on the resource map (e.g., staffing concerns, time restraints, lack of available programs or materials)
3) Ease of accessing the resource map
4) Readability of the resource map

To obtain data on both the effectiveness of a universal social-emotional program and of the resource map itself, staff may utilize several data sources, such as social-emotional universal screening data, staff interviews, and staff questionnaires (Lever et al., 2014). By collecting a wide variety of data, the implementation team can form a better picture as to whether the resource map is being utilized effectively, whether it has assisted staff in locating available supports, and whether the Tier 1 social-emotional supports and programs put into place have been effective. Exercise 5.6 provides a resource map that can be completed with implementation teams, while Figure 5.1 provides a brief questionnaire that can be distributed to school staff before and after resource mapping process.

Exercise 5.6 School Personnel and Social-Emotional Programs Resource Maps

Directions: Fill out the resource maps below with your implementation teams. For universal social-emotional program descriptions, please see Chapter 6.

Position	Name	What days and times are they available?	Contact information	Grades or populations served?
General Education Teacher			Phone: _____ Email: _____	
Special Education Teacher			Phone: _____ Email: _____	
School Counselor			Phone: _____ Email: _____	
School Psychologist			Phone: _____ Email: _____	
School Administrator			Phone: _____ Email: _____	
Community Partner(s) (If needed)			Phone: _____ Email: _____	

Universal Social-Emotional Programs Resource Map

Available Tier 1 Social-Emotional Programs

Program & Description	Grade(s) Targeted	Areas Targeted	Website	Is this program effective per universal screening and other data?

Desired Tier 1 Social-Emotional Programs

Program & Description	Grade(s) Targeted	Areas Targeted	Website	Why is this program desired?

Resource Mapping Questionnaire

Date: _____

Position: _____

Questions to ask before and after resource mapping has been put into place:

1) What is your current level of awareness of available universal social-emotional resources and programs that your school has?
   ☐ No awareness   ☐ A little awareness   ☐ Some awareness
   ☐ A lot of awareness

2) If you have awareness of some of the universal social-emotional resources and programs that our school has, what are they?

   _____

   _____

   _____

3) What is the level of difficulty you have experienced in accessing information regarding the universal social-emotional resources and programs that our school has available?
   ☐ Very Difficult   ☐ Difficult   ☐ Neither difficult nor easy
   ☐ Easy   ☐ Very Easy

4) How frequently have you reviewed the inventory of universal social-emotional programs and resources that our school has?
   ☐ Never   ☐ Seldom   ☐ Sometimes   ☐ Frequently
   ☐ Always

Questions to ask after resource mapping has been put into place:

1) Did the resource map help facilitate coordination and communication regarding universal social-emotional resources and programs? If so, how so?

   _____

   _____

   _____

Figure 5.1 Resource Mapping Questionnaire

2) Has the resource map increased your awareness of available universal social-emotional resources and programs? Please explain.

_____

_____

_____

3) How would you rate the ease of reading the resource map?
   ☐ Very Difficult   ☐ Difficult   ☐ Neither difficult or easy
   ☐ Easy   ☐ Very Easy

4) How would you rate the ease of accessing the resource map?
   ☐ Very Difficult   ☐ Difficult   ☐ Neither difficult or easy
   ☐ Easy   ☐ Very Easy

5) How would you improve the resource map?

_____

_____

_____

(Lever et al., 2014; Sanetti, 2011)

Figure 5.1 Continued

Program Selection

Selecting a universal social-emotional program is no small task, and there is a tendency for schools to buy new programs marketed as solving all their problems without reference to whether they have been proven to work (Moir, 2018; Slavin, 2002). The process of program selection can be arduous, confusing, and time-consuming if implementation teams do not know what steps to take in program selection. However, if a program is selected correctly and yields the desired response in promoting social-emotional well-being in students, it can lead to more consistent and efficient student progress academically, behaviorally, socially, and emotionally (Leko et al., 2019). Moreover, adequate program selection can minimize educator frustration over wasted time and resources in attempting to implement ineffective supports. In selecting a program, there are generally five steps to consider, which include: 1) identifying evidence-based or evidence-informed programs, 2) assessing the cost of the program, 3) considering the complexity and transferability of the program, and 4) determining the contextual and cultural fit of the program (Leko et al., 2019). Each of these steps must carefully be considered and followed before selecting a program and implementing it in the installation stage.

Step 1: Identifying Evidence-Based Program Candidates

When selecting a universal social-emotional program, it is important for implementation teams and educators using it to be able to identify and know where to find evidence-based or evidence-informed programs (Leko et al., 2019). Over the years, there have been many terms to identify what is believed to be the most effective interventions, supports, and programs. Often the terms "research-based practices" and "evidence-based practices" are used interchangeably by educators (Cook & Cook, 2011). However, even though both of these labels share the same underlying purpose to denote and determine effective practices, each term has a distinct meaning and implies different standards (Cook & Cook, 2011).

As defined in Chapter 1, evidence-based practices are instructional techniques or programs that are empirically supported and that have been proven to be effective at treating a presenting problem (Cook & Cook, 2011; Zyromski et al., 2018). **Empirically supported programs** can be defined as those that have been researched and published in credible outlets that make use of peer reviews, such as scholarly journals (Royse et al., 2016). Evidence-based practice originated in medicine in the 1990s to "up the ante" in terms of research support required to determine whether a practice is effective and works best (Cook & Cook, 2011) and quickly spread to other fields, such as agriculture and education, to describe an intervention, program, or support that has a trustworthy body of research that meets specific standards of rigor (Cook & Cook, 2011). Generally, for an intervention or program to be considered an evidence-based practice, four factors have to be considered and met: research design, quality of the research, quantity of the research, and magnitude of the effect of supporting studies.

Research-based practices differ from evidence-based practices in that the term is used loosely to describe interventions and programs that range from being supported by rigorous and robust research base to those supported by meager and flawed research methods (Cook & Cook, 2011). Therefore, research-based practices may have some of the four factors mentioned for an intervention or program to be considered evidence-based but not all of them. Below is a description of the four factors needed for an intervention or program to be considered evidence-based.

Factor 1: Research Design

In order for an intervention or program to be considered evidence-based, certain study designs are needed to demonstrate whether an intervention or program causes a change in a student's emotional well-being or internalizing behavior. Two of the most common types of research studies that demonstrate a cause-and-effect relationship are group experimental or quasi-experimental designs. Both of these study designs are common in helping to determine whether an intervention or program is effective in obtaining desired results. In short, an **experimental design** randomly assigns participants to either a group receiving treatment from the new program or the control group, which receives either no treatment or the standard course of treatment before the new program has been implemented (Miller et al., 2020). For example, to run a true experimental design, the MindUP curriculum is implemented in a classroom with a group of 25 students, while another group of 25 students does not receive the MindUP curriculum.

Like a true experimental design, a **quasi-experimental design** aims to establish a cause-and-effect relationship but does not randomly assign individuals to groups often due to ethical or practical reasons. Ultimately, for a universal social-emotional program to be considered evidence-based, it has to be evaluated using either experimental or quasi-experimental research designs (Cook & Cook, 2011). By using experimental and quasi-experimental designs, alternative explanations for what may have caused changes in students' social-emotional well-being can be ruled out.

Factor 2: Quality of Research Studies

Outside of having a good research design, the studies that show that the program is effective have to be properly conducted (Cook & Cook, 2011). In other words, a team of researchers may select to use an experimental design in determining whether the MindUP program is effective and reducing anxiety in children but implement the program incorrectly. Moreover, the study may have used the MindUP curriculum alongside that of the Second Step program. Consequently, the results of determining whether the MindUp curriculum is effective at reducing anxiety in children can be drawn into question, and the finding of the study itself may be misleading (Cook & Cook, 2011). Overall, if the studies completed on a program are not designed properly, they draw into question whether a program can be considered evidence-based.

Factor 3: Quantity of Research Studies

Another factor in considering whether a program is evidence-based concerns the number of quality studies published. Although confidence in research findings is never absolute, it is strengthened when multiple studies find similar results on the effectiveness of a program (Cook & Cook, 2011). Therefore, the more quality studies that find that a program is effective and share similar findings, the better. Previously, it has been recommended that a program shows promise for being evidence-based when the following factors are present:

(a)   There are at least five or more studies on the program
(b)   Studies on the program have been published in scholarly journals
(c)   These studies have been conducted in at least three geographical locations
(d)   These studies were conducted by at least three different researchers
(e)   These studies included at least 20 participants across all the research conducted

(Cook & Cook, 2011; Horner et al., 2005)

Ultimately, for a program to be considered evidence-based, a number of studies need to be published that converge on similar findings that the program is effective.

Factor 4: Magnitude of Effect

Finally, in order for a universal program to be considered evidence-based, it has to demonstrate a strong magnitude of effect. **Magnitude of effect** refers to the strength of two variables or how strong the correlation is between the implementation of a program and the desired results (Cook & Cook, 2011). In other words, studying the magnitude of effect allows researchers to move beyond the question of whether a social-emotional program works or not to the question of "How well or how strongly does the program work in producing desired results?" (Cook & Cook, 2011). In thinking about magnitude of effect, readers can use the example of an electric screwdriver. The electric screwdriver may turn and effectively screw into soft surfaces, such as drywall. However, the same screwdriver may not effectively screw into hard surfaces like wood. Therefore, researchers might say it has a low magnitude of effect. It does what it is supposed to do, but it does not do it well. In thinking about this concept of magnitude of effect and social-emotional programs, educators likely would prefer a universal social-emotional program that does what it is supposed to do with a strong magnitude of effect. Therefore, educators want the program to strongly produce positive social-emotional outcomes for all learners as opposed to a program that weakly produces results. Figure 5.2 summarizes some of the key differences between evidence-based and research-based practices.

Distinguishing characteristics	Evidence-based practices	Research-based practices
Design research studies	Supporting studies must establish a cause-and-effect relationship, or causality. Research is typically restricted to group or quasi-experiments.	Supporting studies might use any research design, including those that do not establish a cause-and-effect relationship (i.e. correlational research, case studies, and qualitative research).
Quality of research studies	Supporting studies must address rigorous and robust indicators of methodological quality.	Quality of supporting studies may not be systemically evaluated.
Quantity of research studies	Typically supported by >1 studies of acceptable quality and design.	Might be supported by a single study.
Magnitude of research studies	Supporting studies must meet a prescribed level of effect, such as statistical significance.	No criteria applied for minimum effect.

(Adapted from Cook & Cook, 2011)

Figure 5.2 Differences Between Evidence-Based and Research-Based Practices

Step 2: Assessing the Cost of the Program

Step two in selecting a universal social-emotional program involves assessing the cost of implementing the program. Although cost is usually associated with monetary value, the **cost** in the implementation of a social-emotional program is defined as any resource used to employ an intervention (Hunter et al., 2018). Therefore, costs may have a dollar value, such as purchasing tangible supplies or the program itself, or they also might take the form of opportunity costs (Hunter et al., 2018). **Opportunity costs** are resources used in implementation of a program that could have been utilized in another capacity if the program was not put into place, such as teachers' time being used to implement the support (Hunter et al., 2018).

To fully evaluate the cost of implementing a program, four factors should be considered: (a) personnel, (b) facilities, (c) materials and equipment, and (d) other program inputs. **Personnel** refers to the human resources required to implement a program, such as school staff, trainers, consultants, or even volunteers (Hunter et al., 2018). Generally, acquiring, sustaining, and utilizing personnel to implement a universal program that make up most of the costs of employing it. **Facilities** are defined as the physical space needed for implementing a program, such as lighting, classroom space, and storage (Hunter et al., 2018). **Materials and equipment** are tangible items required for program implementation, such as program manuals, technological resources, and office supplies (Hunter et al., 2018). Lastly, **other program inputs** refer to other categories necessary to ensure the fidelity of program implementation like professional development and in-service training (Hunter et al., 2018).

To help calculate the costs of implementing a program, the Center for Benefit-Cost Studies of Education at Columbia University created an online application, CostOut, to assist in estimating the costs and cost-effectiveness of educational programs (Hollands et al., 2015). The CostOut program is set up with US prices and geographical inflation indices (Hollands et al., 2015). Moreover, market prices, such as salaries for educational staff, are kept up to date within the CostOut database. The CostOut program takes into consideration many factors associated with program implementation that have been reviewed in this chapter, such as materials, equipment, personnel, and facilities (Hollands et al., 2015).

Step 3: Considering Program Complexity and Transferability

In considering universal social-emotional programs, implementation teams should take into account the complexity of the program to be implemented and whether it can be easily transferred to other educators (Leko et al., 2019). **Program complexity** considers the number of steps needed to successfully implement the program along with the number of materials required for program implementation, data collection demands, and training needed to achieve fidelity (Leko et al., 2019). **Transferability** refers to the degree to which a program can be transferred to another educator and paraprofessional (Leko et al., 2019). Overall, programs that have fewer steps, materials, data collection demands, and training are less complex and more transferable than programs that have more components, materials, data collection demands, and training.

Step 4: Determining the Contextual and Cultural Fit of the Program

The final step in selecting a universal social-emotional program is considering whether it is contextually appropriate. In selecting a contextually appropriate program, implementation teams and educators should consider potential mismatches between the features of the program and factors such as student characteristics and needs, materials and existing infrastructure, and available time. Therefore, in selecting a social-emotional program, educators should choose one that is based on the students' social, emotional, cultural, and language needs (Leko et al., 2019). For example, a universal social-emotional program that is only available in English may not work well in a school where most of the students are English Language Learners. Some questions that educators can ask themselves when selecting a Tier 1 social-emotional programs for diverse populations include:

1) What is the cultural, racial, ethnic, socioeconomic status, religious, etc. composition of the students in my school?
2) What Tier 1 social-emotional programs have been used with diverse learners?

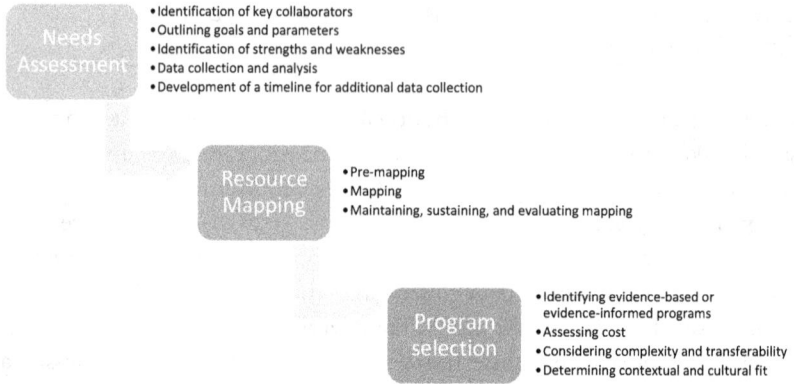

Needs Assessment
- Identification of key collaborators
- Outlining goals and parameters
- Identification of strengths and weaknesses
- Data collection and analysis
- Development of a timeline for additional data collection

Resource Mapping
- Pre-mapping
- Mapping
- Maintaining, sustaining, and evaluating mapping

Program selection
- Identifying evidence-based or evidence-informed programs
- Assessing cost
- Considering complexity and transferability
- Determining contextual and cultural fit

Figure 5.3 Key Components of Exploration Stage

3) If there are Tier 1 social-emotional programs that have been used with diverse learners, are they evidence-based or evidence-informed?
4) What modifications or adaptations may have to be made to existing Tier 1 social-emotional programs for the diverse populations at my school?

In addition to culture, implementation team members and educators should consider whether the school already has existing materials and infrastructure to implement the program. For example, should a universal social-emotional program require the use of tablets, computers, or smartboards, a school may have to consider whether they can afford these materials or whether they are already in possession of them. Additionally, a school should consider whether their existing time blocks fit well with a program that they are selecting (Leko et al., 2019). For instance, a program that requires a 90-minute block of instruction would not fit well in a high school in which class periods are only 55 minutes long (Leko et al., 2019). Ultimately, there are many contextual factors to consider in selecting a universal social-emotional program. Figure 5.3 provides an overview of the key components of the exploration stage.

Resources for Selecting Programs

Although selecting a universal social-emotional program can be a daunting task, there are many resources available to assist implementation teams and educators. For example, CASEL has compiled two guides to assist schools in selecting social-emotional programs. One guide is designed for the preschool to elementary school population, and the other program is designed for the middle-to-high-school population. The program guides consist of lists of CASEL SELect social-emotional programs that are well-designed to promote mental well-being in students (Lawson et al., 2019). Therefore, these programs meet CASEL standards to be considered evidence-based in promoting social-emotional learning (Lawson et al., 2019). More specifically, all CASEL SELect programs address the five SEL competencies of self-awareness, self-management, social awareness, relationship skills, and responsible decision-making (Lawson et al., 2019).

Outside the CASEL and their SELect guides, a comprehensive registry of social, emotional, and behavioral programs has been compiled by the Blueprints for Healthy Youth Development (Blueprints for Healthy Youth Development, 2020). One of the goals of the registry is to promote programs with the strongest scientific evidence to best benefit children (Blueprints for Healthy Youth Development, 2020). Similar to the registry developed by the Blueprints for Healthy Youth Development, What Works Clearinghouse (WWC) is a federal registry of evidence-based programs and policies (Hunter et al., 2018). The mission of What Works Clearinghouse is to be a central and trusted source of evidence for what works in education (What Works Clearinghouse, n.d.). Figure 5.4 provides readers a list of resources to find information on evidence-based social-emotional programs, and the next chapter describes universal social-emotional programs and screeners.

Resource	Type of Resource	Website
CASEL SELect Program Guides	Guide/Registry	https://casel.org/guide/
Blueprint for Healthy Youth Development	Registry	www.blueprintsprograms.org/
What Works Clearinghouse	Registry	https://ies.ed.gov/ncee/wwc/
Google Scholar	Search Engine	https://scholar.google.com/
Microsoft Academic	Search Engine	https://academic.microsoft.com/home
Intervention Central	Resource website	www.interventioncentral.org/

Figure 5.4 Resource Matrix for Selection of Social-Emotional Programs

Implementation teams are encouraged to narrow their searches to three or four programs of interest and explore them in greater detail to come to a final decision as to which are best for their schools. Therefore, Exercise 5.7 is designed to assist educators in program selection.

Exercise 5.7 Program Selection Chart

Directions: Answer the questions to the questions below to assist you in determining which universal social-emotional program is the best fit for your school. You may use this worksheet to compare and contrast your responses to different programs that you or your implementation team is considering. Chapter 6 provides readers detailed descriptions of common universal social-emotional programs.

Name of Program: _____

Mission, Vision, and Goals	Yes	No	Not Sure	N/A
1. Does the program fit with your school's vision?				
2. Does the program align with your school's values?				
3. Is the program compatible with the school's current focus?				
Implementation Capacity	Yes	No	Not Sure	N/A
4. Does your school have enough personnel to implement the program?				
5. Are the personnel prepared or ready to take on the implementation of the program?				
6. Does your school have the material resources to implement the program?				
7. Does your school have the appropriate funding to implement the program?				
8. Can you implement the program in the manner that it was designed?				

Cultural Relevance	Yes	No	Not Sure	N/A
9. Is the program appropriate for the culture and characteristics of the students being served?				
10. Does the program take into account the values and traditions of the students being served and how their families may regard the promotion of mental wellness?				
Evidence-Based and Effectiveness	Yes	No	Not Sure	N/A
11. Is the program or practice based on a well-defined theory or model (e.g., based on cognitive-behavioral therapy or mindfulness)?				
12. Does the program have documented evidence of effectiveness through the scholarly literature or is the program endorsed by a highly regarded registry, such as What Works Clearinghouse?				
13. Does the program have documented evidence of effectiveness with the cultural and ethnic needs of your student population?				
14. Has the program been shown to be effective for areas similar to those that your school wants to address?				

(Adapted from White-Bissot, 2012)

Final Program Selection

Once the implementation team has selected one or two prominent universal social-emotional programs to use with their student population, it is important for them to comprehensively describe such programs. Comprehensively describing the elements of the program will later be important to evaluating its effectiveness, which will be described in Chapter 9. However, for now, comprehensively describing the program will provide the implementation team and those employing the universal program a better understanding of its components. In describing a universal program, readers may find it helpful to reference the program manual, website, scholarly literature, Chapter 6 in this book, or registries, such as the What Works Clearinghouse.

In addition to describing the program, the implementation team should seek to identify its goals and objectives. **Goals,** in the context of this book, are defined as the overarching destinations that explain what a school wants to ultimately achieve through implementing a universal social-emotional program (Giancola, 2014). For example, a goal for a school implementing a universal social-emotional program may be to ensure that 80% of its students are not at risk for mental health concerns within the first four years of employing the program. **Objectives** are precise actions or measurable steps needed to attain the identified goals (Giancola, 2014). For instance, an objective might state that within the first three months of obtaining the new universal social-emotional program, all three first-grade teachers will be trained in its implementation. Schools should attempt to write goals and objectives in a specific, measurable, achievable, relevant, and time-based manner (SMART) (Giancola, 2014). Exercise 5.8 will assist readers in comprehensively describing their universal social-emotional program along with their main goal and objectives.

Exercise 5.8 Formulating a Comprehensive Program Description

Directions: Answer the following questions to formulate a comprehensive program description. In describing a universal program, readers may find it helpful to reference program manuals, websites, scholarly literature, registries, or Chapter 6 in this book.

Program name: _____

1) What does your program purport to accomplish?

_____

_____

_____

2) What is your program's age or grade range?

_____

_____

_____

3) How much time does it take to implement your program in minutes or hours?

_____

_____

_____

4) How many sessions is your program?

_____

_____

_____

5) What are the main components of implementing your program?

A) _____

B) _____

C) _____

D) _____

E) _____

6) What resources are needed to implement your program successfully (staff, technology, materials)?

_____

_____

_____

What is your school's overarching goal(s) for implementing the program?

A) _____

B) _____

What short- and long-term objectives will help you meet your overarching goal(s)?

_____

_____

_____

_____

_____

_____

(CDC, 2012; Giancola, 2014)

Conclusion

The first stage of implementing a new program is known as the exploration stage. During the exploration stage, schools determine their readiness to move forward with employing new programs. Critical to the exploration stage is that implementation team members create a shared vision about the promotion of mental wellness and prevention of social-emotional concerns within their schools (Teague & Anfara, 2012). Additionally, implementation teams need to judge the feasibility of whether Tier 1 social-emotional programs fit into their schools by completing a needs assessment. A needs assessment is a systemic process for identifying gaps between current and desired conditions (Altschuld & Watkins, 2014). The five steps to completing a needs assessment entail identifying key stakeholders, outlining goals and parameters, noting strengths and weaknesses, analyzing and collecting data, and developing a timeline for additional data collection.

After analyzing the results from the needs assessment, the implementation team can begin the process of resource mapping. Resource mapping is an ongoing process to identify, visually represent, and share information about internal and external supports and services to the school (Lightfoot et al., 2014; Skalski et al., 2015). The three stages to resource mapping entail that of pre-mapping, mapping, and maintaining, sustaining, and evaluating mapping. Pre-mapping involves the implementation team establishing a clear vision, defining goals, and coming to an agreement on what will be mapped (Lever et al., 2014). The mapping stage involves the implementation team brainstorming what programs are available and the staff needed to implement such programs (Lever et al., 2014). Finally, the maintaining, sustaining, and evaluating mapping stage assesses the effectiveness of resource mapping and allows the team to evaluate whether or not progress has been made toward achieving their goals (Lever et al., 2014; Sanetti, 2011).

Once implementation teams have engaged in completing a needs assessment and resource mapping, they are in an ideal place to select a social-emotional program. There are generally four steps that educators should be aware of when selecting a program of which include: identifying evidence-based or evidence-informed programs, assessing the cost of the program, considering the complexity and transferability of the program, and determining the contextual and cultural fit of the program. Each of these steps must be followed before selecting a program and implementing it in the installation stage. Aside from following these steps, educators are highly encouraged to consider whether a program is evidence-based over that of research-based. Evidence-based programs are those that have been empirically supported through scholarly literature and have followed a rigorous research design (Cook & Cook, 2011; Zyromski et al., 2018). Ultimately, the four factors educators should consider in determining whether a program is evidence-based include that of considering the research design of the program, quality of the research studies conducted on the program, quantity of the research studies conducted on the program, and magnitude of effect Cook & Cook, 2011; Leko et al., 2019). By being aware of these four factors and familiar with the steps to completing the exploration stage, educators will be best positioned to begin determining which social-emotional programs best fit their schools' needs.

Universal Social-Emotional Programs and Screeners

6

Learning Objectives

After reading this chapter, you should be able to:

- Compare various universal social-emotional programs
- Understand the duration and time needed to implement different universal social-emotional programs
- State the age ranges and demographic information for which different universal social-emotional programs are appropriate
- Compare various universal social-emotional screeners
- Identify the resources needed to administer different universal screeners

Chapter Overview

With readers having a firm understanding of the steps to exploring and selecting universal social-emotional programs, this chapter is dedicated to providing detailed descriptions of such Tier 1 supports. Readers should recall that universal social-emotional programs tend to share three common features: (a) increasing students' knowledge of social and emotional skills, (b) utilization of social and emotional skills in daily interactions with others, and (c) reliance on social and emotional skills to prevent disruptive, antisocial, or harmful behaviors (Moy & Hazen, 2018). Therefore, in considering

DOI: 10.4324/9781003343479-6

universal social-emotional programs, it is important to evaluate whether potential program candidates are meeting these three features. After providing descriptions of select universal social-emotional programs that are widely used in schools, the second half of the chapter is designed to provide readers an overview of common universal social-emotional screeners. Before moving onto the installation stage, readers are encouraged to use this chapter to assist them in completing Exercises 5.1 and 5.2 from Chapter 5. Figure 6.1 provides an overview of common Tier 1 social-emotional programs. Readers should note that although the number of Tier 1 social-emotional programs available to schools is growing, there remains a large gap in the scholarly literature of adapting these programs for use with children from diverse and marginalized backgrounds. Additionally, readers should note that there is a lack of scholarly literature in adapting these programs for use with students with neurodiversity, such as intellectual disabilities. Consequently, schools may have to be innovative in their adoptions and adaptations of Tier 1 social-emotional programs to best meet the needs of diverse learners.

Universal Social-Emotional Programs

Promoting Alternative Thinking Strategies (PATHS)

Promoting Alternative Thinking Strategies is a universal social-emotional program designed to improve children's abilities to discuss and understand emotions, manage behavior, promote peaceful conflict resolution, and develop social competencies (Humphrey et al., 2016). The PATHS program can be delivered to students in pre-kindergarten through sixth grade and is designed to be implemented by classroom teachers (Humphrey et al., 2016). The PATHS program is delivered two to three times weekly, with each scripted lesson lasting 30 to 40 minutes (Humphrey et al., 2016). Lessons from the PATHS program are divided for the following grades: preschool/kindergarten, first through fourth grades, and fifth/sixth grades (Humphrey et al., 2016).

PATHS targets five domains, including emotional understanding, self-control, positive self-esteem, relationships, and interpersonal problem-solving skills (Humphrey et al., 2016). Lessons covered in PATHS include those of controlling impulses, identifying and labeling feelings, understanding others' perspectives, and reducing stress (Humphrey et al., 2016). To extend learning into the home environment, the curriculum includes parent materials, which are available in English and Spanish. PATHS is only one of 14 interventions to be designated as a "model program" by the Center for the Study and Prevention of Violence, and multiple studies have demonstrated PATHS's effectiveness on academic attainment, social-emotional competence, and mental health (Humphrey et al., 2016). The PATHS program can be used in conjunction with the Good Behavior Game known as PATHS to PAX (Humphrey et al., 2016).

Good Behavior Game

The Good Behavior Game (GBG) is designed as a classroom-based behavior management support for students in first through sixth grades, however it has been found to have many social-emotional benefits for youth (Foley et al., 2019). The game assigns students to teams that are balanced based on disruptive behavior, gender, and socially isolated behavior. Subsequently, classroom rules are posted and reviewed. Each team is rewarded if their members commit a total of four or fewer violations of the classroom rules during game periods. It should be noted that the GBG is not a curriculum but is rather embedded into particular areas of the existing curriculum pre-determined by the teacher, such as an existing lesson (Foley et al., 2019; Humphrey et al., 2016). Existing literature has found that children who played the Good Behavior Game showed lower rates of drug and alcohol use disorders, regular smoking, antisocial personality disorder, delinquency and incarceration for violent crimes, suicide ideation, depression, and use of school-based services among students who had played the GBG (Bowman-Perrott et al., 2015; Foley et al., 2019; Kellam et al., 2011). The GBG is often used in conjunction with the PATHS program and is known as PATHS to PAX (Humphrey et al., 2016).

MindUP Curriculum

The MindUP curriculum is a comprehensive evidence-based program that aims to promote students' ability to reduce stress and increase self-awareness, attention, self-regulation, and empathy (Crooks et al., 2020; de Carvalho et al., 2017; Schonert-Reichl et al., 2015). The program is organized into three levels: preschool to second grade; third to fifth grades; and sixth to eighth grades (de Carvalho et al., 2017). Program manuals are adapted for each level and provide implementers detail instructions for employing the program (Crooks et al., 2020; de Carvalho et al., 2017). Each level of the MindUP curriculum consists of four units with 15 sequenced lessons that are taught once a week for approximately 45 to 60 minutes.

The lessons found in the MindUP curriculum are comprised of mindfulness practices along with different activities that allow children to learn about their brains and how their feelings and thoughts influence their actions and learn ways of becoming altruistic and caring people (de Carvalho et al., 2017). Therefore, in units one and two, children learn how becoming aware of their surroundings might help focus their brains (de Carvalho et al., 2017). Subsequently, children then practice exercises such as mindful smelling or seeing (de Carvalho et al., 2017). In unit three, children learn social-emotional understanding through the practice of optimism, perspective-taking, and savoring happy experiences (de Carvalho et al., 2017; Schonert-Reichl et al., 2015). Finally, unit four provides children the opportunity to put mindful awareness into practice through performing acts of kindness and social projects to benefit their school communities (Crooks et al., 2020; de Carvalho et al., 2017; Schonert-Reichl et al., 2015). In-person training for the MindUP curriculum varies, depending on factors such as the number of schools and participants involved and the locations of the schools (de Carvalho et al., 2017; Schonert-Reichl et al., 2015). However, a virtual full year of training now exists that includes five different virtual training sessions with a MindUP curriculum consultation (de Carvalho et al., 2017; Schonert-Reichl et al., 2015). Beyond the 15 lessons, the MindUP curriculum consists having students practice mindfulness activities three times a day for three minutes (de Carvalho et al., 2017). The MindUP curriculum is available in English and Spanish (de Carvalho et al., 2017). Training to implement the program takes approximately one to four hours and is not required but advised.

Second Step

Second Step is a program designed to promote interpersonal and intrapersonal competencies and reduce the development of behavioral, social, and emotional problems in children in preschool through eighth grade (Moy & Hazen, 2018). The program is influenced by social learning theory, cognitive-behavioral therapy, and social information processing (Moy & Hazen, 2018). Second Step is designed to be implemented over the course of 22 to 28 weeks, with lessons focusing on emotion management, empathy, problem-solving, and friendship skills (Moy & Hazen, 2018). The curriculum can be delivered by classroom teachers or school mental health providers. Lessons usually begin with warm-up activities that are followed by an audio-visual media presentation (Moy & Hazen, 2018). Second Step uses four key strategies to reinforce skill development: 1) weekly themed activities, 2) brain builder games to build executive function, 3) home links, and 4) reinforcing activities (Moy & Hazen, 2018). Research has demonstrated that students who participated in Second Step demonstrate increased prosocial outcomes and social-emotional skills (Moy & Hazen, 2018). Second Step is available in both English and Spanish (Moy & Hazen, 2018).

FRIENDS Programs

FRIENDS is a series of resilience programs that incorporate cognitive and behavioral strategies for children, adolescence, and adults placed at risk for anxiety and depression (Anticich et al., 2013; Macklem, 2011). The FRIENDS acronym stands for **F**eeling worried, **R**elax and feel good, **I**nner thoughts, **E**xplore plans of actions, **N**ice work, **R**eward yourself, **D**on't forget to practice, and **S**tay cool (Macklem, 2011). The programs aim to promote resilience, prevent anxiety and depression, and increase social and emotional skills across the lifespan (Anticich et al., 2013; Kozina, 2021; Macklem, 2021).

The FRIENDS series of programs are available for different age ranges, which include: Fun FRIENDS (ages 4 to 7), FRIENDS for Life (ages 7 to 13), My FRIENDS Youth (ages 11 to 16), and Adult Resilience (age 16 years and over). Across the FRIENDS programs, the standardized curriculum is typically delivered over ten weekly sessions with two booster sessions that typically last between 60 to 75 minutes in length (Anticich et al., 2013; Lizuka, 2015; Macklem, 2011). Two information sessions are conducted with caregivers that last approximately 90 to 120 minutes and are designed to enhance resilience at home, behavior management techniques, and the reinforcement of program strategies (Anticich et al., 2013; Lizuka, 2015; Macklem, 2011). To deliver the FRIENDS program, educators must be trained and accredited under a FRIENDS licensee. Accreditation as a facilitator of the FRIENDS programs is valid for three years Anticich et al., 2013; Lizuka et al., 2015; Macklem, 2011). FRIENDS programs can be delivered at Tier 1 or Tier 2 within social-emotional RTI.

The Incredible Years: Parent, Teacher, and Child Training Series

The Incredible Years: Parents, Teachers, and Children Training Series is a set of three empirically validated and integrated program for parents, teachers, and students designed to promote social competence, interpersonal relationships, problem-solving, feeling recognition, prosocial behaviors, and anger management (Webster-Stratton, 2001; Thompson et al., 2017). The program is designed for children three to eight years of age (Pre-K through second grade). The universal childhood program, known as the Classroom Dinosaur Curriculum, consists of 60+ classroom lessons that tend to be delivered by the teacher on a twice-weekly basis (Webster-Stratton, 2001; The Incredible Years, 2013; Thompson et al., 2017). Each classroom lesson consists of 20–30 minutes of circle time, followed by small-group activities to practice skills taught (The Incredible Years, 2013). At Tier 2, the Incredible Years series includes a child treatment program, known as Small Group Dinosaur, which is to be used by school counselors and psychologists to assist children with more severe internalizing and externalizing concerns.

Aside from the universal Classroom Dinosaur Curriculum, the Incredible Years series contains the Teacher Classroom Management Program. This program aims to provide instructors with skills to effectively manage their classrooms and promote social-emotional competence (The Incredible Years, 2013; Thompson et al., 2017). Finally, the Incredible Years Series provides groups for parents. These groups are delivered in 12–20 weekly group sessions and last 2–3 hours (Webster-Stratton, 2001; The Incredible Years, 2013). The focus of these groups is to assist children through fostering parent-child interactions, reducing harsh discipline, and promoting parents' abilities to enhance children's social, emotional, and language development (The Incredible Years, 2013). Existing literature on the Incredible Years suggests that the curriculum improves social-emotional and behavioral outcomes for children (Webster-Stratton et al., 2008). Moreover, the Incredible Years programs have been delivered with racially and ethnically diverse children and families in the United States, including those those who identify as Black, Asian, White, and Hispanic (The Incredible Years, 2013). Additionally, programs have been implemented transnationally across countries such as Canada and the United Kingdom. Training for the Incredible Years Classroom Dinosaur Curriculum takes three days (The Incredible Years, 2013).

Penn Resilience Program (PRP)

The Penn Resilience Program is a cognitive-behavioral curriculum that focuses on building resilience and reducing feelings of sadness in children between ages 10 to 14 years (Macklem, 2011; Sapthiang et al., 2019). Each session within the PRP is 90 minutes across 12 weekly sessions or can be delivered in 60 minutes across 18 to 24 weekly sessions (Hamza, 2018; Sapthiang et al., 2019). Within the PRP, each session is utilized to increase competencies in the areas of self-awareness, self-regulation, and optimism (Macklem, 2011; Sapthiang et al., 2019). To increase these competencies, the PRP uses games, discussions, role-playing, short stories, and cartoons (Macklem, 2011; Sapthiang et al., 2019). Through this, students learn how to challenge maladaptive thought patterns, such as "mind-traps," and develop skills to "bounce-back" from negative situations (Hamza, 2018).

Like other programs discussed within this chapter, the Penn Resilience Program can be used as both a Tier 1 or Tier 2 program (Macklem, 2011). At Tier 1, the program can be used in a classroom of 15 to 30 students (Macklem, 2011). At Tier 2, the program can be used in a group of three to six students (Macklem, 2011). Studies suggest that the Penn Resilience Program has demonstrated some efficacy for improving resilience in adolescents, reducing depression, and decreasing anxiety (Macklem, 2011; Hamza, 2018; Sapthiang et al., 2019). Exercise 6.1 will have readers consider two universal social-emotional programs that are of interest to them.

Exercise 6.1 Selecting Universal Social-Emotional Programs

Directions: List two universal social-emotional programs that are of interest to you below that either have been discussed in this chapter or provided in any of the registries or guides listed in Chapter 5. Subsequently, if you have not completed Exercises 5.7 and 5.8 from the previous chapter, complete them using the programs that you have selected below.

Program of interest #1: _____

Program of interest #2: _____

Why are these programs of interest to you?

_____

_____

_____

Promoting Alternative Thinking Strategies (PATHS) Pre-K to Sixth Grade
DESCRIPTION: • PATHS is a program designed to promote social-emotional learning through assisting all students develop emotional understanding, self-control, social skills, and problem-solving strategies (Macklem, 2011). • Students learn how to discuss basic feelings and feeling management (Daly et al., 2014). • The program guides students in generalizing social-emotional conceptualization of social information, as well as decreasing aggressive behaviors (Crean & Johnson, 2013). • PATHS has shown promise in reducing externalizing behaviors and depressive symptomology in special education students (Daly et al., 2014). • A middle school curriculum known as Emozi was recently developed, but empirical evidence is not yet available.
SETTING: • Classroom
TIME: • Academic year • Five 30-minute sessions per week, with incorporations of lessons throughout the school day • Recommended implementation: School-wide, for duration of each school year, through fifth grade
FACILITATED BY: • General Education Teacher • School-Based Mental Health Professionals
AREAS TARGETED: • Social-emotional understanding • Aggression and behavior • Self-control   problems • Problem-solving   • Oppositional behaviors • Feeling recognition management • Conduct problems   • Impulsivity and hyperactivity
COST AND CONTENTS: • Price ranges from $439 to $669, depending on grade level • Kits for each grade level from preschool/kindergarten to sixth grade • Kits include lesson binders, instruction manual, and supplementary materials for activities (posters, photographs, pictures, stickers, books, puppets, feelings charts, etc.) • Lessons include goals, scripts, and directions

Figure 6.1 Universal (Tier 1) Social-Emotional Learning (SEL) Programs

- Teachers are encouraged to alter lessons in ways that best meet their classroom climates and student needs

TRAINING
- Training for the PATHS programs lasts two days and is not required
- Minimum provider qualifications include: Teacher training or certification, school counselor hours, paraprofessional training, bachelor's degree, and/or experience with children recommended
- Manuals available that explain programming in detail can be purchased through the publisher
- Additional training is available through their website

CULTURAL SENSITIVITY:
- PATHS has yet to be evaluated on What Works Clearinghouse standards for cultural sensitivity

WEBSITE:
- https://pathsprogram.com
- www.cebc4cw.org/program/ promoting-alternative-thinking-strategies/

Good Behavior Game (PAXGBG) First Through Sixth Grades

DESCRIPTION:
- The PAX Good Behavior Game (PAXGBG) is a classroom-based behavior management intervention for elementary school students.
- The game assigns students to teams that are balanced based on gender, disruptive behavior, and socially isolated behavior (Kellam et al., 2011).
- Classroom rules are posted and reviewed. Each team is rewarded if team members commit a total of four or fewer violations of the classroom rules during game periods.
- As the year progresses, the duration of time increases when good behavior is expected.
- Through short-term and long-term follow-ups, PAXGBG has been found to reduce drug and alcohol use, criminal behavior, mental health concerns, and suicide in adolescents and young adults (Bowman-Perrott et al., 2016; Foley et al., 2019; Kellam et al., 2011).
- The PAXGBG is not a curriculum; it is embedded into particular areas of curriculum pre-determined by the teacher

SETTING:
- Classroom

Figure 6.1 Continued

TIME:
- Academic year (three times a week for ten minutes; increases over time)
- Instructor decides during what classes the game will be played
- Instructors are advised to play the game when the whole class is together and when good behavior is expected
- Instructors also choose when to implement daily and weekly rewards for good behavior and what those rewards will be
- The amount of time spent playing the GBG is intended to increase as the school year progresses

FACILITATED BY:
- General Education Teacher
- School-Based Mental Health Professionals

AREAS TARGETED:
- Self-regulation
- Self-control
- Cooperation and compliance
- Socialization
- Aggression or disruptive classroom behaviors
- Oppositional behaviors
- Shyness and social isolation
- Risk for suicide

COST AND CONTENTS:
- Materials to play the PAXGBG are distributed during Initial Teacher Training (see below)
- Contact via website to discuss training prices

TEACHER TRAINING:
- *PAX Good Behavior Game Initial Training*: Teachers are taught skills and strategies to implement PAX GBG. Materials are distributed during training. Training also emphasizes creating a welcoming classroom climate to meet needs of all students.
- *PAX Sustainability Training*: Provides training to individuals to be a PAXGBG expert, guiding other teachers and classrooms in implementing PAXGBG seamlessly.
- *PAX Next Steps Training (PBIS/SEL)*: Provides information about how PAXGBG implementation can be embedded in social-emotional learning curricula and Positive Behavioral Interventions and Supports (PBIS) frameworks.
- *PAX Heroes Training*: Provides already trained PAXBGB instructors with approaches to support students still exhibiting behavior difficulties. PAX Heroes manual offers guidance on identifying difficult behaviors and Tier 2 and Tier 3 strategies to alleviate problem behaviors.

Figure 6.1 Continued

- *PAX Tools Community Educator Training*: Provides instructors with 9 evidence-based strategies for working with youth within their communities and establishing family-team partnerships within these communities

CULTURAL SENSITIVITY:
- PAXGBG has yet to be evaluated on What Works Clearinghouse standards for cultural sensitivity.

WEBSITE:
- www.goodbehaviorgame.org/

PATHS to PAX (PATHS + PAXGBG) 1st—6th Grade

DESCRIPTION:
- An integrated model combining PATHS with the PAX Good Behavior Game.
- Both programs focus their attention on equipping teachers with effective classroom management practices.
- PAXGBG offers staff means to manage inhibitory, off-task, disruptive, and aggressive behaviors through a game (Becker et al., 2013).
- PATHS offers staff explicit ways to guide students in achieving better emotion regulation, conflict resolution, social problem-solving, and self-control skills (Becker et al., 2013).
- The implementation of PATHS to PAX has resulted in reductions in internalizing and externalizing symptoms (Becker et al., 2013).

SETTING:
- Classroom

TIME:
- Academic year.
- PATHS is implemented five times a week through 30-minute sessions. Instructors should incorporate lessons within the school day as well.
- PAX Good Behavior Game (PAXGBG) is implemented in specified classes (determined by the instructor), beginning with ten minutes and increasing to 30–40 minutes by the end of the school year.

FACILITATED BY:
- General Education Teacher
- School-Based Mental Health Professionals

Figure 6.1 Continued

AREAS TARGETED:

- Self-regulation
- Self-control
- Social-emotional understanding
- Feeling recognition and management
- Conduct problems
- Interpersonal relations
- Socialization
- Cooperation with others
- Oppositional Behaviors
- Aggressive or disruptive classroom behaviors

COST AND CONTENTS:

- See PATHS and PAXGBG sections for information on cost and contents

TRAINING:

- See the PATHS and PAXGBG sections for information on training; both are required for PATHS to PAX implementation

CULTURAL SENSITIVITY:

- PATHS to PAX has yet to be evaluated on What Works Clearinghouse standards for cultural sensitivity

WEBSITE:

- No website available for PATHS to PAX

MindUP Curriculum

DESCRIPTION:

- The MindUP curriculum is a comprehensive evidence-based program that aims to promote children's abilities to reduce stress and increase self-awareness, attention, self-regulation, and empathy (Crooks et al., 2020).
- Throughout the MindUP curriculum, children learn how their feelings and thoughts influence their actions and learn ways to become caring and altruistic people.

SETTING:

- Classroom

TIME:

- 15 sequenced lessons that are taught weekly for approximately 45 to 60 minutes

FACILITATION:

- General Education Teacher
- School-Based Mental Health Professionals

Figure 6.1 Continued

AREAS TARGETED:
- Feeling Recognition
- Emotional Regulation
- Empathy
- Assessment of one's
- Perspective-taking

- Managing stress
- Working toward and achieving goals
- Conflict resolution
- Cooperation strengths and limitations
- Nonviolent and constructive conflict resolution

COSTS AND CONTENTS:

Three books are available for the MindUP curriculum based on grade. Each book contains activities, posters, songs, games, activities, and exercises. The grade-level books for the MindUP curriculum are as follows:
- *MindUP Curriculum—Preschool through Second Grade*
- *MindUP Curriculum—Third through Fifth Grade*
- *MindUP Curriculum—Sixth through Eighth Grade*

Each book for the curriculum costs $24.99 and can be ordered through Scholastic Publishing at http://teacher.scholastic.com/products/mindup/index.html.

TRAINING:
- In-person training for the MindUP training varies depending on factors such as the number of schools and participants involved and the location of the schools. To find out more about in-person training and the cost of such training, readers can visit https://mindup.org/request-consultation/.
- Virtual training for the MindUP curriculum is now available and includes five different virtual training sessions that can be spread throughout the school year based on the school's needs. To find out more about the training and the cost of the training, readers can visit https://mindup.org/mindup-for-schools/.

CULTURAL SENSITIVITY:
- At present, more research is needed to determine whether the MindUP curriculum is culturally sensitive. There are existing studies that it has been used in English-, Spanish-, and Portuguese-speaking populations (de Carvalho et al., 2017).
- English and Spanish versions exist of the MindUP curriculum.

WEBSITE:
- https://mindup.org/

Figure 6.1 Continued

Second Step Pre-K to Eighth Grade

DESCRIPTION:
- Second Step is a set of classroom-based curricula that provides instruction in social-emotional learning, inter- and intrapersonal relationship building, and self-regulation (Moy & Hazen, 2018).
- Second Step lessons model competencies through song, games, videos, activities, discussion topics, and take-home materials.
- Teachers are provided a facilitation guide that outlines vocabulary, role plays, and discussion topics. Lessons involve songs, games, activities, videos, and take-home materials (Moy & Hazen, 2018).
- Second Step social-emotional learning packages include Early Childhood (Pre-K), Elementary (K–5), Middle School (6–8), Out-of-School Time (K–5), and SEL for Adults (K–12).
- They also offer Bullying Prevention and Child Protection units (secondstep.org).
- Computer screens necessary or utilizing online lessons and viewing videos

SETTING:
- Classroom

TIME:
- 22–28 weeks (Depending on grade level, each lesson takes between 20 to 35 minutes each)

FACILITATION:
- General Education Teacher
- School-Based Mental Health Professionals

AREAS TARGETED:
- Attention and listening
- Impulsive and aggressive behaviors
- Self-talk and metacognition
- Feeling recognition and management
- Prosocial behavior
- Interpersonal relations
- Socialization
- Problem-solving
- Academic and learning skills

COST AND CONTENTS:
- Bundles range from $1,949 to $8,799, depending on whether the package spans school-wide use, on the grade levels selected, and on whether the SEL curriculum is paired with the Bullying and Child Protection programming.
- Packages generally include a teacher's manual, lesson plans, scripts, online access to videos and lessons, posters, theme cards, and games.

Figure 6.1 Continued

- Visit the Second Step website for more specific information about what each package contains.

TRAINING:
- Training varies for each package between one to four hours but is not required.
- *Early Learning Package*: Two to three hours of material to review, including presentations, videos, and infographics.
- *Kindergarten through 5th Grade*: 60–90 minutes required to review three video training modules. Paper resources include strategies for teaching each lesson, tips on classroom management, summative and formative assessments, forms to track student progress, and home links to connect with families.
- *Middle School*: Classroom instructors review provided "Quick Start Guides," requiring five to seven minutes. Each guide is specific to a grade level and offers strategies related to that developmental level. Individuals leading Second Step implementation school-wide present four different presentations to staff (30–45 minutes each). The four presentations acknowledge a staff overview, responding to bullying and harassment, mid-year check-ins, and end-of-year check-ins.
- Visit the Second Step website for more information about the Bullying and Child Protection trainings.

CULTURAL SENSITIVITY:
- A Spanish version of Second Step is available
- Second Step has yet to be evaluated on What Works Clearinghouse standards for cultural sensitivity

WEBSITE:
- www.secondstep.org
- www.secondstep.org/help/second-step-training

FRIENDS Programs

DESCRIPTION:
- FRIENDS incorporates cognitive and behavioral strategies for children and adolescents at risk for anxiety and depression and has also been utilized as a prevention program (Macklem, 2011).
- Parent training programs are an integral part of FRIENDS. The FRIENDS acronym stands for **F**eeling worried, **R**elax and feel good, **I**nner thoughts, **E**xplore plans of actions, **N**ice work, **R**eward yourself, **D**on't forget to practice, **S**tay cool (Macklem, 2011).

Figure 6.1 Continued

- Different programming is available based on different age ranges: Fun FRIENDS (ages 4 to 7), FRIENDS for Life (ages 7 to 13), My FRIENDS Youth (ages 11 to 16), and Adult Resilience (ages 16+).

SETTING:
- Classroom
- Pull-out group (3–6 students)

TIME:
- Child component: 10 sessions, 2 booster sessions (60–75 minutes each)
- Parent component: 4 sessions (6 hours total)
- ***Sessions can be adapted as long as the sequence and structure are adhered to**

FACILITATION:
- General Education Teacher
- School-Based Mental Health Professionals
- Allied Health Professionals

AREAS TARGETED:
- Feeling recognition and management
- Stress management
- Interpersonal relations
- Socialization
- Resiliency development
- Parent involvement and training

COST AND CONTENTS:
- Licensure cost is dependent on the size of the organization, the plan selected, and number of individuals receiving the services
- When licensure expires (after three years), license fee is required for renewal
- Non-profit organizations do not have extra costs; for-profit organizations are required to pay royalty fees
- Different programs are available depending on the age range; contents vary for each program
- Materials are available through the FRIENDS Resilience hub, an online platform
- Activity books are required for every student; electronic versions cost approximately $11 USD (5 Australian dollars), whereas hard copy books vary in price
- Program manuals are made available for each program the instructor was trained in

Figure 6.1 Continued

TRAINING:
- Instructors are required to have a health profession or education profession (doctors, medical specialists, teaching professionals, speech therapists, occupational therapists, psychologists, counselors, childcare workers).
- Instructors must become licensees with selected packages in order to deliver a Friends program effectively; licenses are valid for three years.
- Online trainings are available to teach required skills for service delivery. PowerPoint slides are provided for instructors in training.
- Once trained and licensed, instructors select programs relevant to their clientele. These instructors can also train other staff in their organizations to become facilitators for no additional cost.

CULTURAL SENSITIVITY:
- FRIENDS Resilience has yet to be evaluated on What Works Clearinghouse standards for cultural sensitivity

WEBSITE:
- www.friendsresilience.org/about
- https://friendsresilience.org/getstart
- www.thepsychologytree.com/friends
- www.thepsychologytree.com/ordering-friends-books

The Incredible Years: Parent, Teacher, and Child Training Series

DESCRIPTION:
- Incredible Years provides parent, teacher, and child training to promote social, emotional, and academic competence, as well as decrease conduct behaviors (Webster-Stratton & Reid, 2017; Macklem, 2011).
- Incredible Years strives to boost parent confidence, strengthen positive approaches to parenting, bolster attachment, and address social, emotional, academic, and verbal needs through play (Webster-Stratton & Reid, 2017). Incredible Years also targets parent mental health by providing resources for parent depression and communication and problem-solving tactics with their children (Webster-Stratton & Reid, 2017).
- Incredible Years aims to replace violent discipline measure with positive interventions. Among these include planned ignoring, redirection, time-outs, and problem-solving (Webster-Stratton & Reid, 2017).

Figure 6.1 Continued

- Incredible Years seeks to create strong family-team partnerships and increase parent voice and presence in student activities (Webster-Stratton & Reid, 2017).
- Tier 2 interventions are available for Incredible Years, which includes lessons aimed toward pull-out groups for students already displaying behavior and social-emotional difficulties. The Tier 2 intervention works best with groups of five to six students (Macklem, 2011).
- Access to electronic devices to view DVD lessons is highly recommended

SETTING:
- Classroom
- Pull-out group (three to six students)
- Parent groups

TIME:
- Tier 1—60+ sessions Dinosaur curriculum (20-to-30-minute classroom circle time followed by small-group activities to practice the skills taught in circle time)
- Tier 2—Child program: 18–22 weeks (two-hour sessions)
- Parent program: 12–20 weeks (two-to-three-hour sessions)

FACILITATION:
- General Education Teacher
- School-Based Mental Health Professionals

AREAS TARGETED:

• Oppositional behaviors	• Social-emotional skills
• Conduct problems	• Academic and learning skills
• Antisocial behavior	• Parent involvement and training
• Aggressive behavior	• Internalized problems (e.g., depression)

COST AND CONTENTS:
- Prepaid orders can be paid by check, or Incredible Years can provide an invoice with a purchase number with payment "due upon receipt"
- Invoice payments are made online through convergepay.com
- Parent training programs range from $450 to $2,070, depending on the program selected
- Parent bundle packages are available and range from $1,170 to $5,240, depending on the programs included in the bundle
- Teacher training programs range from $250 to $1,760, depending on the program selected

Figure 6.1 Continued

- Child training programs range from $65 to $1,550, depending on the program selected
- Online video streaming subscriptions are available for certain training programs
- Books, CDs, videos, home guides, and other supplemental items are available for purchase

TRAINING:

- Incredible Years instructors are recommended to be experienced in one of the following: social work, psychology, education, nursing, psychiatry, or experience working with families and children.
- Training is not required, but instructors are highly recommended to attend in order to implement programming more effectively. Training for the Dinosaur Classroom Curriculum is three days.
- Training programs are dependent on what groups the instructor is leading (parents, children, or teachers).
- Trainings are primarily Seattle based and range from $250 to $550, depending on the number of days selected for training (options are one, two, or three days).
- Organizations can contact Incredible Years to schedule a training at their organization/agency site. At least 15 individuals need to be interested in training. Costs range between $1,500 and $2,500, depending on site location and trainer leading instruction,
- Training sessions are available online. Costs range from $310 to $930 per person, depending on the program selected for training.
- Visit the Incredible Years website for specific training options.

CULTURAL SENSITIVITY:

- What Works Clearinghouse reports that the program has been used with diverse populations.
- Incredible Years programs have been delivered to multi-cultural groups in USA, Canada, and UK. Research showing comparable results and positive outcomes for diverse racial and ethnic groups, including those from Black, White, Asian, and Hispanic youth, can be found on the Incredible Years website.
- Supplemental materials for the Dinosaur program are available in Spanish and can be purchased on the Incredible Years website.

WEBSITE:
www.incredibleyears.com

Figure 6.1 Continued

Penn Resilience Program (PRP) Middle School
DESCRIPTION: • The Penn Resilience Program (PRP) is a cognitive behavior-therapy program designed to proactively identify depression and associated externalized and internalized symptoms in middle aged students (Macklem, 2011; Hamza, 2018; Sapthiang et al., 2019). • PRP aims to equip students with cognitive, behavioral, and social skills strategies in order to cope with various stressors encountered in their transition to adolescence (Macklem, 2011; Hamza, 2018; Sapthiang et al., 2019). • The model utilizes Albert Ellis's ABC model, which stresses that beliefs about events impact emotions and behaviors (Macklem, 2011; Hamza, 2018; Sapthiang et al., 2019). • Classroom and small-group sessions incorporate discussions, skill training, and role plays. Students are also given take-home work for further reinforcement (Macklem, 2011; Hamza, 2018; Sapthiang et al., 2019). • Studies suggest that the Penn Resilience Program has demonstrated some efficacy for improving resilience in adolescents, reducing depression, and decreasing anxiety (Macklem, 2011; Hamza, 2018; Sapthiang et al., 2019).
SETTING: • Classroom (15 to 30 students) • Small group (three to six students)
TIME: • Can be delivered in 12 sessions, 90-minute sessions, or 18–24 60-minute sessions
FACILITATION: • General Education Teachers • School-Based Mental Health Professionals
AREAS TARGETED: • Depression • Feeling recognition management • Anxiety • Coping • Emotional competency • Decision-making • Social competency • Problem-solving

Figure 6.1 Continued

COST AND CONTENTS:
- Cost was not provided
- The full PRP program includes 21 skills identified as essential to fostering cognitive and emotional fitness, character building, and strong relationship building
- Skills will vary by program and based on the needs of the students being served
- Skill target identified resilience competencies (mental agility, optimism, self-awareness, self-regulation, strengths of character, and connection)
- Emphasis on "learn by doing," group presentations, and breakout groups
- Group presentations review resilience skills in detail through conversations, videos, question and answer sessions, and acting out the skill
- Breakout groups support modeling of skills with peers through exercises and instructor feedback
- Individual, partner and group exercises support modeling resilience skills within their own life and school contexts

TRAINING:
- PRP utilizes a "train-the-trainer" approach, where school instructors are trained on effective delivery of resilience programming to their students
- Training program attendance is encouraged to increase effectiveness in resilience curriculum delivery
- Trainings are conducted by University of Pennsylvania instructors

CULTURAL SENSITIVITY:
- Facilitators must consider how depression is defined in different cultures, what coping mechanisms are most salient, how acculturation affects the individual and their experiences with depression. It is important to avoid generalizing race and ethnicity with particular socioeconomic statuses, and tend to within-group differences (Lopez et al., 2002)
- PRP has yet to be evaluated on What Works Clearinghouse standards for cultural sensitivity

WEBSITE:
- https://ppc.sas.upenn.edu/research/resilience-children

Figure 6.1 Continued

Universal Screeners

As mentioned earlier in this book, universal screening involves the system brief assessment of the school population to identify children placed at risk for academic, behavioral, or social-emotional deficits (Gresham et al., 2010). Readers of this text may be familiar with universal screeners in the area of academics, such as AimswebPlus Number Naming Fluency or DIBELS Oral Reading Fluency, to quickly determine children's abilities to quickly identify numbers, letters, or words. On the contrary to academic universal academic screeners, which identify children that may need additional support for reading, writing, or math deficits, universal social-emotional screeners are meant to quickly detect children who may be placed at risk for mental health concerns (Kilgus et al., 2018). Despite being quick to administer, only about one in eight schools conducts universal social-emotional screening to identify children who may be at risk for mental health concerns (Bruhn et al., 2014). Still, universal screening to identify mental health concerns in children is critical, as results of these measures allow the implementation team and school-based mental health professionals to make data-based decisions about the level of support needed by youth (Frederick et al., 2019). Additionally, these measures evaluate the degree to which existing supports, such as a universal social-emotional program, are meeting the needs of students (Frederick et al., 2019).

Like academic universal screening, social-emotional screening typically takes place in the fall, winter, and spring of each school year (Fredrick et al., 2019). However, screener schedules may vary per instrument. For instance, the DESSA-Mini only has to be administered one time per year for universal screening purposes (Kilpatrick et al., 2018). Ultimately, when reviewing and selecting universal social-emotional screeners, readers should select measures based off many of the features discussed for selecting evidence-based social-emotional programs. Therefore, readers should take into account the research design that the universal screener was developed under, the quality of research studies that exist on the screener, and the quantity of research studies (Cook & Cook, 2011; Miller, 2020).

Additionally, readers should take into account whether a universal social-emotional screener is strengths-based. **Strengths-based universal screeners** examine components of student wellness, such as raters' perceptions of student competencies and assets, as opposed to only social-emotional deficits (Nickerson & Fishman, 2013). Using universal strengths-based universal screeners leads to a focus on enhancement of student functioning rather than just focusing on the reduction or elimination of student deficits (Nickerson &

Fishman, 2013). Consequently, this more positive focus is more likely to lead to improved parent-student-professional relationships characterized by supportiveness, mutual trust, and goal seeking (Nickerson & Fishman, 2013). The Behavioral and Emotional Rating Scale-2 and Devereux Student Strengths Assessment-Mini are two of the most common strengths-based universal screeners (Nickerson & Fishman, 2013).

Behavior Intervention Monitoring Assessment System (BIMAS-2)

The **Behavior Intervention Monitoring Assessment System-2 (BIMAS-2)** is a universal screener and progress monitoring measure of behavioral and social-emotional functioning in children and adolescents between 5 and 18 years of age (McDougal et al., 2016). The BIMAS-2 is a nationally norm-referenced assessment and is available in two versions: BIMAS Standard and BIMAS Flex. The BIMAS-2 Standard form comes in a teacher, parent, and student form and contains 34 items used for universal screening of behavior (McDougal et al., 2016). The 34 items on the BIMAS-2 include three Behavioral Concern Scales, which include conduct, negative affect, and cognitive attention, and two Adaptive Scales, including social and academic functioning (Behavior Intervention Monitoring System 2; McDougal et al., 2016). On both the Behavioral Concern and Adaptive Scales, cut scores are identified through the use of T-scores. Therefore, T-scores that are above 70 fall in the high-risk range on the Behavioral Concern Scales (Jenkins et al., 2014). T-scores between 60 and 69 fall within the some-risk range (Jenkins et al., 2014). Lastly, T-scores below 60 fall in the low-risk range (Jenkins et al., 2014). For the Adaptive Scales, T-scores higher than 60 are classified as strengths. T-scores between 41 and 59 are classified as typical. Finally, T-scores below 40 are identified as concerns (Jenkins et al., 2014). The standard form of the BIMAS-2 takes approximately five to ten minutes to complete.

For progress monitoring, the BIMAS-2 Flex is an optional extension of the BIMAS-2 Standard version. The BIMAS-2 Flex is used to target specific interventions for concerns identified with the standard form (Behavior Intervention Monitoring System 2; Jenkins et al., 2014). Like the BIMAS Standard, the BIMAS Flex comes in teacher, parent, and student forms (Behavior Intervention Monitoring System 2; Jenkins et al., 2014). A unique feature of the BIMAS-2 Flex is that it allows users to customize items that are specific to student need for progress monitoring (BIMAS-2, n.d.). Overall, the BIMAS-2 is a promising universal screening and progress monitoring measure for students.

Behavioral and Emotional Rating Scale-Second Edition (BERS-2)

The **Behavioral and Emotional Rating Scale-Second Edition (BERS-2)** is a nationally normed and standardized assessment of social and emotional functioning that has parallel forms that can be completed by students, caregivers, and teachers for students ages 11 to 18 years of age (Duppong Hurley et al., 2015). The measure can be used as both a universal screener and progress monitoring tool and takes approximately ten minutes to complete per student or 200 minutes per class of 20 children (Duppong Hurley et al., 2015; January et al., 2015). The BERS-2 consists of 52 positively worded items on the teacher form and 58 items on the parent and student forms. These items comprise five subscales, which include Interpersonal Strengths (ability to interact with others), Intrapersonal Strengths (youth's perception of their accomplishments), Family Involvement (relationships with family), School Functioning (competence in school), and Affective Strengths (ability to give and receive affection (Duppong Hurley, 2015; January, 2015). Scores from the five subscales combined to produce a Strength Index, which provides an estimate of the youth's overall emotional and behavioral strengths affection (Duppong Hurley, 2015; January, 2015). The five subscales on the BERS-2 have a mean standard score of ten with a standard deviation of 3, while the Strength Index has a mean of 100 and a standard deviation of 15 (Duppong Hurley, 2015; January, 2015). Overall, the BERS-2 is viewed as a reliable and valid measure of social and emotional functioning in children and, as mentioned, is a strengths-based universal screener (Duppong Hurley et al., 2015; January et al., 2015).

Behavioral and Emotional Screening System (BESS)

The **Behavioral and Emotional Screening System (BESS)** is a standardized, norm-referenced, and abbreviated version of the *Behavioral Assessment System for Children*, third edition (Kilgus et al., 2018). The BESS is utilized as a universal screener and consists of 25 to 30 items. The measure comes in a teacher, child, and parent form, which takes approximately five to ten minutes per student to complete (about 100 to 200 minutes to complete for a class of 20 students). The teacher and parent forms are available for children ages 3 through 5. The student form is designed for children in grades third through 12th (Kilgus et al., 2018).

The BESS assesses children in the following four areas: externalizing problems, internalizing problems, school problems, and adaptive skills. Scores on the aforementioned four areas are derived from a four-point Likert scale from 0 (Never) to 3 (Almost Always) and summed to yield a raw single score that suggests a child's behavioral and emotional risk (Kilgus et al., 2018). Higher scores on the BESS are indicative of greater concerns regarding general behavior and emotional functioning. Many educators and school psychologist like the BESS due to its ease of use and being familiar with the longer version of the *Behavioral Assessment System for Children*, third edition.

Devereux Student Strengths Assessment-Mini (DESSA-Mini)

The **Devereux Student Strengths Assessment-Mini (DESSA-Mini)** is a strengths-based and norm-referenced social-emotional scale that can be utilized as a universal screener or progress monitoring measure for students who are in kindergarten through eighth grade (Kilipatrick et al., 2018). For students in grades nine through 12, the DESSA-High-School Edition-Mini (DESSA-HSE Mini) has been created. The DESSA-Mini and DESSA-HSE-Mini are abbreviated forms of the more comprehensive and longer Devereux Student Strengths Assessment (DESSA). Due to the DESSA consisting of 72-items, it was impractical for screening purposes. Therefore, the DESSA Mini was created to save educators financial resources and time (Maras et al., 2015). The DESSA Mini consists of four brief, eight-item parallel forms designed to be completed by teachers or other school staff to assess optimistic thinking, social awareness, goal-directed behavior, relationships skills, personal responsibility, self-management, and decision-making in students (Kilipatrick et al., 2018; Maras et al., 2015). The DESSA Mini utilizes items that are positively worded, strengths-based, and rated on a five-point scale that are based on how often the student has demonstrated each behavior in the past four weeks. Examples of DESSA-Mini items include how often the child shows appreciation for others and how often the child speaks about positive things (Kilipatrick et al., 2018). The DESSA-Mini offers digital administration and data management with educators having the ability to complete the DESSA-Mini online. Families can complete ratings online, alongside the educator, or traditional paper and pencil.

Ratings on the DESSA-Mini items yield a Social-Emotional Total, which indicates the child's level of social-emotional competence. Scores on the DESSA-Mini are reported as T-scores, which have a mean of 50 and a standard deviation of 10 (Maras et al., 2015; Kilpatrick et al., 2018). Higher scores on the DESSA-Mini suggest areas of strength, and lower scores suggest an area of need. Consequently, T-scores of 60 and above are considered strengths. T-scores of 41 to 59 are considered typical scores (Maras et al., 2015; Kilpatrick et al., 2018). Lastly, T-scores of 40 and below are described as needs for instruction. Students whose Social-Emotional Total falls below the 25th percentile are considered to be at high risk (Maras et al., 2015). Therefore, these students are regarded as being in need of additional social-emotional support beyond those core interventions provided at Tier 1 (Maras et al., 2015; Kilpatrick et al., 2018). Unlike other social-emotional universal screeners measures that are used three times per year for universal screening, the DESSA-Mini has been found to be relatively stable over time and, as a result, does not need to be re-administered for universal screening beyond fall benchmarking (Kilpatrick et al., 2018).

Social, Academic, and Emotional Behavior Risk Screening (SAEBRS)

The **Social, Academic, and Emotional Behavior Risk Screening (SAEBRS)** is a brief universal screening tool for students displaying both behavioral and emotional risk (Taylor et al., 2018). The SAEBRS takes approximately one to three minutes per student or about 30–40 minutes for a class of 20 to complete (Taylor et al., 2018). Moreover, the universal screener is designed to be used up to five times per year across grades K–12 (Taylor et al., 2018). The SAEBRS consists of 19 items and is divided into three subscales: Social Behavior (six items), Academic Behavior (six items), and Emotional Behavior (seven items) (Taylor et al., 2018). By summing the items, a Total Behavior score is obtained, which indicates whether the child is at risk for academic, social, or emotional behavior deficits (Taylor et al., 2018). The SAEBRS can be administered online or through paper-pencil. Both online scoring and hand scoring are possible, and online data management is available.

Through the SAEBRS, raters indicate how frequently the student has displayed behaviors over the course of the previous month using a four-point Likert scale (0 = never, 1 = sometimes, 2 = often, 3 = often, 4 = almost always) (Kilgus et al., 2018, 2018; Taylor et al., 2018). Scores that are higher on the SAEBRES suggest more positive and appropriate behavior. Cut scores indicating whether students fall in the at-risk range are as follows: Total Behavior Scale: ≤ 36, Social Behavior: ≤ 12, Academic Behavior: ≤ 9, and Emotional Behavior: ≤ 16 (Kilgus et al., 2018). Research on the SAEBRES supports its use as a valid, reliable, and diagnostically accurate tool in identifying students at behavioral and emotional risk (Kilgus et al.,

2018; Taylor et al., 2018). Consequently, the SAEBRES is a useful tool for universally screening students but is not designed to be a progress monitoring tool.

Strengths and Difficulties Questionnaire (SDQ)

The **Strengths and Difficulties Questionnaire (SDQ)** is a brief, norm-referenced universal screener for social, emotional, and behavioral concerns in children ages 2 to 17. The measure is not recommended as a progress monitoring tool but can be used as a universal screener (Deutz et al., 2018; Jenkins et al., 2014). The SDQ consists of 25 items across the following five subscales: Emotional Symptoms, Conduct Problems, Hyperactivity/Inattention, Peer Relationship Problems, and Prosocial Behavior (Deutz et al., 2018; Jenkins et al., 2014). Each subscale on the SDQ consists of five items. By summing all the scores on the SDQ except the Prosocial Behavior Subscale, a Total Difficulties score can be generated. Computer scoring and hand scoring (although not recommended by the publisher) is available.

The items on the SDQ ask parents, teachers, or the student, via self-report, to what extent positive and negative items were true over the past six months. Informants rate items on the SDQ using a three-point scale. Items rated zero indicate attributes that informants believe are "not true" of the child. Item rated one suggest attributes informants believe are "somewhat true" of the child. Finally, items scores rated two suggest attributes informants believe are "certainly true" of the child. The Total Difficulties score ranges from 0 to 40, with each one-point increase corresponding with an increase in the risk of a child developing a mental health disorder (Deutz et al., 2018; Jenkins et al., 2014). Suggested cut-off scores and risk ranges for the SDQ vary based on whether the parent, teacher, or student form was utilized. Cut-off and risk ranges can be found on the SDQ website at www.sdqinfo.org.

Student Risk Screening Scale-Internalizing and Externalizing (SRSS-IE)

The **Student Risk Screening Scale-Internalizing and Externalizing (SRSS-IE)** is a free universal screening and progress monitoring measure that is an adapted version of the Student Risk Screening Scale (SRSS) (Drummond, 1994; Taylor et al., 2018). The new adapted version of the SRSS added additional items to increase the measures utility in measuring patterns of internalizing problems. Consequently, the SRSS-IE includes a total of 12 items and takes approximately one to three minutes per student or 30–40 minutes per class of 20 students. On the SRSS-IE, the first seven items are devoted to externalizing maladaptive behaviors and include the following: (a) steal; (b) lie, cheat, sneak; (c) behavior problem, (d) peer rejection; (e) low achievement, (f) negative attitude; and (g) aggressive behavior (Drummond, 1994; Taylor et al., 2018). The subsequent five items of the SRSS-IE are designed to assess internalizing problems, which happen to be the focal point of this text, and are as follows: (a) emotionally flat; (b) shy, withdrawn; (c) sad, depressed; (d) anxious; and (e) lonely (Oakes et al., 2016; Taylor et al., 2018). The SRSS can be completed paper-pencil or directly on the Excel file that is free for download. Hand scoring or use of the Excel file can be used to facilitate scoring.

To complete the SRSS-IE, teachers use a four-point Likert-type scale to rate the frequency with which students display each behavior, from 0 (never) to 3 (frequently) (Taylor et al., 2018). The SRSS-IE scores are then calculated by obtaining the sum of item ratings within the internalizing and externalizing scales (Taylor et al., 2018). Higher scores are indicative of more problematic behavior and social-emotional concerns, while lower scores suggest less problematic behavior and social-emotional concerns. The SRSS-IE comes in elementary and middle-high school versions. For the elementary school SRSS-Externalizing scale (SRSS-E), cut score risk levels are as follows: 0–3 (low), 4–8 (medium), and 9–21 (high). For the elementary SRSS-Internalizing scale, cut score risk levels are as follows: 0–1 (low), 2–3 (moderate), and 4–15 (high) (Oakes et al., 2016; Taylor et al., 2018). The SRSS-IE is regarded by research as a well-established screening and progress monitoring measure and has been utilized to predict short-term (1.5 years) and long-term (10 years) negative behavioral and social-emotional outcomes for children (Oakes et al., 2016; Taylor et al., 2018). Exercise 6.2 has readers identify two universal screeners that are of interest to them that have been discussed in this chapter, while Figure 6.2 provides a helpful table for each of the universal screeners discussed.

Exercise 6.2 Selecting Universal Screeners

Directions: List two universal screeners that are of interest to you that have been discussed in this chapter.

Universal Screener #1: _____

Universal Screener #2: _____

Screening Measure	Informant(s): Age	Completion Time	Online Completion/ Data Storage	Cost	# of Items	Scales/Subscales/Constructs Assessed
BASC-3 Behavioral and Emotional Screening System (BESS)	T: 3:0–18:11 P: 3:0–18:11 S: 8:0–18:11	5–10 min.	Q-global—individual score report, multi-rater report Review360—individual and group level analysis, multi-rater report, progress report, good for large group screening at building/district level Note: Paper/pencil admin and scoring avail	Q-global—$3.10-$3.40 (with interv. recs) per student Review360—need to contact them for info	25–30 items	◆ Behavioral and Emotional Risk Index ◆ Externalizing Risk Index ◆ Internalizing Risk Index ◆ Adaptive Skills Risk Index ◆ Self-Regulation Risk Index ◆ Personal Adjustment Risk Index **Universal Screener** ☒ Yes ☐ No **Progress Monitoring** ☒ Yes ☐ No
BIMAS-2 Link: www.edumetrisis.com/products/282-bimas-2						

BESS-3 Link: www.pearsonassessments.com/store/usassessments/en/Store/Professional-Assessments/Behavior/Comprehensive/BASC-3-Behavioral-and-Emotional-Screening-System/p/100001482.html

Screening Measure	Informant(s): Age	Completion Time	Online Completion/ Data Storage	Cost	# of Items	Scales/Subscales/Constructs Assessed
Behavior Intervention Monitoring Assessment System-2 (BIMAS-2)	T: 5:0–18:11 P: 5:0–18:11 S: 12:0–18:11	5–10 min.	Online Data Management System has dynamic analysis, graphing, and reporting options Universal Assessment Reports and Progress Monitoring Reports available	$2.00–$4.00 per student after license purchase $90.00 one-time set-up fee $100.00 annual license fee	34 items	◆ Behavioral Concern Scales: o Conduct o Negative affect o Cognitive/Attention ◆ Adaptive Scales: o Social functioning o Academic functioning **Universal Screener** ☒ Yes ☐ No **Progress Monitoring** ☒ Yes ☐ No

BIMAS Link: www.edumetrisis.com/products/282-bimas-2

Measure	Age/Grade	Time	Administration	Cost	Items	Features

Behavioral and Emotional Rating Scale-2 (BERS-2)	T: 5:0–18:11
	P: 5:0–18:11
	S: 11:0–18:11
		10 min.	Paper-and-pencil administration. Hand scored	ParInc: $208.00 for introductory kit; includes: BERS-2 Examiner's Manual, 25 Teacher Rating Scales, 25 Parent Rating Scales, 25 Youth Rating Scales, and 50 Summary Forms	52–58 items	◆ Overall Strength Index
						◆ Single Summary Score of Strengths
						◆ Five subscales:
						  o Interpersonal Strength
						  o Family Involvement
						  o Intrapersonal Strength
						  o School Functioning
						  o Affective Strength
						Universal Screener ☒ Yes ☐ No
						Progress Monitoring ☒ Yes ☐ No
						*The BERS-2 is a strengths-based measure

BERS-2 Link: www.parinc.com/Products/Pkey/18

Measure	Age/Grade	Time	Administration	Cost	Items	Features
*Devereux Students Strengths Assessment-Mini (DESSA-Mini)	T: grade K–8 P: grade k-8 S: N/A	1–2 min.	Online administration and data management Student reports, classroom reports, and site reports available	Request a quote from publisher Packaged together with DESSA (i.e., the costs are the same)	8 items	◆ Self-Awareness ◆ Social Awareness ◆ Self-Management ◆ Goal-Directed Behavior ◆ Relationship Skills ◆ Personal Responsibility ◆ Decision-making ◆ Optimistic Thinking **Universal Screener** ☒ Yes ☐ No **Progress Monitoring** ☒ Yes ☐ No *Only has to be used one time per year for universal screening and is a strengths-based measure

DESSA-Mini Link: https://apertureed.com/dessa-overview/the-dessa-mini/

Figure 6.2 Universal Screening and Progress Monitoring Measures

Screening Measure	Informant(s): Age	Completion Time	Online Completion/Data Storage	Cost	# of Items	Scales/Subscales/Constructs Assessed
Social, Academic, and Emotional Behavior Risk Screener (SAEBRS)	T: grade K–12 P: N/A S: N/A	1–3 min.	Paper/pencil administration and hand scoring are possible Online administration and data management through *FastBridge*	No cost for paper version (see link below). $3 per student for online completion and data management via *FastBridge*	19 items	◆ Social Behavior ◆ Academic Behavior ◆ Emotional Behavior **Universal Screener** ☒ Yes ☐ No **Progress Monitoring** ☐ Yes ☒ No

SAEBRS Link: www.fastbridge.org/products/product-behavior/behavior/

SAEBRS tool: http://ebi.missouri.edu/wp-content/uploads/2014/03/SAEBRS-Teacher-Rating-Scale-3.3.14.pdf

Screening Measure	Informant(s): Age	Completion Time	Online Completion/Data Storage	Cost	# of Items	Scales/Subscales/Constructs Assessed
*Strengths and Difficulties Questionnaire (SDQ)	T: 2:0–17:11 P: 2:0–17:11 S: 11:0–17:11	5 min.	Hand or computer scoring available	No cost to download and manually score $0.25–$0.75 per assessment score if done through website	25 items	◆ Emotional symptoms subscale ◆ Conduct problems subscale ◆ Hyperactivity/inattention subscale ◆ Peer relationships problem subscale ◆ Prosocial behavior subscale **Universal Screener** ☒ Yes ☐ No **Progress Monitoring** ☐ Yes ☒ No

SDQ Link: https://youthinmind.com/products-and-services/sdq/

| Student Risk Screening Scale–Internalizing and Externalizing (SRSS-IE) | T: grade K–12
P: N/A
S: N/A | 1–3 per student
30–40 minutes per class of 20 (universal screener) | Hand scored (Excel may be used to facilitate scoring) | No cost, available for download online | 12 items | ◆ Internalizing behaviors
◆ Externalizing behaviors
Universal Screener ☒ Yes ☐ No
Progress Monitoring ☒ Yes ☐ No |

SRSS Link: www.ci3t.org/screening

Assessment available here: www.ci3t.org/screening

SSBD Link: www.ancorapublishing.com/wp-content/uploads/2018/08/SSBD_Portfolio.pdf

Figure 6.2 Continued

Why are these universal screeners of interest to you?

_____

_____

_____

Conclusion

In this chapter, an overview of commonly used, evidence-based, social-emotional programs and screeners was provided. When reviewing social-emotional programs and screeners, it is important for educators to be aware of the age and grade ranges these supports and measures target, time needed to implement such supports and measures, skills taught or assessed, and cultural appropriateness. Additionally, it is important for educators to be able to identify whether a universal social-emotional screener is strengths-based. Strengths-based measures, such as the BERS-2 and DESSA-Mini, emphasize a student's strengths rather than solely focusing on their social-emotional deficits (Nickerson & Fishman, 2013). Through being aware of each of the aforementioned areas and the evidence base surrounding universal social-emotional programs and screeners, schools will be best prepared to meet the needs of their students and move onto the next stage of universal implementation, the installation stage.

Installation Stage

7

Learning Objectives

After reading this chapter, you should be able to:

- Describe the importance of implementation drivers
- Understand the leadership, competency, and organizational implementation drivers that are most relevant for school-based SEL implementation
- Determine what type of training is most appropriate for your team
- Identify common challenges that arise during this stage and ways to problem-solve the challenges
- Describe additional program considerations to improve successful implementation

Installation Stage

It is an exciting time when a program has been selected and the team decides to implement it! However, there are several key tasks that must be in place before implementation actually begins. Teams may be tempted to rush into the implementation phase since, for some teams, it may have taken quite a bit of time to decide to implement and select a program. However, the National Implementation Research Network (NIRN) reports that the **installation stage** occurs when resources are incorporated into the structural supports necessary to implement the new program. During this stage, organizational and personnel competencies and as well as infrastructure development must be aligned. This stage allows for assessing for this alignment and considering

DOI: 10.4324/9781003343479-7

how to improve or change these areas before the next stage (initial implementation). The resources that help to improve the likelihood of success are called implementation drivers. **Implementation drivers** are core components that are associated with successful employment of evidence-based practices (Freeman et al., 2015). The following section will describe the three major implementation drivers that help outline and streamline efforts in implementing a universal SEL program, including leadership, competency, and organization (Freeman et al., 2015; Eagle et al., 2015).

Implementation Drivers

Leadership Drivers

Leadership drivers focus on management strategies that may arise when implementing MTSS and involves decision-making and providing guidance in the process of employing evidence-based programs (Eagle et al., 2015; Freeman et al., 2015; Owens et al., 2014). Within implementation science, two types of leadership styles are identified: technical leadership and adaptive leadership (Freeman et al., 2015; Eagle et al., 2015). **Technical leadership** utilizes an established protocol to respond to concerns that are often defined without ambiguity, and a clear solution is evident (Freeman et al., 2015; Eagle et al., 2015). Within MTSS, an action plan may be utilized to provide clarification how (e.g., Who implements? Using what materials?), when (e.g., What time of day? What class period?), and for how long (e.g., Once a day for 15 minutes? Once a week for 40 minutes?) to implement SEL in classrooms. **Adaptive leadership** refers to guiding others through complex and more difficult-to-recognize challenges that are typically not resolved through traditional approaches (Freeman et al., 2015; Eagle et al., 2015). Freeman et al. (2015) suggests that adaptive leadership may be needed when districts encounter resistance to program implementation from educators within the school.

One of the first steps in ensuring that leadership has been developed to lead universal SEL program implementation is for schools to assemble a team and identify who will provide leadership to the team. A **social-emotional team** is a group of school and community members that meets regularly, uses data-based decision-making, and relies on action planning to support student mental health, including improving school climate, promoting student and staff well-being, and addressing individual student strengths and needs (National Center for School Mental Health, 2020a, 2020b). Exercise 7.1 asks readers to identify how members can contribute to the social-emotional team. The purpose of the social-emotional team is to:

- Shape district guidelines and standards for school mental health
- Communicate and coordinate between the team and serve as a liaison
- Provide training, coaching, and implementation support
- Implement mental health practices
- Maximize limited mental health resources to address needs of students

Exercise 7.1 Contributing to the Team

Directions: In the table below, brainstorm ways you think the team could achieve each of these purposes.

Purpose of the Team	How would the TEAM contribute to this?	How will YOU contribute to this?
Shape district guidelines and standards for school mental health		
Communicate and coordinate between the team and serve as a liaison		
Provide training, coaching, and implementation support		
Implement mental health practices		
Maximize limited mental health resources to address needs of students		

Competency Drivers

Competency drivers seek to build the knowledge of educators in understanding and implementing SEL programming through activities, in-service trainings, and district-wide resources (SEL trainings, videos, books, etc.).

A helpful way to examine competence of educators' knowledge of SEL program implementation involves designing a self-assessment tool to determine what educators know about SEL and program implementation and what they would like to learn about it. There are several considerations to take into account when implementing competency drivers. First is the composition of the team (as discussed above). Ensuring diverse voices and a variety of perspectives and skills that can uniquely contribute to the process is important. A second aspect is the plan for training. Using a brief assessment tool to evaluate educators' knowledge, skills, comfort, and areas they'd like to learn more about could help inform training. This information could be gathered from the needs assessment (discussed in Chapter 5) and is not something additional that the team needs to complete. Additionally, the program that is selected will likely require training for most, if not all, team members, teachers, other school personnel involved in implementation, and possibly families. Training may require a cost (above and beyond cost of the program; some training may come with the program), time, and commitment. Training, or lack of training, can also be a major reason for resistance, so thoughtful planning about how knowledge and skills will be provided to the implementers of a new program is imperative for buy-in, successful delivery, and maintenance. Figure 7.1 provides examples of common training modalities.

Related to initial training, ongoing coaching has been linked to enhanced fidelity and outcomes for implementation (March et al., 2016). Although initial training is important, there are often questions and areas of problem-solving that may need to be worked through when the actual implementation of the program takes place. A question implementation teams may ask is: How can in-person or virtual coaching from leadership or team members be provided to those who need it? Considering a system for formal or informal coaching, having a contact person and communicating that ongoing coaching will be available can be helpful.

When selecting a modality of training, here are some questions to consider:

- What intensity of training do the team and personnel need? Does the team have prior experience in SEL implementation?
- What training modality would be most motivating to teach members and school personnel?
- How can the team and administration provide resources (e.g., time, cost of training, devices to access virtual training, incentives) toward training?
- Is the goal to train the team and personnel all at once or in phases? How does this affect the modality selected?

Common training modalities	Example	Advantages	Disadvantages
In-person (face to face)	A trainer of the program or someone with experience with the program's implementation conducts a workshop with those training to be implementers of the program	• Live, in-person training • Can possibly be tailored for the trainees (e.g., educators, administrators)	• May be costly • Scheduling difficulties between trainer and trainees • May be difficult to schedule and coordinate a large number of trainees to attend one training
Virtual or remote (synchronous, online)	Real-time class	• Live training • Possibly less costly • Less (or no) travel for trainer and trainees • Can flexibly attend training	• Less accountability • Internet access needed • Device to view and listen to training needed (e.g., computer, tablet)
Virtual or remote (asynchronous, online)	Pre-recorded webinar or series of webinars	• Possibly less costly • Less (or no) travel for trainer and trainees • Can flexibly attend training • Can be completed on trainees' own time	• Less accountability • No opportunity to receive feedback • If questions arise, trainees have to seek answers out on their own • Internet access needed • Device to view and listen to training needed (e.g., computer, tablet)
Reading, self-study	Reading training manual	• Cost effective • Can be completed on trainees' own time	• Less accountability • No opportunity to receive feedback • If questions arise, trainees need to seek answers out on their own

Figure 7.1 Training Modalities for SEL Program Implementation

- How could a survey be administered to school personnel to get a sense of their overall preference of training and use that to guide the type of training modality selected?

Organizational Drivers

Organizational drivers involve building an infrastructure to facilitate the implementation of universal SEL programs through developing internal and external partnerships, locating funding, allocating resources, and using data for decision-making (Freeman et al., 2015). Needs assessments (discussed in Chapter 5) and resources for organizational drivers to be utilized effectively are often developed and employed through administrators who have a sound understanding of the evidence-based program to be implemented (Eagle et al., 2015). School mental health teams and other school personnel charged with implementing SEL programs may work together to build a sound infrastructure for program implementation.

Organization is an important consideration during an even earlier stage (exploration stage) and should have been considered. However, as we have emphasized throughout this text thus far, this is a cyclical, problem-solving process, meaning that these factors that are highly influential of successful program implementation should be revisited and monitored closely. One aspect of organization to consider is the larger community and state-level context and policies, as well as sociopolitical factors that may be influential to the team's decision-making and programming. It is important to consider if any of these landscapes (e.g., organization, community, state-level context, federal-level context, sociopolitical factors) have changed since first deciding on program implementation, whether there are anticipated changes, and how the school can we plan for the likelihood of implementation and sustainability over time. Addressing social-emotional concerns for students in schools has become more recognized as a need not only during the pandemic but also seen as something that will need to be addressed in the aftermath of the pandemic. It is imperative to consider how pandemic is influencing the team's decision-making (e.g., more resources allocated toward mental health for students and staff, considering what grade levels to target in the initial program rollout, how to provide accessibly for families to share their perspective on mental health programming in schools). If a school had a universal SEL program in place prior to the pandemic, or a team was considering the implementation of a program before the pandemic, it is imperative to revisit what was implemented and how this may change as a result of this unprecedented event. Exercise 7.2 asks readers to reflect on data collection.

Exercise 7.2 Data Collection

Directions: Read the following case example and answer the questions below.

Last year, Motivated School District determined that they wanted to implement a universal, SEL program that targeted peer relationships with a focus on anti-bullying. Since those initial discussions a year ago, much has changed in terms of modality of school attendance, increased concern of students' social-emotional health, and increased awareness of police brutality and systemic racism. It would be problematic to ignore how school, society, resources, etc. have changed and to not include these considerations in decision-making.

Position	What data do you want to collect?	How would it be collected?
Administrator		
School mental health provider		
Teacher(s)		
Student(s)		
Family member(s)		
CMH provider(s)		
Community member(s)		

- It is not to say that the program should not be implemented, but rather how can the team incorporate the needs of students, teachers, and families and use data to inform whether this is the most appropriate program to implement this upcoming school year?
- Would you move forward with the program? Why or why not?
- Could it be adapted?

An imperative organizational component to consider is what type of data the team wants to collect, possibly before and certainly during implementation. Planning early and considering what you (and other stakeholders) want to learn from the data, how the data will be used, who the key players will be in the data system creation and maintenance, and how it will be presented to stakeholders are questions that may help guide the team in their decision-making.

It is important to ask these questions and consider the type of data that will be collected and process for collecting it because data will let the team know whether the SEL program is effective and contributes to meeting goals that have been set forth for the students/school. To add to these decisions, it is beneficial to determine how data will be managed and who the point person(s) will be for the data. The data management system that is used should be informed by the type of data the team determines is appropriate to collect (Gottfredson et al., 2015). For example, a cloud-based storage system could be used with the DESSA-Mini, given that the publishing company provides this service with the purchase of the screener. If visits to the nurse due to somatic complaints (e.g., stomachache, headache, loss of appetite) are data that is collected, determine whether the number of nurse visits and reasons for the visits could be tracked by the nurse. Similar to the training mentioned above for implementers, there is often training in data management systems (depending on what is selected), and it is encouraged that if training is offered, those who are the key players in managing data be involved with training. In the example with the school nurse, the team should create the system of data collection for somatic complaints and in collaboration with the nurse, determine whether it is feasible for them to collect, and adjust as necessary. Exercise 7.3 will take readers through types of data related to social-emotional concerns, while Exercise 7.4 will help readers identify reasons to resistance in implementation.

Exercise 7.3 Types of Data Related to Social-Emotional Health

Directions: Take a few moments, begin to brainstorm what type of data each team member wants to collect regarding student social-emotional health, and complete the following chart. To assist you in your efforts, examples of data that could be collected can be found below. Is your team or school already collecting any of this data? What would be helpful to collect?

Types of data related to student social-emotional health	Descriptions and examples	Is my team or school collecting this data?	If so, how is it being collected? Should it be changed?	Would this data help us determine program effectiveness?
Academic records	Grades, standardized test scores	☐ Yes ☐ No ☐ Not sure		☐ Yes ☐ No ☐ Not sure
Attendance	Attendance records, records indicating that student is arriving at school late or leaving school early	☐ Yes ☐ No ☐ Not sure		☐ Yes ☐ No ☐ Not sure
Behavior Monitoring and/or Discipline Referrals	Records of discipline referrals (e.g., infraction, type of discipline received)	☐ Yes ☐ No ☐ Not sure		☐ Yes ☐ No ☐ Not sure
Demographic Information	Records of race, ethnicity, student who are English Language Learners, free and reduced school lunch program	☐ Yes ☐ No ☐ Not sure		☐ Yes ☐ No ☐ Not sure
Program-Specific Surveys	Surveys that are specific to measuring outcomes of a particular program	☐ Yes ☐ No ☐ Not sure		☐ Yes ☐ No ☐ Not sure
School Climate Survey	Survey assessing perceptions of school environment completed by students, teachers, staff, and/or parents	☐ Yes ☐ No ☐ Not sure		☐ Yes ☐ No ☐ Not sure

Types of data related to student social-emotional health	Descriptions and examples	Is my team or school collecting this data?	If so, how is it being collected? Should it be changed?	Would this data help us determine program effectiveness?
Social-Emotional/Behavioral (SEB) Screening	SEB screening completed by teachers, parents, or student self-report	☐ Yes ☐ No ☐ Not sure		☐ Yes ☐ No ☐ Not sure

Adapted from Durlak (2016) and National Center for School Mental Health (2020a, 2020b)

Preparing for Successful Installation: Starting to Think Ahead and Problem-Solve

According to previous research, this stage is exciting, but it can also lead to frustration and resistance to change (change is hard!). Knowing this and being proactive in steps to reduce frustration and resistance can improve your success in implementation!

Exercise 7.4 Reasons for Resistance

Directions: Complete the following chart that will help you proactively identify reasons for resistance in implementation.

Who might resist?	Reason for resistance	Ideas to overcome resistance	What is needed for ideas to take place?

Common Barriers to Implementation

There are many barriers that may hinder efforts in implementing a universal social-emotional program. The first of these barriers is buy-in. **Buy-in** can be defined as commitment to the model (Vernez et al., 2006), and in this case it is commitment to the social-emotional program and processes of implementation. Reasons for lack of buy-in could be that educators and school personnel do not view universal SEL implementation as a priority (given everything else they have to do!), see it as time-consuming, may not understand the benefits, or may lack the skills to implement. Through initial and ongoing training and professional development, a clearer understanding and skill building can help improve buy-in. *Additionally, educators need reassurance and sound rationale that adopting a universal SEL prevention program is not just another passing educational trend but one that has real-life implications for bettering the lives of children.* Educators and school personnel may also be more likely to engage in universal SEL implementation if they are reinforced for their efforts (Pinkelman et al., 2015). Therefore, educators and school personnel may be more likely to adhere to program implementation if they receive public acknowledgment for their work. Some suggestions for public acknowledgment include rewards such as gift cards, class coverage, or even continuing education units (CEUs) for their participation in trainings and implementation (Pinkelman et al., 2015). Educators may be even more likely to support efforts if they see their efforts paying off through improved student outcomes or if their ideas regarding program implementation are put into place (Bambara et al., 2009; Pinkelman et al., 2015). Through district newsletters and staff meetings, positive examples can be provided in which grades or schools within the district that have met a goal of a certain percentage of implementation or have experienced a decreased percentage of behavior challenges, as evidenced by universal social-emotional/behavioral screening or behavioral referrals. By receiving training to grow knowledge and skills, reviewing data, and being recognized for their efforts, educators' knowledge and acceptance of implementation is likely to increase.

A second barrier to implementing a universal social-emotional program is that of fidelity. As mentioned earlier, **fidelity** or integrity refers to the degree to which a practice, such as a universal SEL intervention, is implemented as intended (McKenna & Parenti, 2017). *In order for universal SEL programming to be implemented with fidelity, school personnel need to commit to the notion that all children have the best opportunity to learn, grow, and succeed under such a framework.* When practices or interventions are delivered as they are intended, they have the best chance of succeeding. Even with an exemplary needs assessment, resource mapping, and educator "buy-in," a great challenge to implementing universal social-emotional centers on being able to execute the model with fidelity (King-Sears et al., 2018; McKenna & Parenti, 2017). In order to best ensure that program implementation is being carried out as an effective framework for preventative practice, the school mental health team and educators should work together to break the program down into its component parts. This allows each aspect of program implementation to be explicitly described, step by step, in words, and helps to ensure that all parts of the program are being implemented with integrity. A fidelity checklist can be formulated on key areas of the intervention and implementation and subsequently scored to determine the integrity of execution. In Chapters 9 and 10, the text will describe breaking down a universal SEL program into its component parts to assess fidelity. Also, an example of a fidelity checklist is provided and can be adapted to meet the needs of various programs.

Another barrier to effectively implementing universal SEL programming involves possessing adequate school resources (Bambara et al., 2009; Marrs & Little, 2014; Pinkelman et al., 2015). For purposes of this discussion, **school resources** are defined as time and funding. Educators and school personnel may find time constraints for effectively planning and implementing a universal intervention due to their primary job responsibilities, differing schedules between team members, school holidays, weather-related days off, and summer break. A study by Bambara et al. (2009) revealed that participants view the leading time barriers to be school schedules that provide few opportunities for school personnel to collaborate and plan. In order to overcome time restrictions, educators in previous studies have suggested that aligning, combining, and adapting new endeavors with already existing school protocols and teams may prove useful solutions (Bambara et al., 2009; Pinkelman et al., 2015). For instance, an ongoing evaluation of Tier 1 data across the academic, behavioral, and social-emotional domains may be incorporated into monthly instructional support team meetings. Funding has also been identified as a challenge to intervention implementation (Bambara et al., 2009; Marrs & Little, 2014; Pinkelman et al., 2015). Initial and ongoing trainings and materials such as books, videos, and computer programs all may be cost-prohibitive to districts that receive little financial support from their respective states. Adequate funding needs to be secured and allocated. Without adequate school resources, it will be very difficult for educators to establish buy-in and engage in program implementation.

Readiness of a school or organization for SEL program implementation is an important aspect of implementation. **Readiness** is defined as the ability and capacity to implement an SEL program or intervention effectively.

Research has suggested that there is a variety of factors that are linked to readiness of implementation, which then in turn links to high-quality implementation. Where are the team, school, and stakeholders in these areas (Bumbarger, 2015)?

Adapting SEL programming may occur due to interaction with contextual features and individual needs. It is encouraged that the program fit the population, meet the needs of the population, and be culturally appropriate. Therefore, adaptations may need to be made! However, what adaptations are made and the rationale for making them, how adaptations are made, communication with implementers about adaptations, and feedback from stakeholders must be considered. If not, it could lead to variation in implementation activity. This variation can stem from (Evans et al., 2015):

- Intervention training—How do those who are implementing the intervention/program acquire the knowledge about the program?
- Intervention assessment—Do those who are implementing the program think that the intervention is contextually appropriate?
- Intervention clarification—How is knowledge shared, and is support available for implementation?
- Intervention responsibility—What is the process of assigning accountability?

Clearly answering these questions and addressing them early in the installation process may help to improve consistency of implementation across implementers and fidelity of implementation. It is important to note that adaptation does not equate to automatic effectiveness (Durlak, 2016). Chapter 8 will go into more detail about types of program adaptations, how to make adaptations, and how to monitor them. However, it is important that possible adaptations are considered during this installation stage.

Conclusion

The installation stage is the stage at which organizational and personnel competencies and infrastructure are examined, and possibly changed, to improve the likelihood of SEL implementation success. The three implementation drivers—leadership, competency, and organization—are core components associated with the successful employment of evidence-based practices. Leadership, often in the form of administrators and the school mental health team, and leadership strategies are necessary, with two types described in this chapter (technical and adaptive). Competency drivers seek to build the knowledge of implementers through planned trainings and resources. Organizational drivers contribute to infrastructure by developing both internal and external partnerships to help strengthen resources and increase sustainability. This stage is the last one before implementing the program, and there are common barriers that arise. Understanding what common barriers are, reflecting on whether these may be true for your school/district, and proactively employing strategies to reduce those barriers are steps that are necessary before moving forward to the next stage.

Initial Implementation Stage   **8**

Learning Objectives

After reading this chapter, you should be able to:

- Summarize what the initial implementation stage is
- Identify quality indicators of successful implementation
- Describe the importance of cultural adaptation to SEL programs
- Define the three domains of cultural adaptation for SEL programs
- Describe the two ways ongoing evaluation should occur during implementation
- Describe the importance of ongoing team meetings and professional development

Initial Implementation Stage

Implementation refers to the initiation and delivery of the SEL program to students. This stage occurs when educators and other stakeholders are applying the newly learned knowledge and skills to the system. The initial implementation stage entails taking the previously agreed upon purpose, strategically utilizing the supports identified, and using the training of the SEL program received, and putting into practice. Due to this, the National Implementation Research Network (2017) reports that the initial implementation stage "is the most fragile stage where the awkwardness associated with trying new things and the difficulties associated with changing old ways of work are

DOI: 10.4324/9781003343479-8

strong motivations for giving up and going back to comfortable routines (business as usual)" (National Implementation Research Network, 2017).

Example: The purpose of implementing an SEL program in Sunny School District was to improve students' self-regulation skills and decrease stress for students and teachers. Given that the school mental health team identified that educators would prefer to implement skills regularly and throughout the day in short amounts of time (rather than one time per week for 45 minutes), the team selected a mindfulness-based program. A mindfulness program was selected because research has shown that mindfulness can be embedded within typical academic school curriculum and has been found to be effective for students (Janz et al., 2019). Research has also suggested that implementation of mindfulness has been found to be beneficial for teachers (Klingbeil & Renshaw, 2018). After mindfulness program training was complete, the school mental health team and teachers in the elementary school began implementation. Using a mindfulness-based intervention curriculum, teachers first introduced students to mindfulness and explicitly taught various mindfulness skills (e.g., identifying and becoming aware of one's thoughts and feelings, deep breathing, visualization). Throughout the school day, teachers would take brief pre-determined (e.g., morning meeting, when students return from recess or physical education, after lunch, during math lesson, end of school day) mindfulness breaks (2–5 minutes).

The chapters in this book leading up to this one have provided an in-depth discussion on selection and using data to inform decision-making. The purpose of this chapter is to describe components of high-quality implementation and adaptation of SEL programs. Additionally, guidance is provided regarding monitoring implementation and collecting data to determine effectiveness. Finally, a discussion occurs as to the importance of ongoing professional development opportunities for implementers.

Why Is Quality Implementation Important?

Research suggests that some of the most important factors affecting positive outcomes for students are the quality and level of SEL program implementation achieved (Durlak et al., 2011). For example, stronger outcomes are evident when implementation is better, and failure to achieve positive outcomes one sets out to achieve may occur if implementation is poor. This pattern has been found for both social-emotional/behavioral and academic outcomes (Durlak et al., 2011; Dix et al., 2012). While there is a lot of emphasis on SEL program promotion, effective SEL programs are used less widely. When they are used, they are often selected, implemented, and monitored in ways that lack consistency and intentionality, which may impact their success (Elias et al., 2015).

What does it mean for implementation of SEL programs to be "good quality?" According to Durlak (2016), there are several aspects of quality implementation. These include the following:

- Fidelity/integrity—The degree to which the major components of the program have been implemented as intended
- Dosage—How much or to what degree the program was delivered (how many minutes, per day, per week?)
- Quality of delivery—How well was the program implemented?
- Participant responsiveness or engagement—The degree to which the program maintains participants' attention and how much they are actively involved in the intervention
- Program differentiation—The way the program is different from other programs or interventions being delivered in the setting
- Monitoring of control conditions—The ways in which the control conditions (or business as usual conditions) are similar or dissimilar to the program
- Program reach—How much of the eligible population participated in the program
- Adaptation—The changes, if any, that were made to the program

The next chapter describes the importance of fidelity and ways to measure this. During the initial implementation stage, it important to continuously monitor integrity using the tools previously selected and using data to guide decisions. According to research, the integrity of new program implementation significantly decreases in just one to ten days from initial implementation (Sanetti et al., 2014)! This suggests that close and careful monitoring is imperative to increase likelihood of success. Also, by determining what areas are not being implemented fully, additional coaching or training can support implementers and benefit students. Rather than waiting until several weeks or months into implementation and not receiving the outcomes stakeholders hoped for, ongoing fidelity monitoring can improve the use of resources (e.g., time, training) and can strengthen implementation.

Cultural Adaptation of SEL Programs

Adaptations, particularly in schools, are important considerations when implementing SEL programs. Adaptations such as shortening lessons due to time constraints, modifying activities/exercises to tailor to student interest or developmental level, or reducing content that may be less relevant are common (Durlak, 2016). Making these adaptations are acceptable and research suggests that as long as the "effective ingredients" remain included in the program, adaptations do not reduce effectiveness of the program. It is highly recommended, however, that the adaptations made should be intentional, documented, and discussed among the team members.

In addition to the adaptations listed above, there has been a need for considering cultural and contextual factors of students, the community, and schools they are situated within when selecting and implementing an SEL program. The increasing diversity in US schools, coupled with what is known about marginalized students who are disproportionately and harshly disciplined, requires practitioners to increase the use of positive approaches to enhance students' well-being and overall school climates. Furthermore, we know that lack of cultural acknowledgment and lack of cultural responsiveness (of the program, treatment, and implementer) is one of the biggest barriers of service utilization and positive outcomes for marginalized individuals. Extending this to SEL programming for students in schools, it could be hypothesized that if the program, implementer, and team are not aware of or utilize a culturally responsive approach when supporting students, fewer positive outcomes may be experienced. Additionally, children and adolescents who are already disadvantaged and marginalized are disproportionately placed at risk for social-emotional concerns (Fegert et al., 2020). To best support the needs of students, particularly those who are historically and currently marginalized, it is imperative to consider culture and cultural adaptations when implementing programs, including SEL programs.

When we say the term "cultural adaptations," it is important to recognize what the term *culture* means. **Culture** is a set of meanings, behavioral norms, and values shared by members of a societal group or society. Each of us lives our culture all of the time, and therefore it is often considered invisible to us until we are faced with something that is different from our own. Culture is dynamic and fluid and impacts our everyday lives. In regard to SEL, culture influences how we view social, emotional, and behavior (e.g., What is it? What is acceptable or unacceptable? Why is important?) and whether/how we teach SEL skills (e.g., Are challenges with SEL skill indicative of child deficits? Or do students struggle because they haven't been taught the skill, haven't had enough opportunities, or haven't had the skill reinforced?). It is also important to remember that how we assess skills, what programs we implement, how we implement programming, and the type of data collection method we use, again, are all influenced by our culture.

Sometimes when we hear the term "culturally" responsive or when we consider cultural adaptations for programming, it is the belief that one needs to become an "expert" at all "other cultures" in order to be an effective implementer, practitioner, or leader. That is not true. In fact, there is no such thing as being an "expert" in other cultures. Rather than working toward expertise or competence, it is encouraged that school personnel work toward understanding and demonstrating cultural humility. Cultural humility is a change in overall perspective (Foronda et al., 2016) that is described as "a way of being" (Sue & Sue, 2016). One becomes **culturally humble** by being "aware of their own beliefs, biases, values, understanding how such beliefs impact their ability to effectively engage with all people, and approaching all individuals with openness and humility" (Fisher-Borne et al., 2015; Mosher et al., 2017).

According to Castro-Olivo et al. (2016), **cultural adaptation** describes the process of assessing characteristics of the target population and context to inform changes to practices or programming. In terms of SEL curriculum, thoughtful and strategic changes made to the program will help to improve buy-in, implementation, effectiveness, and sustainability in the long term. In a recent review of cultural adaptations (Brown et al., 2018), three domains emerged in which cultural adaptations often occur in SEL programs. Domains and definitions provided by Brown and colleagues (2018) include **content adaptations** ("modifications made to the intervention materials including adapting language, metaphors, goals, and concepts to increase cultural alignment"), **procedural adaptations** ("methods and processes used to inform the selection of particular modifications such as engaging stakeholders and reviewing program components"), and **program delivery adaptations** ("modifications to individuals, methods, and location of an intervention to support culturally sensitive implementation"). In a review of the type of adaptations made, content adaptations were the most common. Figure 8.1 provides an overview of the types of adaptations.

Example. In a large, urban, racially and ethnically diverse middle school, a school mental health team selected Strong Kids as the SEL universal curriculum. To increase representation, relevance, and interest for students, the team carefully reviewed materials (e.g., posters, worksheets) (content adaptations) and sought feedback from students' families (procedural adaptations) to determine whether the program was appropriate. In collaboration with families, the school mental health team adapted scenarios in the curriculum and materials to racially and linguistically connect to students (Doherty Kurtz et al., 2022).

Type of Adaptation	Potential Areas to Adapt	Description
Content Adaptations	• Language • Values • Customs • Goals • Traditions	• The language the materials and content are available or delivered in (e.g., English, Spanish) • Values taught in the program (e.g., teamwork, leadership) • Customs portrayed (e.g., how we greet one another) • Goals of the program (e.g., learn how to identify feelings) • Traditions portrayed (e.g., holidays, events attended)
Procedural Adaptations	• Evaluate program for appropriateness for population • Document what and how adaptations were made	• Engage stakeholders and community members to review program and materials to ensure cultural relevancy • Discuss whether program's purpose, mechanisms of change are consistent with culture • Consider consulting with program developer about recommendations for adaptation
Program Delivery Adaptations	• Consider characteristics of implementer • Consider characteristics of implementation setting	• Ensure the implementer understands the culture of students and cultural adaptations made to the program • Consider methods of delivering the program (e.g., whole class, small group, face to face, virtually)

Figure 8.1 Types of Cultural Adaptations

Example: In a mid-size urban school, an SEL team selected an SEL program to implement with their elementary school students that also included a trauma focused component. They were aware that a high number of students in the community have been exposed to trauma. Within the curriculum, SEL goals were emphasized and curriculum taught at the school- and class-wide levels. The curriculum also suggested that mental health clinicians facilitate small counseling consisting of students that have experienced first-hand, recent trauma. Although this format preserved resources, the SEL team and clinicians decided that individual counseling for students would be more appropriate (program delivery adaptation). It was also fortunate that the clinicians available to facilitate counseling were from the community and had both personal and professional experiences that some of the students were currently experiencing (program delivery consideration).

Example: With schools increasingly adopting virtual learning platforms in addition to in-person instruction, the implementation of SEL curriculum is required to be adapted. Some programs, such as Second Step, have already created the procedural adaptations for educators and teams. Other programs may not have done so already. It could also be the case that the program that your school or district has been implementing will continue to being implemented, with limited guidance for individual implementers on how to adapt to a remote learning environment. It is important for SEL implementation teams and leaders to discuss what and how adaptations should be made to both meet the needs of students as well as make it as feasible as possible for implementers. Decisions for adaptations should be carefully documented and closely monitored to ensure that adaptations are consistent so that data collected is both meaningful and interpretable.

When determining whether adaptations should be made and what adaptations to make, it is essential to have discussion with the team, stakeholders, community members, and those who may have knowledge about the culture or how to improve the relevancy for the target student population. Additionally, the rationale for adaptation should be considered, and the intention of the adaptation should be made clear. Furthermore, documentation of the type of adaptations made, how they were implemented, and what data were collected to determine effectiveness is imperative. This helps to better understand what works for students and improves the likelihood of replication if positive outcomes are achieved. The Framework for Reporting Adaptations and Modifications-Expanded (FRAME) suggests documenting adaptations to evidence-based interventions and the process of implementation (Wiltsey Stirman et al., 2019). FRAME suggests reporting:

- When and how the modification to the intervention or process was made
- Whether the modification was planned/proactive or unplanned/reactive
- Who determined the need for the modification
- What was modified
- The level of delivery the modification was made
- Type or nature of context or content-level modification
- Extent to which modification was consistent with fidelity of implementation
- Reasons for modification

This is a great way to systematically consider adaptations and raises questions to consider when deciding if a change is to occur. Exercise 8.1 takes readers through considerations for cultural program adaptation. Figure 8.2 is a chart that allows readers to document adaptations made to the SEL curriculum.

Exercise 8.1 Cultural Program Adaptation

Directions: Individually or with your team, consider what adaptations may be necessary to improve the representation, relevancy, effectiveness, and sustainability of the SEL program that is going to be implemented.

What adaptation needs to be made?	How will it be made?	Type of adaptation	Rationale
Ex. Storybooks suggested in SEL program contain only White characters.	Substitute suggested storybooks with those that include characters who are racially, ethnically, and linguistically diversity. Ensure that new storybooks selected are teaching a similar topic (e.g., empathy, friendship)	Content	Students are racially, ethnically, and linguistically diverse. Representation of characters is necessary

Use the chart below to document program adaptations made to the SEL curriculum.

Describe adaptation	Type of adaptation	When did the adaptation occur?	Who participated in the decision to adapt?	Rationale	Goal of adaptation	Data collected to determine effectiveness of adaptation

Figure 8.2 Chart Documenting Adaptations Made to an SEL Curriculum

Evaluation During Implementation

During implementation, evaluation of the SEL program should occur in two ways. The first is the ongoing monitoring and measuring of the components that contribute to implementation, or in other words, evaluating fidelity of implementation. If implementation is not evaluated, teams/schools run the risk of poor implementation, which can lead to not achieving desired outcomes. Many resources, such as personnel, trainings, time, resources, and commitment, have been put into planning this far into the process, so it would be waste of resources if implementation is poor! It can also lead to a reduced likelihood in the future for personnel to buy into SEL program implementation if they have had negative experiences (or no outcomes). If limited desired outcomes are achieved, is it that the program is ineffective, or is it that implementation was poor? This will be further discussed in Chapter 9, in which implementation fidelity is described, and Chapter 10, in which program effectiveness is featured.

The second way is the ongoing monitoring of desired outcomes that the SEL program was intended to target. In earlier chapters of the book, we discussed the importance of identifying and prioritizing the outcomes desired as well as selecting a tool to measure these outcomes. It is recommended to continuously collect data on this and evaluate it so that progress can be monitored, and the ongoing evaluation of effectiveness is documented. It would be discouraging if an SEL program were implemented for months and months, and at the end of the school year, it is determined that it was less effective or not targeting the outcomes desired.

Sharing data among team members is important, but be sure to share it with families, students, community members, and others who collaborated and are invested in this process, implementers. For SEL programming to be implemented, many people were involved in the process. Therefore, sharing what is going well and what is continuing to be improved can be motivating for all to hear about. For example, inviting families, students, and community members to meetings in which data will be shared is one way to deliver information and seek feedback. Another is to include helpful visuals of data (e.g., pie graphs, charts) in family or school-wide newsletters highlighting improvements in student outcomes (e.g., aggregated social-emotional/behavioral screening data), percentage of educators implementing the SEL across the district (e.g., all kindergarten, first, and second grade teachers are now implementing the program; in the upcoming weeks, the third, fourth, and fifth grade teachers will begin), and successes in the process. This is especially important, given that momentum can be a challenge to maintenance and sustainability (Akin et al., 2017). More information about this will be discussed in the following chapter (Chapter 9, "Full Implementation").

Ongoing Team Meetings, Professional Development, and Technical Assistance

Professional development, training about the SEL program selected, and technical assistance were likely implemented for team members, implementers, and support personnel earlier in the process and before implementation. As we highlighted in chapters earlier in the book, it is recommended that ongoing team meetings and professional development be planned for (e.g., time, cost, support) throughout implementation and not just when introducing SEL or the SEL program. It should be considered an ongoing part of the implementation process. Often, targeted support or ongoing support can be offered as part of the purchase of different SEL programs (e.g., Second Step Elementary Classroom kits), or schools can contact the authors for professional consultation. It is helpful for implementers to come together to refresh skills, problem-solve challenges, and celebrate successes. If there are updates to the program (e.g., technology updates) or data collection procedures, pre-planned meetings provide an opportunity to seamlessly share information with those who are involved. Some teams prefer to schedule meetings that are specific to this purpose, others may set aside time during already existing team meetings to dedicate time to discuss these issues. Figure 8.3 provides readers a checklist to use in determining whether meetings are scheduled and accessible to team members.

See the checklist below to determine whether ongoing meetings are scheduled and accessible for the team:

	Yes or No	If yes, when are they scheduled?	If no, when could they be scheduled?
Are regular meetings or professional development scheduled for the team?			
Are regular meetings or professional development scheduled for the implementers?			

Are the following addressed in ongoing team meetings?	Yes or No
Information and updates about the program or data collection procedures	
Data sharing and interpretation	
Problem-solving	
Time for coaching and mentoring	
Decision-making about ongoing data collection	

Figure 8.3 Meeting Scheduling

Conclusion

The National Implementation Research Network (n.d.) reports that the initial implementation is the most fragile stage of implementation, given that is a time when educators, implementers, and team members are applying the newly learned knowledge and skills to the school system. Within this stage, initial implementation refers to the initiation and delivery of the SEL program to students and occurs on a small scale. While it is important to consider this stage as extension of the previous (Installation), and the foundation of the next (Full Implementation), there are unique features that must be carefully considered during this phase to improve likelihood of success. It is important to consider the quality indicators of successful implementation (which will be discussed further in Chapter 9) and consider when and how to consider culture and adapt SEL programming accordingly. Lastly, it is recommended that the team continuously schedule regular times to meet as well as consider who will be involved with ongoing data collection throughout implementation and how data will be collected and analyzed.

Full Implementation Stage

9

Learning Objectives

After reading this chapter, you should be able to:

- Summarize what the full implementation stage is
- Describe the four critical indicators that suggest whether a school has entered the full implementation stage
- Define scaling up
- Identify the four important components to scaling up a universal social-emotional program
- Describe why depth and a shift in ownership are important to scaling up a universal social-emotional program

Full Implementation Stage

Arguably, the most difficult stage for schools to reach when employing new supports is that of full implementation. Therefore, implementation team members and educators who reach this stage should rejoice but also realize that employing a universal social-emotional program, or any new intervention or practice, is an ongoing and fluid process. Consequently, it often takes two to four years for schools to move from the exploration stage to the full implementation stage when employing a new intervention or program, (Brown et al., 2014; Fixsen et al., 2007; National Implementation Research Network, n.d.).

DOI: 10.4324/9781003343479-9

During the full implementation stage, the employment of universal social-emotional supports has become part of everyday practice and is incorporated into a standard routine (Metz & Bartley, 2012; Sanetti et al., 2019a). Therefore, the adoption of a universal social-emotional program and supporting mental wellness within a school becomes integrated into educator, school, and district practices, policies, and procedures (Bertram et al., 2015; Metz & Bartley, 2012). Throughout the full implementation stage, the skillful use of a universal social-emotional program is well integrated into the repertoire of teachers and other educators implementing the support (Duda & Wilson, 2015). Moreover, a full discontinuation of non-evidence-based practices and beliefs should have taken place through de-implementation. Recall that de-implementation involves the elimination of faulty and non-evidence-based practices. For example, the belief that children cannot be taught social-emotional skills is a common misguided belief. In thinking about de-implementation, educators should ask the following questions:

1) What ineffective or non-evidence-based practices are currently in place in our school that could be hindering students social-emotional development?
2) What is allowing these ineffective or non-evidence-based practice to continue?
3) How can we prevent the continuation of ineffective and non-evidence-based practices in our school?

Upon reaching the full implementation stage, a primary focus of the implementation team is to sustain the implementation infrastructure put into place during the installation stage and refined in the initial implementation stage (Metz et al., 2015). A secondary focus of implementation teams during the full implementation stage is to develop strategies for improving the effectiveness of the universal social-emotional programs and/or the efficiency of implementation to improve outcomes (Metz et al., 2015). For example, the implementation may examine the schedules of teachers to determine the best time of the day to provide them ongoing training and support in implementing a universal social-emotional program. There are four critical indicators that educators can use to tell whether they have entered the full implementation stage. These four critical indicates are proficiency, staffing, fidelity, and data collection (Fixsen & Blase, 2011; Fixsen et al., 2019).

Indicator 1: Proficiency

The first key indicator as to whether a school has reached the full implementation stage is when at least 50% of allocated educators are routinely employing the universal social-emotional program with fidelity (Brown et al., 2014; Fixsen et al., 2007; National Implementation Research Network, n.d.). Therefore, to reach the full implementation stage, at least half of the allocated educators designated to deliver the universal social-emotional program should be practitioners who currently meet the fidelity criteria for employing the support. For example, if a school has allocated ten teachers to employ a universal social-emotional program, and eight of the ten teachers have not demonstrated adequate proficiency on the fidelity checklist for implementing the universal social-emotional program, the full implementation stage has not been reached (Fixsen & Blase, 2011). For schools to reach the full implementation stage of employing a universal social-emotional program, staff must be trained and well-versed in using the support effectively. As a result, staff will need to be adequately trained by someone proficient in using the program who can offer ongoing coaching and feedback (Brown et al., 2014; Fixsen et al., 2007; National Implementation Research Network, n.d.).

Indicator 2: Staffing

A second indicator as to whether a school has reached the full implementation stage revolves around having adequate staffing. For example, if a school has allocated ten teachers to employ a universal social-emotional program, and there are seven instructor vacancies, the full implementation stage cannot be reached (Fixsen & Blase, 2011). Similarly, if a school has ten well-trained teachers implementing a universal social-emotional program with fidelity, and six of those instructors retire, the school is no longer in the full implementation stage, as it now has less than 50% of their allocated staff able to employ the universal social-emotional program (Brown et al., 2014; Fixsen et al., 2007; National Implementation Research Network, n.d.). Overall, to reach the full implementation stage, schools need to maintain staff who are well-versed in universal social-emotional support and can implement it with fidelity. If schools cannot maintain or meet staffing needs, they will either not be able to reach the full implementation stage or will no longer meet the criteria for being in the full implementation stage. Therefore, the overall job of the implementation team at the full implementation stage is to ensure that effective practices continue to be improved and maintained over time in light of transitions in school leadership and staff (National Implementation Research Network, n.d.).

Indicator 3: Fidelity

As mentioned earlier, aside from adequate staffing and proficiency in employing the universal social-emotional program, schools need staff who can implement the support as intended (Fixsen & Blase, 2011; Fixsen et al., 2019). Therefore, schools whose staff are unable to implement the universal social-emotional program with integrity are unable to reach the full implementation stage. Moreover, schools that have not developed or put a fidelity assessment into place cannot enter the full implementation stage (Fixsen & Blase, 2011; Fixsen et al., 2019). Consequently, implementation teams should work together to maintain fidelity by developing their integrity assessment or utilizing the sample integrity checklist found in Chapter 9 to determine which staff are delivering the universal social-emotional program as intended (Fixsen & Blase, 2011). For ease of reference, a brief preview of the fidelity checklist provided in Chapter 9 is provided in Figure 9.1, and a more in-depth discussion on implementation integrity will also take place in the same chapter. It is generally advised that schools complete a fidelity assessment or checklist on staff implementing the universal social-emotional program at least bi-annually or quarterly throughout the school year (Halle et al., 2015).

In conjunction with a fidelity checklist, Fixsen and Blase (2009) developed a brief implementation quotient measure. The brief measure not only takes into account practitioner competency in delivering a universal social-emotional program but also considers staff turnover and can be used at any point during the school year (Fixsen & Blase, 2009; Fixsen et al., 2019). The implementation quotient measure can be used to better determine whether half of the educators or school staff implementing a universal social-emotional program are doing so as intended. Figure 9.2 shows a completed implementation quotient measure, and Exercise 9.1 has readers complete the implementation quotient measure on their own. It is worthy to note that implementation teams should complete the implementation quotient measure after collecting data from their universal social-emotional program fidelity checklist.

Adherence

Definition:
- Whether or not the specific components of the program were implemented as planned

Key:
- 2 points = High level of implementation integrity
- 1 point = Inconsistent level of implementation integrity
- 0 points = Instructional element not implemented
- N/O = Not observed

Before Program Implementation

Area being Evaluated	Rating				Comments
Materials are ready	2	1	0	N/O	
Materials for students are ready	2	1	0	N/O	
Materials are presented in an organized fashion	2	1	0	N/O	
The purpose of today's social-emotional lesson is introduced	2	1	0	N/O	

Instructional Presentation

Area being evaluated	Rating				Comments
Follows steps in program lesson	2	1	0	N/O	
Follows standardized/prescribed wording in program (if provided)	2	1	0	N/O	
Models skills/strategies appropriately	2	1	0	N/O	

Figure 9.1 Fidelity Checklist Preview

Exercise 9.1 Implementation Quotient Exercise

Directions: Referencing the example above, complete the implementation quotient measure below. To best ensure that school staff are employing the universal social-emotional program with fidelity, use this implementation quotient measure in conjunction with an integrity checklist (see Figure 10.2 found in Chapter 10 for an example fidelity checklist).

Number of positions in your school allocated to use the universal social-emotional program: 10

Status of Practitioner	Score for status of position		How many practitioners in position?		Total
Practitioner Position vacant	0	+	1	=	1
Practitioner in position, untrained in program implementation	1	+	1	=	2
Practitioner completed initial training	2	+	0	=	2
Practitioner trained receives weekly coaching	3	+	2	=	5
Practitioner met fidelity criteria on integrity checklist as of this month	4	+	3	=	7
Practitioner met fidelity criteria on integrity checklist 10 of past 12 months	5	+	3	=	8
Total	—		**10**	=	**25**

10	÷	**25**	=	**40%**
Practitioners in Position	÷	Total	=	40% < 50% Full implementation stage criteria not met

Figure 9.2 Example of Completed Implementation Quotient Measure (Fixsen & Blase, 2009)

Number of positions in your school allocated to use the universal social-emotional program: _____

Status of Practitioner	Score for status of position	How many practitioners in position?	Total
Practitioner Position vacant	_____ +	_____ =	_____
Practitioner in position, untrained in program implementation	_____ +	_____ =	_____
Practitioner completed initial training	_____ +	_____ =	_____
Practitioner trained receives weekly coaching	_____ +	_____ =	_____
Practitioner met fidelity criteria on integrity checklist as of this month	_____ +	_____ =	_____
Practitioner met fidelity criteria on integrity checklist 10 of past 12 months	_____ +	_____ =	_____
Total	—	_____ =	_____

_____	÷	_____	=	_____
Practitioners in Position		Total		Are at least 50% of staff employing the universal social-emotional program with fidelity? ☐ Yes ☐ No

Indicator 4: Data Collection

The last key indicator of whether a school has entered the full implementation stage is that it has developed adequate data collection methods and is regularly referring to the information that it has collected to make data-based decisions (Halle et al., 2015). Therefore, data-collection and data-based decision-making are utilized frequently to assess fidelity, the responses of students taking part in the universal social-emotional program, and areas in need of improvement

(Halle et al., 2015; Prenger & Schildkamp, 2018; Schildkamp, 2019). Ideally, schools that have reached the full implementation stage of employing a universal social-emotional program have developed and outlined what types of data will be collected, how often data will be collected, what times of the year will this data be gathered, and how this data will be used to improve student, teacher, and program outcomes (Halle et al., 2015; Prenger & Schildkamp, 2018; Schildkamp, 2019). Moreover, schools that have reached the full implementation stage have created tools and systems for quickly collecting data, monitoring fidelity, identifying problems in program delivery, and solutions to address such problems (Halle et al., 2015; Prenger & Schildkamp, 2018).

By analyzing data regularly in the full implementation stage, schools can effectively gain knowledge and learn new lessons on how to sustain and improve upon efforts to effectively implement their universal social-emotional program (Halle et al., 2015). Therefore, at the full implementation stage, the data is collected regularly and is used to guide modifications or adaptations to the universal social-emotional program in place (Halle et al., 2015). Subsequently, the data can be used to carefully evaluate whether such changes ensure that fidelity to critical elements of the program are not compromised (Halle et al., 2015). In the following chapter, utilizing data-based decisions will be discussed in greater detail. For now, readers are encouraged to complete Exercise 9.2 to gauge whether or not their schools have reached the full implementation stage. Figure 9.3 provides an overview of the four indicators of full implementation.

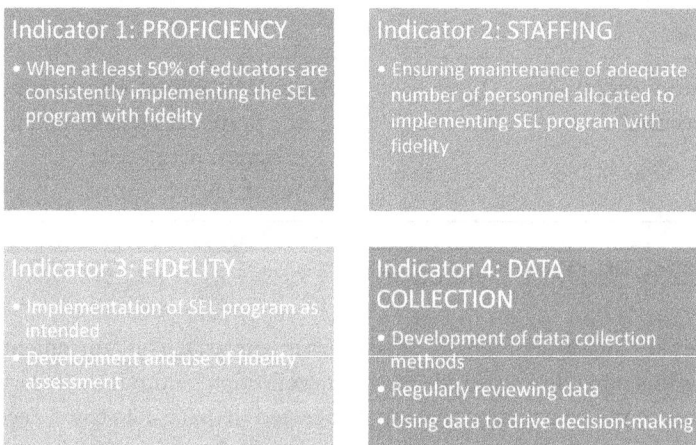

Indicator 1: PROFICIENCY	Indicator 2: STAFFING
• When at least 50% of educators are consistently implementing the SEL program with fidelity	• Ensuring maintenance of adequate number of personnel allocated to implementing SEL program with fidelity
Indicator 3: FIDELITY	Indicator 4: DATA COLLECTION
• Implementation of SEL program as intended • Development and use of fidelity assessment	• Development of data collection methods • Regularly reviewing data • Using data to drive decision-making

Figure 9.3 Four Indicators of Full Implementation

Exercise 9.2 Full Implementation Stage Checklist

Directions: Complete the checklist below to gauge whether your school has reached the full implementation stage. *If any answers to the questions in each area are a "no" response, the school implementing the universal social-emotional program has not reached the full implementation stage.*

Proficiency	No	Yes
• Have staff had adequate training on utilizing the universal social-emotional program?		
• Was the training completed with someone proficient in using the program, such as a consultant to the company selling the program?		
• Was frequent and ongoing feedback provided to staff utilizing the program to assist them in becoming proficient?		
• Do at least 50% of the allocated school staff designated to deliver the universal social-emotional program do so with fidelity (utilize the fidelity checklist and the implementation quotient measure)?		
Staffing	No	Yes
• Does the school have an adequate number of staff to implement the universal social-emotional program?		
• Does the school anticipate any staff proficient at delivering the universal social-emotional program to be leaving within the next year (e.g., retirement, moving to a different school within the district, switching positions, taking a leave of absence, etc.)?		
Fidelity	No	Yes
• Does the school have an assessment or fidelity checklist to determine whether the universal social-emotional program is being delivered with integrity?		
• Is this fidelity assessment or checklist being used bi-annually or quarterly throughout the school year?		
• Has the implementation quotient measure been completed to determine if 50% of the allocated school staff are delivering the universal social-emotional program with fidelity?		

Data Collection Methods	No	Yes
• Has the school outlined what types of data it will be collecting to determine whether the universal social-emotional program is being delivered with fidelity (see Chapter 9 for further information)?		
• Has the school outlined what types of data it will be collecting to determine whether the universal social-emotional program is effective and is benefiting students (see Chapter 9 for further information)?		
• Has the school created tools and systems for quickly collecting data on the fidelity to which the universal social-emotional program is being delivered?		
• Has the school created tools and systems for quickly collecting data on whether the universal social-emotional program being implemented is effective and is benefiting their student population?		
• Is data regularly being collected on the fidelity of program implementation?		
• Is data regularly being collected on whether the universal social-emotional program is effective (see Chapter 9 for more information)?		
• Is the data regularly being utilized to make decisions as to whether the universal social-emotional program is being implemented with fidelity?		
• Is the data regularly being utilized to make decisions as to whether the universal social-emotional program is benefiting students?		
• Is the data collected regularly being disseminated to staff using the universal social-emotional program to provide them feedback?		

Scaling Up Universal Social-Emotional Programs

Once schools have successfully reached the full implementation stage, implementation teams can begin to focus on scaling up the use of a universal social-emotional program beyond that of a single classroom, grade level, or even school. **Scaling up** refers to the process by which educators move from initially implementing and showing an intervention or program is successful on a small scale to its widespread adoption across multiple classrooms, grade levels, schools, or even districts (Bacon, 2011; Klinger et al., 2013). Scaling up a new social-emotional program involves more than just frequently using routines, activities, and materials associated with it (Klinger et al., 2013). Instead, scaling up also involves the ubiquitous buy-in of norms, beliefs, and principles underlying the program or practice to be undertaken (Klinger et al., 2013).

Although scaling up an intervention, program, or practice can be a daunting task, educators have completed such adoptions in the past. Arguably, the most widely scaled up interventions and programs have come under the intervention service delivery model of school-wide positive behavior support (Spaulding et al., 2008). For instance, in 2008, it was reported that nearly 8,000 schools across the United States were at various stages of adopting and implementing interventions and programs under school-wide positive behavior support and that many of these schools sustained implementation beyond 10 years (Spaulding et al., 2008). By 2018, over 26,000 schools across America had adopted and were employing interventions and programs under School-Wide Positive Behavior Supports (SWPBS; Sugai & Horner, 2020). Given these figures, it is extremely possible for schools to not only adopt but sustain the implementation of a universal social-emotional program using the stages of implementation science. Coburn (2003) suggested that there are four important components to scaling up interventions, programs, and school reform efforts: depth, sustainability, spread, and a shift in ownership.

Depth

For schools to effectively scale up implementation of a universal social-emotional program, deep change needs to occur. **Depth** or deep change refers to the fundamental alteration of attitudes, behaviors, assumptions, and expectations of educators employing universal social-emotional programs (Coburn, 2003). Therefore, during the full implementation stage, educators should have a firm understanding as to why they are employing a universal social-emotional program and how that social-emotional program will benefit the students they teach academically, behaviorally, emotionally. Therefore, as discussed throughout this text, implementation teams need to establish "buy-in" from those implementing the universal social-emotional program (Choi et al., 2019; Kennedy, 2019).

Coburn (2003) indicates that because educators draw on their prior beliefs, knowledge, and experience, they tend to gravitate toward approaches that are congruent with their prior practices or what they know. Therefore, educators who have not fully bought into implementing a universal social-emotional program may simply focus on the surface-level attributes of it, such as the materials or activities, as opposed to deeper pedagogical principles as to how the program can truly impact students mental health, well-being, and development of interpersonal relationships (Coburn, 2003). Therefore, when implementing a universal social-emotional program, an educator should not simply view themselves as a passive instructor of mental health and wellness practices. Instead, the educator should view themselves as an active facilitator whose efforts instill social-emotional learning in students. Consequently, educators implementing social-emotional programs need to understand the history of children's mental health efforts in education and how children's social-emotional well-being impacts not only their feelings and emotions but everyday interactions with people and academic performance (Brännlund et al., 2017; Kang-Yi et al., 2018; Murphy et al., 2015; Teo et al., 1996).

Educators tasked with implementing social-emotional programs tend to go "above and beyond" the program by showing empathy, appropriate social interactions, and incorporating mental wellness into their daily classroom routine. In other words, educators who have a deep understanding as to why they are teaching social-emotional learning do so even outside the allocated times in which the program is being implemented (Coburn, 2003). To put it simply, these educators "just get it." To capture depth, Coburn (2003) recommends completing in-depth interviews with educators, conducting observations, collecting student work samples, or even letting those implementing the program present what they have learned in using it.

Sustainability

To successfully scale up a universal social-emotional program, its use in the full implementation stage must be sustained. **Sustainability** refers to the ability of a program to be implemented with fidelity over time (Coburn, 2003; Klinger et al., 2013). Therefore, the distribution and adoption of a universal social-emotional program are only significant if its use can be sustained in subsequent classrooms, schools, or districts (Coburn, 2003). For instance, if a universal social-emotional program cannot be used with fidelity over time, it is unlikely to have a considerable impact on many children. Often even if a school successfully implements a universal social-emotional program, it may find it difficult to sustain its use due to competing priorities, changing demands, and staff turnover (Coburn, 2003; Klinger et al., 2013). Therefore, it is important for educators to be able to use the universal social-emotional program over a long period.

Of particular vulnerability to schools sustaining a program or reform effort is whether or not it is viewed as being externally developed or forced upon educators (Coburn, 2003). For example, if educators are not aware of why mental health is important to student learning, or if they do not view mental health as a problem their students face, they may feel as though implementing a universal social-emotional program is being forced upon them. Likewise, educators may view a local university's efforts to work with the school on improving social-emotional learning in children as externally developed. Consequently, educators may believe that the academic scholars attempting to promote social-emotional learning in children at their school are dictating to them what to do from an "ivory tower."

To sustain universal social-emotional program efforts, schools should utilize a needs assessment, resource mapping, distributed leadership, and open dialogue to increase buy-in, interest, and obtain ongoing support. Educators implementing universal social-emotional programs are better able to overcome competing priorities, changing demands, and staff turnover if communication and dialogue remain open and when there are mechanisms in place to support their efforts (Coburn, 2003). Overall, the key to sustainability is to best prepare and become aware of potential changes in priorities, demands, and staff turnover and to address such difficulties through a professional community of colleagues who have developed a plan for such alterations (Coburn, 2003; Klinger et al., 2013). Consequently, the implementation team is a vital support to educators employing a universal social-emotional program.

Spread

Outside of sustainability, a program's spread is important to scaling up its use across classrooms, schools, and districts (Coburn, 2003). **Spread** refers to both the social-emotional program being used across classrooms and schools along with the distribution of underlying beliefs, norms, and principles that come with the program (Coburn, 2003). For example, if another school within the district begins implementing the universal social-emotional program without buying into the concept that internalizing concerns can be prevented and mental wellness can be taught, there is less a chance for the program to be sustained. Rather than thinking about spread in terms of expanding social-emotional programs to more classrooms and schools, a focus on distributing statistics, facts, and information on why mental health and wellness programs are needed in education (Coburn, 2003; Klinger et al., 2013) is an effective strategy to improve spread. Additionally, educators looking to scale up the use of universal social-emotional programs may have to inform their colleagues and district administrators on the history and statistics regarding childhood mental health and wellness. Therefore, to scale up the use of a universal social-emotional program across classrooms or schools, efforts need to be made to reform norms and principles that influence district procedures, policies, and professional development (Coburn, 2003). Exercise 9.3 will have readers answer questions as to how they can increase the spread of a universal social-emotional program beyond their classrooms or schools.

Exercise 9.3 Spread Questionnaire

Directions: As discussed throughout this text, there are many variables to consider in why a fellow educator, school, or even district may not want to buy into utilizing a universal social-emotional program. Either individually or with a team, answer the questions below to come up with solutions as to how you can help the spread of implementing a universal social-emotional program.

1) What is the name of the universal social-emotional program that you would like either your co-worker, school, or district to use?

   _____

2) What information do you feel is important for your co-worker, school, or district to know about the program that will help them buy into using it?

   _____

   _____

   _____

3) What information do you feel is important for your co-worker, school, or district to know about regarding childhood mental health and well-being that may increase their understanding of why a universal social-emotional program is needed?

   _____

   _____

   _____

4) How will you effectively present information on the universal social-emotional program to a co-worker, school, or district? Do you feel that verbally presenting the information is enough, or is a presentation of data from your use of the program important to better inform others?

_____

_____

_____

5) Other than a presentation, how else can you inform others about the universal social-emotional program you are using with your student population in your school or district?

_____

_____

_____

6) Within your school, how can you work to reform norms and principles that may influence policies, procedures, and professional development regarding the universal social-emotional program and student mental health and wellness?

_____

_____

_____

Shift in Ownership

Lastly, to scale up the use of a universal social-emotional program, a shift in ownership needs to take place. A **shift in ownership** refers to the alteration of the universal social-emotional program from being viewed as an "external effort" to it being viewed as part of internal reform (Coburn, 2003). Therefore, the employment of a universal social-emotional program is no longer seen as an external effort by a select few within the school or even consultants outside of the school but now is viewed as an undertaking by professionals within the school (Coburn, 2003). Through a shift in ownership, educators within the school building see it as their responsibility to sustain, spread, and deepen reform efforts using the universal social-emotional program (Coburn, 2003).

One of the critical components of scaling up the use of a universal social-emotional program is to shift authority and knowledge of the reform from external efforts and professionals to that of internal efforts and school staff (Coburn, 2003). To shift authority, schools one again must turn to the data gathered in their needs assessments, observations of staff, interviews, and information provided through resource mapping. By utilizing this information, implementation teams can develop a plan to shift ownership to internal and more distributed efforts across a school.

Coburn (2003) outlines three methods for shifting ownership to further scale up a program's use. The first being to increase the knowledge of staff regarding why a universal social-emotional program has been put into place to create "buy-in." Through increasing staff knowledge regarding student mental health and how the universal social-emotional program promotes social-emotional wellness, educators are more likely to buy into why the support has been put into place.

Secondly, to shift ownership, there needs to be a change in transferring substantive and strategic decision-making from the implementation team to educators within the school (Coburn, 2003). Although the implementation team will still help guide decision-making regarding the universal social-emotional program, educator's views outside the implementation team will be further be considered. By further including educators into the decision-making process, they are more likely to take an increasing interest in seeing the universal social-emotional program succeed and feel a sense of ownership for its success.

Finally, to shift ownership, schools and districts may be required to develop the capacity to generate continued funding for the program (Coburn, 2003). Although external grant funding may initially support efforts to afford training, professional development, and outside consultation for the universal social-emotional program, schools and districts should strive to be self-sufficient in case funding diminishes (Coburn, 2003). Overall for a shift in ownership to occur, several indicators have to be present, including (a) the presence of mechanisms for ongoing educator learning about the universal social-emotional program being implemented (e.g., professional development); (b) the presence of established strategies to provide ongoing funding for mental health and wellness reform efforts and implementing the universal social-emotional program; (c) the degree to which schools or districts have taken responsibility for the continued spread of the reform and the universal social-emotional program; (d) the use of methods to incorporate school or district personnel in decision-making, such as through completing a needs assessment or staff interviews (Coburn, 2003). Exercise 9.4 has readers evaluate whether their school has taken effective steps toward a shift in ownership in regard to implementing a universal social-emotional program.

Exercise 9.4 Indicators for Shift in Ownership

Directions: Answer the questions below to gauge whether your school has made progress toward the process of shifting ownership for implementing the universal social-emotional program.

1) What mechanisms are in place for ongoing educator learning about social-emotional wellness within the school and the universal social-emotional program being implemented (e.g., professional development, book study on child mental health, etc.)?

_____

_____

_____

2) What established strategies are in place to provide ongoing funding for social-emotional wellness efforts and implementing the universal social-emotional program?

_____

_____

_____

3) How is your school or district taking responsibility for the continued spread of social-emotional efforts and use of the universal social-emotional program?

_____

_____

_____

4) What efforts has your school or district made to incorporate staff into the decision-making regarding social-emotional wellness in your school

and use of the universal social-emotional program (e.g., needs assessment, staff interviews, etc.)?

_____

_____

_____

Conclusion

The full implementation stage is arguably the most difficult to reach when employing a new universal social-emotional program in schools. Consequently, it typically takes two to four years for schools to arrive at this stage and integrate the use of a social-emotional program into everyday use with fidelity. Several key indicators can inform implementation teams and educators of whether they have entered for full implementation stage that revolves around proficiency, staffing, fidelity, and data collection (Fixsen & Blase, 2011; Fixsen et al., 2019). To reach the full implementation stage, at least half of the allocated educators designated to deliver the universal social-emotional program are filled with practitioners who meet the fidelity criteria for employing in the support (Brown et al., 2014; Fixsen et al., 2007; National Implementation Research Network, n.d.). In addition to proficiency, schools who reach the full implementation stage have enough staffing to sustain employing the social-emotional program. Therefore, schools that successfully implement a universal social-emotional program at the full implementation stage are not short on staff who are proficient in utilizing the support (Fixsen & Blase, 2011; Fixsen et al., 2019). Aside from staffing needs, and as mentioned, schools that have reached the full implementation stage have staff who can deliver the program with fidelity and possess a fidelity checklist for the support (Fixsen & Blase, 2011; Fixsen et al., 2019). Finally, schools that have reached the full implementation stage have developed adequate data collection methods and are frequently referring to the information that they have collected to make data-based decisions (Halle et al., 2015).

After reaching the full implementation stage, implementation teams and educators can turn their attention to scaling up the use of a universal social-emotional program. Scaling up is defined as the process by which educators move from employing a universal on a small scale to the widespread adoption across multiple classrooms, grade levels, schools, or even districts (Bacon, 2011; Klinger et al., 2013). There are four important components to scaling up a universal social-emotional program: depth, sustainability, spread, and shift in ownership (Coburn, 2003). Depth refers to the fundamental change of beliefs, behaviors, assumptions, and expectations of educators employing the universal social-emotional program (Coburn, 2003). Sustainability is defined as the ability of a program to be implemented with integrity over time (Coburn, 2003). Universal social-emotional programs that are difficult to implement or are unable to be implemented over time due to competing priorities are likely to be prematurely abandoned by educators (Coburn, 2003; Klinger et al., 2013). Spread refers to both the social-emotional program being used across classrooms and schools along with the distribution of underlying beliefs, norms, and principles that come with the program. Finally, for a universal social-emotional program to be scaled up, there needs to be a shift in ownership. A shift in ownership refers to the alteration of the universal social-emotional program from being viewed as an "external effort" to it being viewed as part of internal reform (Coburn, 2003). Ultimately, to scale up the use of a universal social-emotional program, implementation teams should seek to involve their fellow educators by using their input from needs assessments and interviews and through completing resource mapping.

Evaluating Program Effectiveness 10

Learning Objectives

After reading this chapter, you should be able to:

- Define a program evaluation
- Explain what a process evaluation is and how fidelity relates to completing a process evaluation
- Summarize the steps to completing a process evaluation
- Describe an outcome evaluation
- Paraphrase the steps to completing an outcome evaluation

Program Evaluation

A **program evaluation** is defined as a systemic investigation to determine what a program does and how well it does what it is intended to do (Arora et al., 2016). It seeks to routinely and deliberately gather information to uncover and/or identify what contributes to the success or failure of a program and how effective the program is (Frye & Hemmer, 2012). This process of conducting a program evaluation is still relatively new in the field of education, although it has commonly been used in medicine and business (Tusing & Breikjern, 2017). Due to schools increasingly experiencing budgetary constraints, there is a need to know whether the programs they are providing are maximizing positive outcomes for students in the most cost-effective ways (Moir, 2018). After all, while good evidence-based programs can be

DOI: 10.4324/9781003343479-10

implemented poorly, bad programs that lack evidence bases can be implemented well (Moir, 2018). Additionally, even if a good evidence base is implemented with fidelity, it may not provide the most desired results due to it not being culturally or contextually relevant for students (Moir, 2018; Tusing & Breikjern, 2017). For example, while the MindUp curriculum has been developed for children who are of average cognitive functioning, research has not been conducted with students experiencing intellectual disabilities, therefore considering the student populations the intervention is intended for is important. It is important for schools to both evaluate whether a universal social-emotional program is being implemented with fidelity and producing desired results.

Through gathering information in a program evaluation, decisions can be made about the design, implementation, and outcomes of a program for the purpose of monitoring and improving the quality of it (Arora et al., 2016; Frye & Hemmer, 2012). Program evaluation differs from program assessment in that it is a much more formal process that involves complying with a set of guidelines, whereas assessment, in this context, is a more informal type of analysis. Therefore, a program evaluation is used to inform policy and guide decisions in areas like determining program effectiveness, identifying areas of improvement, optimizing resource allocation, examining whether the program is meeting educator and student needs, and determining whether program protocols were being followed effectively (Cook, 2010). Through a program evaluation, educators should be able to answer the following questions:

1) To what extent does the program work?
2) How does the program work?
3) In what ways does the program work?
4) For whom does the program work best?
5) Under what conditions does the program work best?

(Giancola, 2014, p. 24)

For the purposes of this book, there are two subtypes of evaluation that will be important to determine whether a program is being implemented with integrity and whether it is effective (CDC, 2012; Giancola, 2014). These two subtypes of program evaluation are known as process evaluation and outcome evaluation. While **process evaluations** are concerned with whether programs are operating as planned, **outcome evaluations** investigate to what extent the goals of the program were met and whether the program was successful (Giancola, 2014).

Process Evaluation and Fidelity

Earlier in this book, the importance of fidelity was discussed. As you may recall, fidelity, also known as integrity, can be described as the degree to which a program is implemented as intended (Carroll et al., 2007; McKenna & Parenti, 2017). A large part of completing a process evaluation entails exploring whether programs are being implemented with fidelity and in accordance with their designed protocols to determine the degree to which they are being employed correctly. For example, a doctor may prescribe a person to take 800 milligrams of ibuprofen per day to eliminate severe back pain. However, if a person only takes 200 milligrams of ibuprofen per day, the medication will not be as effective at alleviating the person's discomfort. Therefore, the individual broke the fidelity of the prescribed plan to take 800 milligrams of ibuprofen per day and instead took a significantly lesser dose, which did not alleviate their pain to the maximum extent possible. Given what readers have learned about fidelity and their knowledge of adhering to a plan or prescribed curriculum, Exercise 10.1 asks readers to brainstorm the major components of employing a program with integrity.

Exercise 10.1 Most Important Fidelity Components

Directions: Think of a time when you followed a recipe in cooking a meal or had to follow a set of instructions to put something together. Given what you know about following a recipe or set of instructions, what do you think are the most five most important components in completing a task with fidelity?

1. _____
2. _____
3. _____
4. _____
5. _____

According to Dane and Schneider (1998), fidelity has five components: (a) adherence, (b) quality of delivery, (c) program differentiation, (d) exposure, and (e) participant responsiveness. Each of these components is important to note and understand in completing a process evaluation. **Adherence** refers to how closely an educator attends and follows the specific steps or procedures as it was designed or written by the program's developer (Carroll et al., 2007; Dane & Schneider, 1998). **Quality of delivery** includes the manner, skill, decisions, choice-making, and judgment in implementing an intervention (Carroll et al., 2007; Gerstner & Finney, 2013). For example, an educator who is new to implementing a program may not deliver it with the same skill and judgment as a teacher who is experienced and well-trained.

Program differentiation can be defined as the unique features of the program that are distinguishable from other existing practices (Dane & Schneider, 1998). In simple terms, program differentiation asks what makes one social-emotional program different and distinct from another. Program differentiation is important because if the implementation team is interested in evaluating the outcomes of a support, they should be aware of the materials and strategies that are distinct from the components of another intervention to know which program is more effective than another (Carroll et al., 2007; Gerstner & Finney, 2013). If implementation team members do not take into account differentiation, it is difficult to determine whether positive or negative outcomes are attributed to the program in place or due to some other environmental factor or support that was being employed (Carroll et al., 2007; Gerstner & Finney, 2013). Therefore, although program differentiation is not evaluated in terms of fidelity, it greatly assists educators to know the specific and unique components, features, and materials of the program. For this reason, Chapter 5 had readers described each of the aforementioned areas.

Aside from program differentiation, fidelity is comprised of exposure or dosage. **Exposure** refers to the extent to which students receive the full amount of the treatment (Gerstner & Finney, 2013). Therefore, exposure takes into account the length, frequency, or duration of the intervention sessions (Dane & Schneider, 1998; Gerstner & Finney, 2013). Lastly, **participant responsiveness** refers to the receptiveness of students exposed to the program (Dane & Schneider, 1998; Gerstner & Finney, 2013). Therefore, participant responsiveness is concerned with whether students are attentive and engaged with the universal social-emotional program. Consequently, even though a program may possess a strong evidence base, if students are not engaged, they are not likely to fully benefit from it. Through evaluating the fidelity in which a program is implemented, educators can be informed about how well the support was employed and what adaptations may be needed to address concerns over integrity.

In the context of implementation science, the evaluation of whether a program is being implemented with integrity or not should take place regularly across the installation, initial implementation, and full implementation stages. Through evaluating fidelity throughout each of these stages, vital feedback can be provided to educators on how to improve implementation or to determine whether the program is effective or not. Overall, since the fidelity of

Program was not implemented as planned and therefore cannot be credited with contributing to students meeting their objectives. Consequently, educators. should *not* claim the program was effective.

The program was implemented as planned. The objectives were met. Consequently, the program may be effective and contributing to meeting the intended objectives.

Favorable Outcomes (+)

Low Fidelity (–)   High Fidelity (+)

Unfavorable (–)

No claims can be made about the program because it was not implemented, nor were the objectives met by students. Educators should *not* claim the program is ineffective because it has not been implemented.

The program was implemented as planned, but the objectives were not met. Evaluating the fidelity of program implementation should lead to informed changes to the employment of the support.

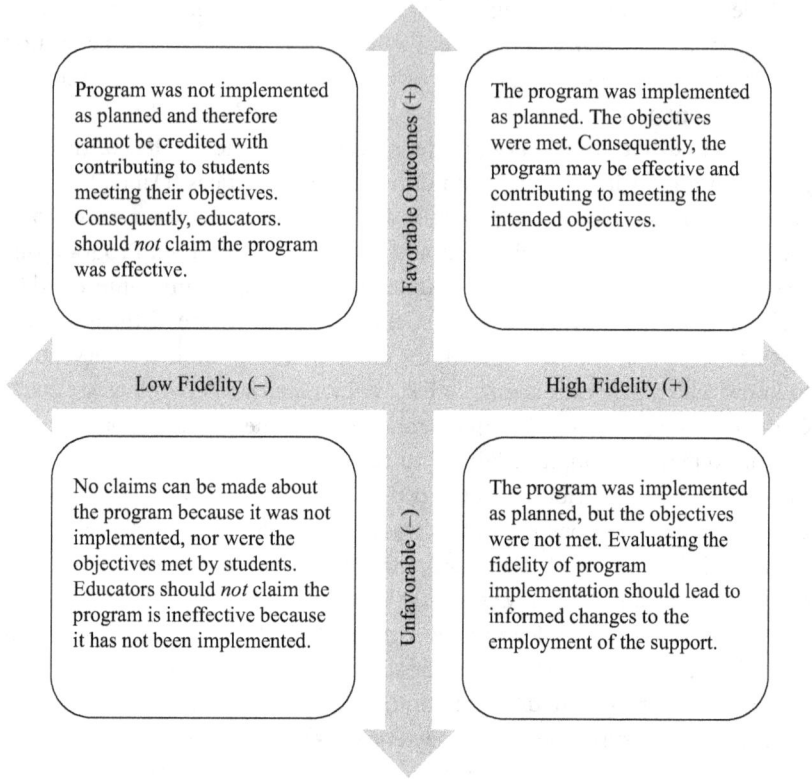

Figure 10.1 Four Potential Outcomes in Completing an Evaluation of Fidelity
Source: (Adapted from Gerstner & Finney, 2013)

implementation can waver throughout the installation, initial implementation, and full implementation stages, the evaluation of whether a program is being implemented with integrity should take place regularly. Figure 10.1 presents four outcomes that can arise in evaluating a program's fidelity. Figure 10.2 provides an example of a fidelity checklist.

Steps to Completing a Process Evaluation

In this next section, readers will walk through the steps of completing a process evaluation. This will help readers understand process evaluation more fully and provide context for how fidelity fits into the overall process evaluation. Moreover, readers will be able to easily complete a process evaluation to determine

Program Name: _____

Program Differentiation
Definition:
• Detailing the specific features of the program that enable students to meet their objectives. Program differentiation is not "evaluated" but involves describing the unique components of the program and materials needed.

What are the main components of implementing your program?

A) _____

B) _____

C) _____

D) _____

E) _____

What resources are needed to implement your program successfully (staff, technology, materials)?

A) _____

B) _____

C) _____

Adherence

Definition:
- Whether or not the specific components of the program were implemented as planned

Key:
- 2 points = High level of implementation integrity
- 1 point = Inconsistent level of implementation integrity
- 0 points = Instructional element not implemented
- N/O = Not observed

Before Program Implementation

Area Being Evaluated	Rating				Comments
Materials are ready	2	1	0	N/O	
Materials for students are ready	2	1	0	N/O	
Materials are presented in an organized fashion	2	1	0	N/O	
The purpose of today's social-emotional lesson is introduced	2	1	0	N/O	

Figure 10.2 Example Fidelity Checklist

Instructional Presentation					
Area Being evaluated	**Rating**				**Comments**
Follows steps in program lesson	2	1	0	N/O	
Follows standardized/prescribed wording in program (if provided)	2	1	0	N/O	
Models skills/strategies appropriately	2	1	0	N/O	
Models skills/strategies with ease	2	1	0	N/O	
Transitions between steps/activities were smooth	2	1	0	N/O	
The program was easy to follow	2	1	0	N/O	

Quality

Definition:

- How well the program was implemented or the caliber to which the program features were delivered. The manner, skill, decisions, choice-making, and judgment in implementing an intervention.

Area Being evaluated	**Rating**		**Comments**
Were there unnecessary stops in the program lesson or apparent confusion due to unfamiliarity with it?	Yes	No	
Was the language used during program implementation clear and easy to understand for students?	Yes	No	
Were any materials missing during program implementation?	Yes	No	
Was the implementer of the program engaging?	Yes	No	
Did the implementer of the program repeat or rephrase parts of the program that students appeared to have difficulty understanding?	Yes	No	
Overall quality of program delivery (e.g., 1 = low to 5 = high)	1 2 3 4 5		

Figure 10.2 Continued

Exposure		
Definition: • The extent to which students receive the full amount of the treatment.		
Was the appropriate amount of time spent on each component of the program?	Yes	No	
Were any parts of the program left out due to time constraints?	Yes	No	

Responsiveness		
Definition: • The receptiveness of students exposed to the program.		

Area Being evaluated	**Rating**	**Comments**
To what degree were students attentive during program implementation? (e.g., 1 = little attention to 5 highly attentive)	1 2 3 4 5	
Were students provided opportunities to ask questions?	Yes	No	
Did the students engage in the materials and activities presented?	Yes	No	
Did the students seem to enjoy the content presented to them?	Yes	No	
Were there any particular components of the program that the students seemed especially engaged in?		
Were there any particular components of the program that students seemed especially disengaged in?		

Figure 10.2 Continued

whether a universal social-emotional program is being implemented as intended or what factors are interfering in adequate program implementation.

Step 1: Assign Personnel to Perform the Evaluation

To complete a process evaluation, schools will need the right personnel to do it. What is meant by this, is that although implementation team members should be involved in the oversight of a process evaluation, it may be best for it to be completed by personnel independent or who do not have a vested interest in the presenting program (Lesesne et al., 2016; Saunders et al., 2005). In an ideal world, it is recommended that process evaluations be conducted by evaluators outside the school to have an unbiased view of whether the program is being implemented as intended (Giancola, 2014; Lesesne et al., 2016). However, given feasibility (e.g., budgetary constraints that schools face, availability, logical barriers), process evaluations can be completed by school personnel who are not actively involved in program implementation or oversight. Moreover, if schools would like evaluators outside of their building to evaluate the process of implementing a program, they can utilize other staff throughout the district. It is imperative that program evaluators remain independent of facilitators, or those who have been implementing the program (Lesesne et al., 2016).

Step 2: Decide What to Measure

Completing a process evaluation does not simply consist of determining whether a program is being implemented with fidelity (Giancola, 2014; Lesesne et al., 2016). Instead, educators must select what factors they believe may be impacting program implementation. Outside of evaluating whether a program is being implemented with fidelity, educators should be aware that student demographics, attendance, and staff and student perceptions all impact whether a program is being implemented as intended (Giancola, 2014; Lesesne et al., 2016). For instance, it would not matter if a school were employing a universal social-emotional with fidelity if their student attendance is low. Moreover, if staff do not buy into the program or find it cumbersome to implement, they may not employ it as intended. Finally, obtaining the perceptions of students over the program is paramount to understanding whether they find it enjoyable, engaging, and beneficial (Lesesne et al., 2016). Therefore, it would behoove schools to develop staff and student satisfaction surveys to determine how educators and youth view the program and its employment during implementation. It may be helpful if some of the questions on staff and student surveys were consistent so that comparisons between the groups could be made. Some questions to consider asking staff and students halfway through program implementation may include:

1) Is the program meeting its objectives so far? Why or why not?
2) Do you find the program helpful so far? Why or why not?
3) Do you find the program engaging so far? Why or why not?
4) Do you find the program easy to follow so far?

5) What do you like about the program?
6) What do you dislike about the program?
7) Is there anything that can be done differently to improve the program?

Step 3: Select Methods for Obtaining Data

Just as important in deciding what to measure in regard to program implementation are the methods for how to measure it. Through selecting and utilizing data collection methods, schools will be supplied with information regarding the quality of their implementation process. Therefore, schools should determine what data they want to collect on program implementation and how they will use that data to better inform practice. Moreover, schools should be aware that there are formal and informal data that can be collected. **Formal data** includes any systemically devised and collected information, such as universal screeners, structured classroom observations, attendance records, and formal questionnaires/surveys (Schildkamp, 2019). **Informal data** is typically collected by educators through everyday practice or less formal measures (Schildkamp, 2019). Examples of informal data may include that of having conversations with students, unstructured observations, student work samples, or simply observing students' learning and interactions with others (Schildkamp, 2019). In collecting data to complete a process evaluation, both formal and informal types of data from staff and students may prove useful, such as attendance records, program satisfaction surveys, interviews, fidelity checklists, and pupil demographic information (Giancola, 2014; Lesesne et al., 2016).

Step 4: Distribution of Data Collection Methods

Once methods have been selected to evaluate the process of program implementation, schools are left with the decisions of when, who, and how to distribute staff and student program satisfaction surveys and when to complete fidelity checklists (Giancola, 2014; Lesesne et al., 2016). Therefore, it would benefit implementation team members to devise a timeline as to when to disseminate satisfaction surveys and conduct evaluations on the integrity of program implementation (Giancola, 2014; Lesesne et al., 2016). Additionally, implementation teams should indicate when they anticipate surveys, interviews, and fidelity checklists to be completed by. Figure 10.3 provides a sample timeline that readers can complete.

Data Collection Method	Data to be Distrib-uted	Date to be Completed	Date to be Collected
Fidelity Checklist			
Teacher Survey or Interview			
Student Survey or Interview			
Student Atten-dance Records	n/a	This will be obtained by this date_____	This will be obtained by this date_____
Student Demo-graphic Information	n/a	This will be obtained by this date_____	This will be obtained by this date_____

Figure 10.3 Timeline for Distribution and Data Collection

Step 5: Data Analysis

After data has been collected, it is time to analyze it to best understand what factors are impacting program implementation. Often educators find data analysis a daunting task, but it is important for them to note that school-based practitioners, such as school psychologists, are well-trained in data collection and analysis (Eagle et al., 2015). **Data analysis** involves educators using data to inform practice and make data-based decisions (Prenger & Schildkamp, 2018; Schildkamp, 2019). Recall that data-based decision-making entails the ongoing collection and interpretation of data to change and improve social-emotional practices to best benefit students (Prenger & Schildkamp, 2018; Schildkamp, 2019). The term "decision" in data-based decision-making indicates that a variety of actions can be undertaken based on data, such as adapting instruction and curriculum, setting goals, evaluating the effectiveness of programs, improving policy, and reallocating time, funds, and resources (van Geel et al., 2016).

When completing a process evaluation, the data is used to determine whether the program is being implemented as planned. If the program is not being implemented accordingly, the data can be used to determine what factors are negatively impacting how the program is being employed (van Geel et al., 2016). From there, steps can be developed to remediate poor implementation practices. In analyzing data, educators may want to ask the following questions:

1) What data is relevant in completing a process evaluation for the social-emotional program the school is using?
2) Are there any common trends or themes across all data?
3) What comparisons can be made between classrooms implementing the program as intended and those that are not implementing the program with integrity?
4) If statistical data is being analyzed, are there any data points that appear to be different from the norm or that could be considered outliers?
5) Does the data indicate that the program is meeting its objectives thus far?

(van Geel et al., 2016; Prenger & Schildkamp, 2018;
Schildkamp, 2019)

Step 6: Dissemination of Findings

The final step in completing a process evaluation includes disseminating findings to the implementation team and to those employing the program (Giancola, 2014). Whether it be through completing a full process evaluation or simply completing a fidelity checklist, findings should be communicated to staff implementing the program on an ongoing and regular basis (Giancola, 2014). Findings need to be reported regularly so that staff can improve their implementation of a program quickly. In reporting findings to educators, it is vital to determine whom the results will be revealed to. For example, do all educators within the school need to know about whether a universal social-emotional program is working or only the grade levels that are currently implementing it? Additionally, what should families know about the universal social-emotional program and how it is working? Therefore, it may be helpful for those disseminating the results to make a list of all the key parties that findings will be revealed to (Giancola, 2014). Additionally, in revealing the results of a process evaluation, those sharing the results should ask themselves the following questions:

1) What is the background of the audience who is receiving the results of the process evaluation?
2) What will the audience want to know?

3) In what format or modality should the results be shared (e.g., letter home, on a website, through a newsletter, during school-wide events)?
4) What do you want the audience to know about the results?
5) How much time and interest will the audience have in the results?
6) What recommendations can be made from the findings from the process evaluation?

(Giancola, 2014)

Lastly, in reporting the results from a process evaluation, readers should remember to present their findings in clear and succinct terms and remove technical jargon to improve accessibility. Therefore, those reporting the results should remember that there is more than one way to disseminate their findings other than a technical report. Other methods that can be used to disseminate results from a process evaluation include presentations, school newsletters, staff newsletters, email, and even creating a brief video for educators (Giancola, 2014). Through disseminating process evaluation results in easily understandable terms, educators implementing the universal social-emotional program should be able to understand what they are doing well and what areas they need to work on. Exercise 10.2 will have readers answer the general questions to completing a process evaluation.

Exercise 10.2 Completing a Process Evaluation

Directions: Answer the questions below to assist you in completing a process evaluation.

1. How many times per year will you complete a process evaluation?

_____

2. What personnel will be completing the process evaluation? List them below.

Name	Title
_____	_____
_____	_____
_____	_____
_____	_____
_____	_____

3. What factors may be negatively impacting program implementation?

_____

_____

_____

4. What methods will you utilize to assess what factors may be impacting program implementation?

☐ Universal Screening Data   ☐ Structured Classroom Observations

☐ Unstructured Observations   ☐ Formal Staff Interviews

☐ Informal Staff Interviews   ☐ Formal Student Interviews

☐ Informal Student Interviews   ☐ Questionnaires/Surveys

☐ Attendance Records   ☐ Disciplinary Records/Reports

☐ Other _____   ☐ Other _____

5. When will you distribute data collection materials?

_____

6. When will the data be collected?

_____

7. When will the data analysis be completed by?

_____

8. Who will complete the data analysis?

_____

9. Whom will the results of the process evaluation be revealed to?

☐ School Staff   ☐ Parents   ☐ State Education Officials

☐ Other _____

10. How will results of the process evaluation be revealed or discussed?

☐ Presentation/In-Service Training   ☐ Newsletter to Staff

☐ Report   ☐ Newsletter to Parents

☐ Email   ☐ Video Report

☐ Other _____

Outcome Evaluation

As mentioned earlier, outcome evaluations examine the extent to which the goals of the program being implemented were met and if it was successful (Giancola, 2014). Therefore, outcomes evaluations are typically completed once the program has been successfully employed for quite some time in the full implementation stage (CDC, 2012; Giancola, 2014). Of course, en route to completing an outcomes evaluation, the school should evaluate whether the program is on track toward meeting its objectives and goals before reaching the full implementation stage. However, the results of completing an outcomes evaluation will provide the larger picture as to whether the program has been successful and to what extent the program has been successful. The CDC (2012) provides several tips that schools can use in determining whether they should move from only completing process evaluations to also conducting outcomes evaluations. These tips include schools evaluating the sustainability, fidelity, stability, reach, and exposure of the program. Descriptions of each of these elements can be found in Figure 10.4.

1) **Sustainability**	There are enough funds and resources to sustain the program throughout implementation so that it is not terminated prematurely.
2) **Fidelity**	The program is being implemented with fidelity and has shown to have been being employed with integrity for some time.
3) **Stability**	There is a high probability that the program is not likely to change during the outcome evaluation being completed.
4) **Reach**	The program has reached a sufficiently large number of students for the school to be able to complete the data analysis.
5) **Exposure**	The students have had sufficient exposure to the program to result in the intended outcome. In other words, students should have been provided the full program before completing an outcome evaluation as opposed to completing one when the program is halfway through or uncompleted.

Figure 10.4 Descriptions of Fidelity Elements

After schools have determined whether they can move onto completing an outcome evaluation, they should determine the design of completing such evaluations. Generally, completing an outcome evaluation can be either experimental or quasi-experimental in design. In an **experimental outcome evaluation,** the aim is to establish a cause-and-effect relationship between students who received the program and their outcomes through random assignment (Frye & Hemmer, 2012). An example of an experimental outcome evaluation would entail a lottery system in which students were randomly selected to either take part in the Second Step or receive a placebo curriculum. This experiment would aim to see if those students that took part in the Second Step curriculum reported more appropriate ways to manage their feelings than students who did not partake in the program. Therefore, the hope would be that a cause-and-effect relationship can be drawn in that students who take part in Second Step have developed more strategies for managing their emotions appropriately.

Where an experimental outcome evaluation uses random assignment to assign students to groups, a quasi-experimental outcome evaluation does not. Therefore, **quasi-experimental outcome evaluations** aim to establish a cause-and-effect relationship between students who receive the program and their outcomes but keeps students in their already existing groups or classes (Frye & Hemmer, 2012). For example, in a quasi-experimental outcome evaluation, students would remain with their assigned class and receive the universal social-emotional program in that class, whereas another class or children at another school may not receive the program. Overall, in schools, quasi-experimental designs are easier to implement and popular than experimental designs (Frye & Hemmer). Nonetheless, the goal remains the same to see if the universal social-emotional program being put into place is meeting its expectations and can be attributed to helping children.

Steps to Completing an Outcome Evaluation

Many of the steps in completing an outcome evaluation are similar to those of a process evaluation. The only real difference in the completion of these steps is what data is being used and how it is being used. Therefore, readers need to keep in mind that, as mentioned, an outcome evaluation is a measure to determine whether the universal social-emotional program is working and to what extent is it working well (CDC, 2012). Additionally, an outcome evaluation helps to determine whether there is a direct cause-and-effect relationship between program implementation and results. Therefore, rather than fully going over many of the similar steps between a process and outcome evaluation in great detail, only steps that are different or that need to be elaborated on when completing an outcome evaluation will be explained extensively below.

Step 1: Assign Personnel to Perform the Evaluation

Just as in completing a process evaluation, the appropriate personnel will be needed to complete an outcome evaluation. As mentioned earlier in this book, whether it be for a process or outcome evaluation, school psychologists may be key personnel to have involved due to their extensive training in program evaluation (Eagle et al., 2015; Splett et al., 2013). Other personnel that should be considered in helping to complete an outcome evaluation include school administrators, school counselors, mathematics teacher for help completing complex statistical analyses, and other personnel who understand the culture and context of the school and its students.

Step 2: Decide What to Measure

The next step in an outcome evaluation entails deciding what to measure (CDC, 2012). To best assist with helping what to measure, educators should revisit their needs assessment to determine what the needs were for selecting the universal social-emotional program and whether the social-emotional program is meeting those needs. Additionally, educators should revisit the goals and objectives of the program and determine how they would like to evaluate whether those goals and objectives were met.

Step 3: Utilize Universal Screener Baseline Data

The third step in completing an outcome evaluation involves utilizing and recognizing the importance of baseline data. **Baseline data** can be defined as a measurement of the student population's social-emotional well-being before the program is put into place (Tusing & Breikjern, 2016). Collecting baseline data on the overall social-emotional well-being of students is important because it allows educators to compare how they were functioning before and after the program went into place to determine if it is working (Tusing & Breikjern, 2016).

In comparing data before and after a program has gone into place, it is important for educators to be aware of certain cut scores on universal screeners like the DESSA-Mini, BIMSAS-2, and BESS. A **cut score** is a predefined score that is used to determine whether a student is at risk for social-emotional concerns (Bernhardt, 2017; Schaffer, 2017). For universal screening, students whose scores fall below the predefined cut score typically receive more intensive intervention services at Tier 2 in addition to still receiving core instruction (Bernhardt, 2017). On the contrary, children who fall at or above the cut score receive only Tier 1 social-emotional supports. For example, higher scores on the BESS suggest more concerns regarding general behavior and emotional functioning with T-scores being classified into three levels of risk, including normal ($T < 60$), elevated ($T = 61$–70), and extremely elevated ($T > 70$) (Kilgus et al., 2018). Therefore, schools may utilize the cut score of 61 and above to determine students who are at elevated risk for social-emotional concerns.

In collecting baseline data for a whole grade level, educators may note that before implementing a universal social-emotional program 40% of the grade was deemed at risk for mental health concerns as suggested by the BESS. However, after implementing a social-emotional program for only one school year, only 32% of the grade was deemed at risk for mental health concerns. Ideally, by the time schools reach the full implementation stage, the school would want to consistently have 20% or less of their student population in the at-risk range for social-emotional concerns on universal screeners, such as the BESS or DESSA-Mini. Utilizing baseline data from universal screeners is critical to determining whether a social-emotional program is producing desired outcomes. At the very least, schools should be comparing their baseline data on universal screeners at the start of each year to how students are performing at the end of each year to determine whether the social-emotional program they are using is working. Additionally, throughout each stage of implementation, schools can compare their universal screening data to determine whether they have made adequate progress to move forward with the next stage. If schools have not made adequate progress in moving from one stage to the next within implementation science, they can re-evaluate what may be hindering successful program employment through looking at their process evaluation results (CDC, 2012).

Step 4: Utilize Other Data Sources

Aside from looking at universal screening data, schools have access to many other sources of information to determine whether a program is effective when completing an outcome evaluation. For example, schools have access to needs assessment data and surveys inquiring about what social-emotional concerns educators want addressed in their students before a program is selected (CDC, 2012). By asking the same or similar questions after a program has been employed, implementation teams can determine whether a social-emotional program that has been put into place is addressing the needs of staff (Altschuld & Watkins, 2014; Morrison & Harms, 2018). In addition to survey data, student and staff interviews and classroom observations can further inform whether a program has met the objectives and goals that were initially outlined before program implantation (CDC, 2012). Taking everything into account, there are many sources of data that can be collected both before and after a program has been fully implemented to determine whether it is effective and the extent to which it has been successful. Therefore, in considering what data to collect, whether it be for a process or outcome evaluation, schools may find Figure 10.5 helpful in providing an overview of data collection measures. Moreover, the following questions may be beneficial for schools to ask:

1) What information is needed to make current decisions about the program?
2) Of this information, how much can be collected and examined in a low-cost and practical manner?
3) How accurate will the data being collected be?
4) Who can and should administer the methods of collecting the data?
5) Is training required to collect and analyze the data (e.g., Will the training be needed to administer a survey or social-emotional universal screener)?

(McNamara, n.d.)

Step 5: Data Analysis

The next step in completing an outcome evaluation involves taking all the data and converting it into a format that summarizes and synthesizes the information (CDC, 2012; Giancola, 2014). Therefore, educators conducting a data analysis should compare data before a program has been implemented to that of data from the full implementation stage (CDC, 2012; Giancola, 2014). Consequently, a determination can be made as to whether the universal social-emotional program being implemented is effective and to what extent it has met the school's objectives and goals.

Method	Overall Purpose	Advantages	Challenges
Universal Screeners	A brief norm-referenced assessment that is typically administered three times per year—fall, winter, and spring	• Brief • Norm-Referenced • Able to obtain lots of data • Quick to administer • Inexpensive • Extremely sensitive to change in student social-emotional well-being	• Does not assess what students like or dislike about the program in particular • Students unable to elaborate on their feelings or why they feel the way they do • Requires training to administer and interpret • Assesses whether the program is working but does not fully take into account the effectiveness to how the program is being delivered or fidelity of delivery • Student-focused
Questionnaires, Surveys, Checklists	Utilized to quickly and easily obtain a lot of information from youth, families, and educators	• Can complete anonymously • Inexpensive to administer • Easy to analyze data • Can obtain lots of data • May be less intimidating than an observation or interview	• Not norm-referenced • Typically created informally • Wording can bias the client's responses • Are impersonal

Figure 10.5 Overview of Data Collection Methods

Method	Overall Purpose	Advantages	Challenges
Interviews	Used to fully understand students, families, and staff's impressions or experiences or to learn more about their answers to questionnaires/surveys	• Obtain full depth and range of information • Develops a relationship with the individual being interviewed • Can be flexible with the client as opposed to a survey	• Not norm-referenced • Must decide on formal vs. informal interview questions • Must code answers to see themes in student and staff responses—hard to analyze • The interviewer can bias the client's responses
Observations	Utilized to obtain accurate information about how a program actually	• Able to view how a program is actually operating and how educators and students are responding to the program	• Difficult to interpret seen behaviors, program response, and complex observations • Can influence behaviors or program participants • Can be time-consuming and expensive

(Adapted from Cahill, n.d.; McNarma, 2017)

Figure 10.5 Continued

Step 6: Dissemination of Findings

The final step to completing an outcome evaluation is to disseminate the findings. Through disseminating findings, educators can obtain a clear understanding as to whether the universal social-emotional program has worked as intended or whether it did not meet its objectives and goals (CDC, 2012; Giancola, 2014). In disseminating these results, schools can provide school staff recommendations for continuing to sustain the positive impact the program has had on students and staff, or they can provide insight as to why the program did not produce desired results.

The ultimate goal of disseminating findings from an outcome evaluation is to show those who were involved in the program implementation process that positive changes in students' social-emotional well-being are associated with the implementation of the program (CDC, 2012; Giancola, 2014). Therefore, in reporting the results, schools should seek to explain why they believe the social-emotional program had a positive impact on students over other factors that may have influenced their well-being (CDC, 2012; Giancola, 2014). On the contrary, if the program did not meet expectations, findings should seek to explain why the program did not work as anticipated if it was implemented accordingly. Figure 10.6 provides an empty chart that readers can use in when completing an outcome evaluation.

Data Sources	Before Program Implementation	After Full Program Implementation
Universal Screener		
Staff Survey Results		
Staff Interview Results/ Summary of Findings		
Student Survey Results/ Summary of Findings		
Student Interview Results/ Summary of Findings		
Were the objectives and goals of the needs assessment met?		

Figure 10.6 Data Sources Chart

Conclusion

Program evaluation is defined as the systemic investigation to determine what a program does and how well it does it (Arora et al., 2016). Program evaluation differs from program assessment in that it is a more formal process that is conducted to a set of guidelines. There are generally two subtypes of program evaluation that are important in determining whether a program is being implemented with fidelity and whether it is effective. These two types of program evaluation are known as process and outcome evaluations (Giancola, 2014). While process evaluations are concerned with whether a program is being implemented with fidelity, an outcome evaluation investigates the extent to which the program is successful (Giancola, 2014).

There are five components to fidelity that educators should be aware of when completing a process evaluation. These five components are adherence to program guidelines, quality of delivery, program differentiation, exposure, and participant responsiveness. Once educators take into account the five factors that impact whether a program is being implemented with fidelity, they can move forward in completing a process evaluation. The recommended steps to completing a process evaluation include assigning personnel to perform the evaluation, deciding what to measure, selecting methods for obtaining data, distributing data collection methods, data analysis, and disseminating findings (Giancola, 2014; Eagle et al., 2015; Lesesne et al., 2016).

In determining whether schools should move from only completing a process evaluation to an outcome evaluation, the CDC (2012) provides several tips for educators. These tips include ensuring that the program in place is both sustainable and stable. Additionally, in moving toward completing an outcome evaluation, the CDC (2012) recommends that the program has been implemented with fidelity, employed with a large number of students, and put into place over a long period of time. Aside from these tips, it is important for educators to use either an experimental and quasi-experimental design in determining the effectiveness of a program (Frye & Hemmer, 2012). Either of these models will help educators conclude whether there is a cause-and-effect relationship between students who received the social-emotional program and their outcomes compared to students who did not take part in it (Frye & Hemmer, 2012). Similar to completing a process evaluation, the steps to conducting an outcomes evaluation include assigning personnel to perform the evaluation, deciding what to measure, utilizing universal screening data, collecting information from other data sources, analyzing the data, and disseminating the findings to key stakeholders (CDC, 2012; Giancola, 2014). Overall, through completing process and outcomes evaluations, schools can best set up programs for success in helping students learn key social-emotional skills.

Appendices

Appendix A

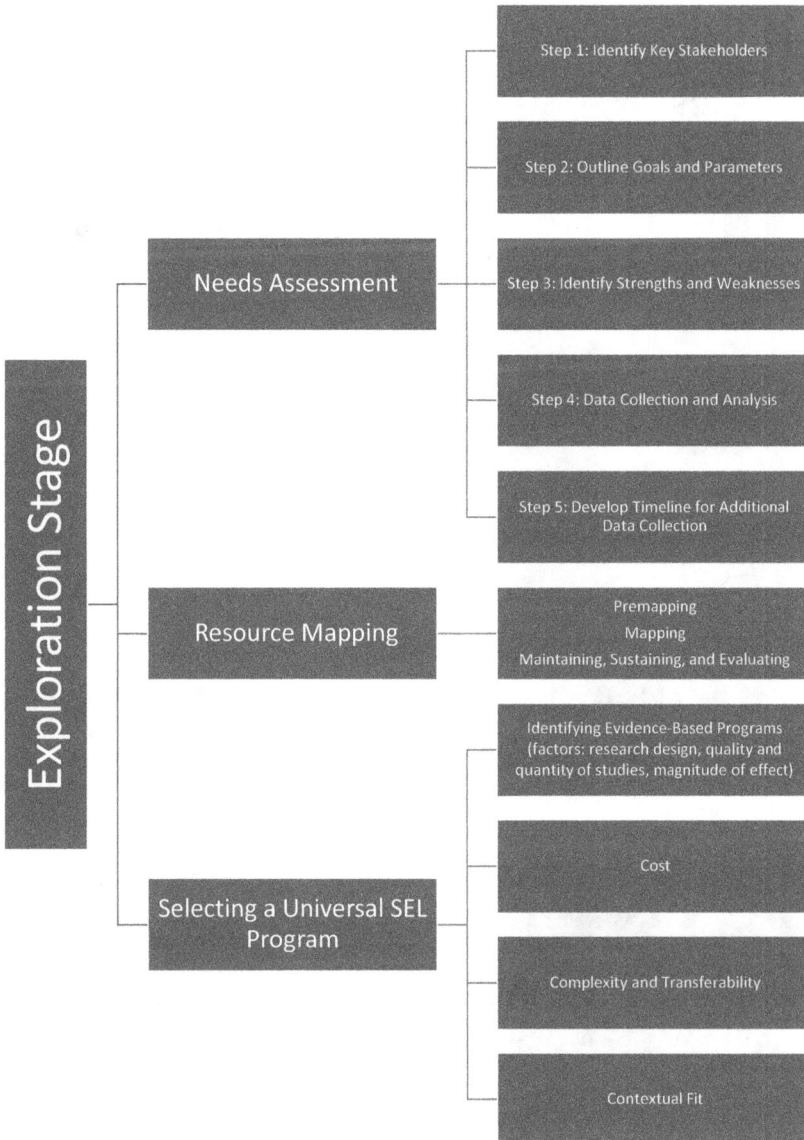

Appendix B

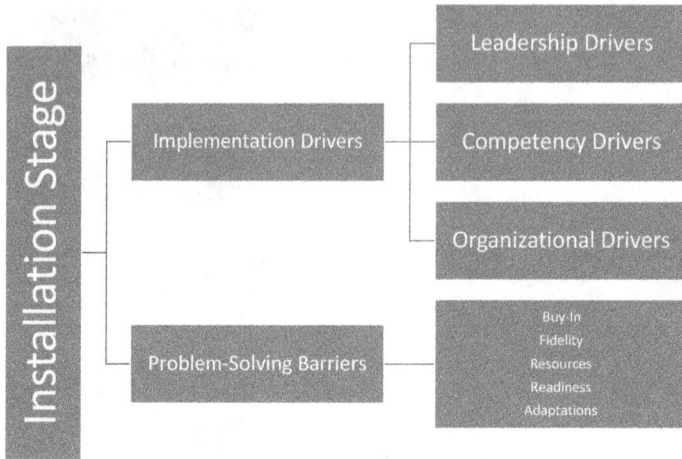

Appendix C

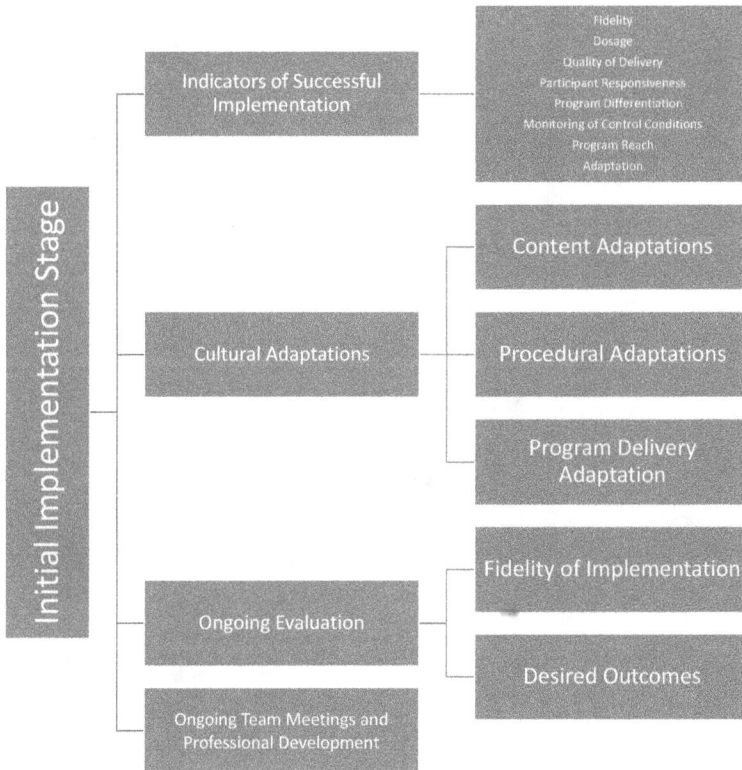

Initial Implementation Stage

- **Indicators of Successful Implementation**
  - Fidelity
  - Dosage
  - Quality of Delivery
  - Participant Responsiveness
  - Program Differentiation
  - Monitoring of Control Conditions
  - Program Reach
  - Adaptation

- **Cultural Adaptations**
  - Content Adaptations
  - Procedural Adaptations
  - Program Delivery Adaptation

- **Ongoing Evaluation**
  - Fidelity of Implementation
  - Desired Outcomes

- **Ongoing Team Meetings and Professional Development**

Appendix D

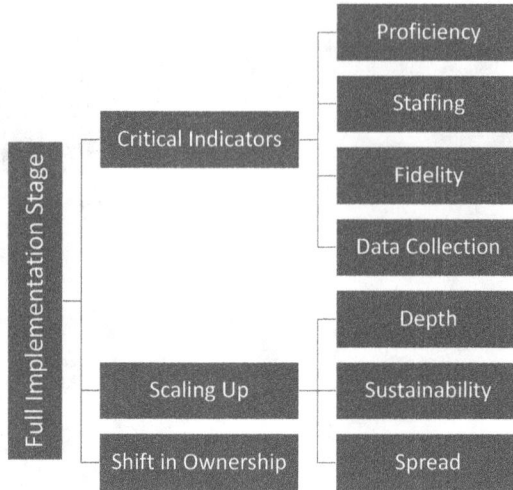

Appendix E

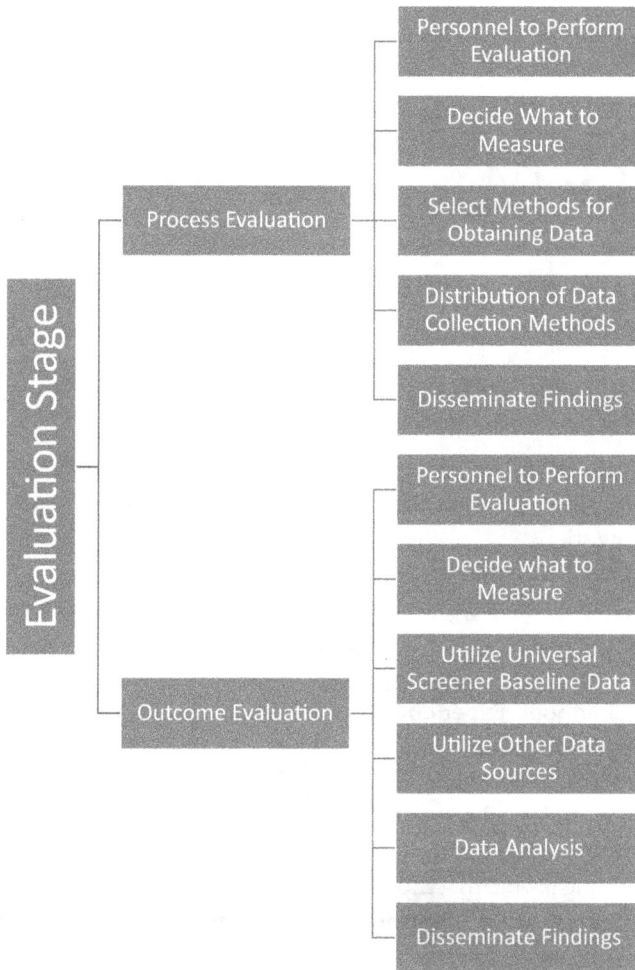

Glossary

Active Team Member—A member of an interdisciplinary team whose responsibilities consist of listening to the opinions of others and responding to questions.

Acculturative Stress refers to the stressors associated with being an immigrant or ethnic minority and going through the acculturation process.

Adherence—How closely an individual attends and follows the specific steps or procedures as it was designed or written by the program's developer.

Adverse Childhood Experiences (ACEs)—Potentially traumatic events that occur in childhood between 0 to 17 years of age.

Behavior and Emotional Screening System (BESS)—A brief norm-referenced universal screener that evaluates whether students are at risk for developing concerns in the following areas: externalizing problems, internalizing problems, school problems, and adaptive skills.

Behavior Intervention Monitoring Assessment System (BIMAS-2)—The BIMAS-2 is both a universal screener and progress monitoring measure for behavioral, social, and emotional functioning in children and adolescents ages 5 to 18 years.

Buy-In—An educator's acceptance and willingness to actively support and participate in a new plan or policy, such as the implementation of a Tier 1 social-emotional program.

C.A.T. Project—An extension of the Coping Cat program use to help children between ages 14 to 17 recognize thoughts, feelings, and bodily actions associated with anxiety.

Collaboration—The process of two or more people working together to achieve a common goal.

Coping Cat Program—A 16-session manualized counseling curriculum designed for children ages 7 to 13 who are exhibiting signs and symptoms of anxiety disorders.

Culture is a set of meanings, behavioral norms, and values shared by members of a societal group or society.

Cut Score—A predefined score that is used to determine whether a student is at risk for social-emotional concerns.

Data Analysis—The use of data to inform practice and make data-based decisions.

Data Analyst—A role that entails collecting and analyzing data before team meetings and to present such data to the implementation team in an easily understandable manner, such as through charts or graphs.

Data-Based Decision Making—The ongoing process of collecting and interpreting data to alter and improve practices to best benefit learners.

Deep-Level Attributes—Underlying psychological characteristics that group members tend to learn about one another over time, such as personality traits, values, attitudes, and abilities.

De-implementation—The decrease and discontinuation non-evidence-based practices and beliefs.

Differentiated Instruction—Refers to teachers tailoring the classroom environment, instructional practices, and teaching environments to create appropriately different learning experiences for students with different interests, needs, readiness, and learning profiles.

Distributed Leadership—An approach to management that purports that the designation and completion of tasks should not be left to a single person in charge, or authority figure, but should be shared among professionals within a workplace based on their area(s) of expertise.

Double-Barreled Question —A question that is comprised of more than two separate issues or topics but which can only have one answer.

Education for All Handicapped Children Act (EAHCA)—An act that required all public schools accepting federal funds to provide equal access to education for children with physical and mental disabilities and thus educate children with disabilities with their non-disabled peers to the maximum extent possible. EAHCA is also known as Public Law 94–142 and later would become known as the Individuals with Disabilities Education Act (IDEA).

Empirically Supported Programs—Programs that have been researched and published in credible outlets that make use of peer-reviews, such as a scholarly journal. These programs are often sold commercially and are also known as evidence-based programs.

Evidence-Based Interventions—Treatments or supports that have been peer-reviewed and demonstrate empirical support for effectiveness in scholarly literature.

Evidence-Based Practice—The use of empirically supported interventions and programs that have been proven effective at treating a presenting problem.

Evidence-Based Programs—Empirically based supports and protocols that are often sold by companies in a standardized and manualized format also known as empirically supported programs.

Every School Succeeds Act (ESSA)—The main federal education law in the United States from 2015 to present. The law reversed many of the provisions outlined by NCLB regarding the federal government's role in education and once again provided leeway to the states in determining academic progress for students.

Experimental Design—A study design that randomly assigns participants to either a group receiving treatment through a new program or the control group, which receives no course of treatment or the standard course of treatment before a new program has been implemented.

Experimental Outcome Evaluation—An evaluation that aims to establish a cause-and-effect relationship between students who received the program and their outcomes through random assignment.

Explicit Instruction—A method of instruction that involves teaching skills or concepts to students directly and in a structured format.

Exploration Stage—A stage in implementation science that consists of the adoption of a new program and development of performance assessment processes, initial training efforts, and the securing of resources.

Exposure—The extent to which students receive the full amount of the treatment.

Facilities—The physical space needed for implementing a program, such as lighting, classroom space, and storage.

Fidelity—The degree to which an intervention or program is implemented as intended.

Formal Data—Any systemically devised and collected information, such as universal screeners or structured classroom observations.

Full Implementation Stage—A stage in implementation science that consists of over half of school personnel changing their practices under MTSS with a high level of fidelity.

Goals—The overarching destination that explains what a school wants to ultimately achieve through implementing a universal social-emotional program.

Informal data—Data that is typically collected by educators through every-day practice or through less formal measures, such as by having conversations with students or simply observing students.

Initial Implementation Stage—A stage in implementation science that entails staff attempting to utilize newly learned skills and is highlighted by the learning curve staff experience as the school district adjusts and integrates new changes into daily work.

Intervention Service Delivery Models—Triangular three-tiered systems that increase in intensity and duration and are utilized to provide evidence-based supports to children in general education.

Implementation—The process or set of activities needed to put a program or practice into place.

Implementation Readiness—The capacity to employ an evidence-based intervention or program effectively.

Implementation Science—The scientific study of methods utilized to promote the systemic uptake of evidence-based practices into everyday practice.

Installation Stage—A stage in implementation science that involves the adoption of a new program and the development of performance assessment processes, initial training efforts, and the securing of resources.

Implementation Team—A group generally consisting of three to five individuals charged with selecting and leading the employment of an intervention, program, or organization-wide procedure.

Interdisciplinary Teamwork—A complex process in which different types of staff work together to share expertise, skills, and knowledge to impact student and school outcomes.

Leadership Drivers—Drivers that focus on management strategies that may arise when implementing MTSS and involve decision making and providing guidance in the process of employing evidence-based programs.

Maintaining, Sustaining, and Evaluating Mapping Stage—A stage that is utilized to assess the effectiveness of resource mapping through monitoring various data sources.

Mapping Stage—A stage within resource mapping that involves convening the implementation team to begin brainstorming about available programs and staff needed to implement such programs.

Materials and Equipment—Tangible items required for program implementation, such as program manuals, technological resources, and office supplies.

Meeting Facilitator—The leader of the implementation team and helps to clarify the aims of the group and ensures that all group members understand the topics to be discussed by the group.

Multi-Tiered Systems of Support (MTSS)—A problem-solving framework that houses and integrates intervention service delivery models and is used to improve learning, behavior, and social-emotional outcomes in children.

Needs Assessment—A systemic process for identifying and prioritizing needs or "gaps" between current and desired conditions.

Note Taker—A role which entails keeping a running record of what has occurred during the meeting and summarize discussions and decisions made by the rest of the group.

Objectives—Precise actions or measurable steps needed to attain the identified goals.

Opportunity Costs—Resources used in the implementation of a program that could have been utilized in another capacity if the program was not put into place.

Organizational Drivers—Drivers that involve building an infrastructure to facilitate the implementation of MTSS through developing internal and external partnerships, locating funding, allocating resources, and using data for decision making.

Other Program Inputs—Refer to other categories necessary to ensure the fidelity of program implementation like professional development and in-service training.

Outcome Evaluation—An evaluation that investigates the extent the goals of the program were met and if the program was successful.

Parental Involvementinvolves the interactions and behaviors parents engage in with the school to benefit and enhance their children's educational outcomes and future success.

Positional Diversity—Refers to those individuals who have represented a greater variety of positions within an organization or who have worked across various schools.

Participant Responsiveness—The receptiveness of students exposed to the program.

Personnel—The human resources required to implement a program, such as school staff, trainers, consultants, or even volunteers.

Pre-Mapping Stage—A stage of resource mapping that entails the implementation team establishing a clear vision, defining goals, and coming to a consensus on what will be mapped and what will be the process for mapping.

Process Evaluations—An evaluation that is concerned with whether programs are operating as planned.

Program Complexity—The number of steps needed to successfully implement the program along with the amount of materials required for program implementation, data collection demands, and training needed to achieve fidelity (Leko et al., 2019).

Program Differentiation—The unique features of the program that are distinguishable from other existing practices.

Program Evaluation—The systemic evaluation of whether a program or intervention that has been introduced directly led to a significant improvement in the performance of students (Shaw, 2016).

Progress Monitoring—The repeated brief assessment of skills and strategies learned to determine whether a child is responding to the interventions and services being provided.

Protective Factors—A condition, event, or life situation that decreases an individual's chances of developing a mental health concern or condition.

Public Health Model—A medical model of practice that emphasizes the overall health of the public through epidemiologic methodology and the prevention of health problems.

Quality of Delivery—The manner, skill, decisions, choice-making, and judgment in implementing an intervention.

Quasi-Experimental Design—A type of study design that aims to establish a cause-and-effect relationship but does not randomly assign individuals to groups often due to ethical or practical reasons.

Quasi-Experimental Outcome Evaluation—An evaluation that aims to establish a cause-and-effect relationship between students who receive the program and their outcomes but keeps students in their already existing groups or classes.

Racial Trauma—Trauma experienced by individuals due to the exposure and re-exposure of race-based adversity, discrimination, stress, and microaggressions, is another type of trauma that negatively affects the mental health and overall development of youth of color.

Risk Factors—A condition, event, behavior, or life situation that increases an individual's chances of developing a mental health concern or condition.

Research-Based Practices—A term used to loosely describe interventions and programs that range from being supported by rigorous and robust research base to those supported by meager and flawed research methods.

Resource Mapping—The process of evaluating programs, personnel, and services that are available to students and identifying how such resources are currently being used.

Relationship skills—An individual's ability to establish and maintain healthy and rewarding relationships with diverse groups and individuals.

Responsible Decision-Making—The ability to make constructive choices about personal behavior and social interactions based on social norms, safety concerns, and ethical standards.

Responsibilities—The specific tasks or duties that team members are expected to complete according to their roles.

Roles—The positions that team members are assigned.

Scaling Up—The process by which educators move from initially implanting and showing an intervention or program is successful on a small scale to its widespread adoption across multiple classrooms, grade levels, schools, or even districts.

School-Family-Community Partnerships—collaborative initiatives and relationships between school professionals, families, and community members to implement programs and resources that address children's needs, increase their educational resilience and strengths, and foster their social-emotional development.

Self-Awareness—The ability to recognize one's own emotions, thoughts, and values and how each of these factors may influence behavior.

Self-Management—The ability to successfully regulate emotions, thoughts, and behaviors across different situations and contexts.

Shared Mental Model—The perception, understanding, or knowledge about a situation or process that is shared among team members through communication.

Shift in Ownership—The alteration of the universal social-emotional program from being viewed as an "external effort" to it being viewed as part of internal reform.

Social Awareness—The ability for one to take on the perspective of others and empathize with them.

Social-Emotional Development—A child's ability to understand the feelings of others, control their own emotions and behaviors, and get along with peers.

Social-Emotional Learning—The presence through which children and adults acquire and effectively apply the knowledge, attitudes, and skills necessary to understand and manage emotions, set and achieve positive goals, feel and show empathy for others, make responsible decisions, and establish and maintain positive relationships.

Social-Emotional RTI—A triangular three-tiered intervention service delivery model focused on promoting mental wellness and preventing mental illness from developing in children.

Social-Emotional Team—A group of school and community members that meets regularly, uses data-based decision making, and relies on action planning to support student mental health, including improving school climate, promoting student and staff well-being, and addressing individual student strengths and needs.

Spread—The distribution social-emotional program being used across classrooms and schools along with the widespread sharing of underlying beliefs, norms, and principles that come with the program.

Student Risk Screening Scale-Internalizing and Externalizing (SRSS-IE)—A twelve item social-emotional and behavior screener and progress monitoring measure that assists in identifying children who are at-risk for internalizing and externalizing behavior problems.

Surface-Level Attributes—Readily detectable categories (e. g., age, sex, race) or easily accessible information (e.g., reputation, role, tenure in position) that shape how team members feel, think, and behavior toward other team members.

Sustainability—The ability of a program to be implemented with fidelity over time.

Team—A group of people who share a common goal and are jointly responsible for the completion of a task

Technical Drivers—Drivers that utilize an established protocol to respond to concerns that are often defined without ambiguity and a clear solution is evident.

Tier 1—Refers to universal supports that are delivered to all students. Approximately, 80 to 85% of students are expected to respond at the Tier 1 level.

Tier 3—Refers to tertiary supports that are designed for one to five present of students with chronic or long-standing deficits that are beyond the capacity of Tier 1 or Tier 2.

Tier 2—Refers to targeted supports that are delivered to approximately 10 to 15% of students with deficits that are beyond the capacity of Tier 1.

Timekeeper—A role that entails assisting the facilitator in maintaining the meeting agenda's order by tracking how much time is allotted for each section of the agenda

Transferability—The degree to which a program can be transferred to another educator and paraprofessional.

Trauma—A real or perceived experience that is significantly distressing and causes feelings of fear, terror, or helplessness.

Trauma-Informed—A phrase used to indicate that a school is prepared and sensitive to respond to children impacted by trauma.

Universal Screening—The systemic brief assessment of the school population to identify children at-risk for academic, behavioral, or social-emotional deficits

References

Aarons, G. A., Fettes, D. L., Hurlburt, M. S., Palinkas, L. A., Gunderson, L., Willging, C. E., & Chaffin, M. J. (2014). Collaboration, negotiation, and coalescence for interagency-collaborative teams to scale-up evidence-based practice. *Journal of Clinical Child and Adolescent Psychology, 43*(6), 915–928. https://doi.org/10.1080/15374416.2013.876642

Aarons, G. A., Hurlburt, M., & Horwitz, S. M. (2011). Advancing a conceptual model of evidence-based practice implementation in public service sectors. *Administration and Policy in Mental Health, 38*(1), 4–23. https://doi.org/10.1007/s10488-010-0327-7

Akin, B. A., Strolin-Goltzman, J., & Collins-Camargo, C. (2017). Successes and challenges in developing trauma informed child welfare systems: A real-world case study of exploration and initial implementation. *Child and Youth Services Review, 82*, 42–52. https://doi.org/10.1016/j.childyouth.2017.09.007

Altschuld, J. W., & Watkins, R. (2014). A primer on needs assessment: More than 40 years of research and practice. *New Directions for Evaluation, 144*(1), 5–18. https://doi.org/10.1002/ev.20099

American Psychological Association. (2016). *County-level analysis of U.S. Licensed psychologists and health indicators.* American Psychological Association. www.apa.org/workforce/publications/15-county-analysis/report.pdf

American School Counselor Association. (2019). *The ASCA national model: A framework for school counseling programs* (4th ed.). American School Counselor Association.

Anticich, S. A. J., Barrett, P. M., Silverman, W., Lacherez, P., & Gillies, R. (2013). The prevention of childhood anxiety and promotion of resilience among preschool-aged children: A universal school based trial. *Advances in School Mental Health Promotion, 6*(2), 93–121. https://doi.org/10.1080/1754730X.2013.784616

Arora, P. G., Conners, E. H., Blizzard, A., Coble, K., Gloff, N., & Pruitt, D. (2016). Dissemination and implementation science in program evaluation: A telemental health clinical consultation case example. *Evaluation and Program Planning, 60*, 56–63. https://doi.org/10.1016/j.evalprogplan.2016.09.003

Augustyniak, K., Kilanowski, L., & Privitera, G. J. (2016). Perceptions of leadership practices of school psychologists: Views of multiple stakeholders. *School Psychology Forum, 10*(4), 371–385.

Averill, O. H., s& Rinaldi, C. (2011). Multi-tier system of supports. *District Administration*, 47(8), 91–95. www.researchgate.net/profile/Claudia_Rinaldi/publication/257943 832_ Research_Brief_Multitier_System_of_Supports_MTSS_Urban_Special_Education_ Leadership_Collaborative_From_RTI_and_PBIS_to_MTSS/links/00b7d52669fb e69ded000000.pdf

Bacon, A., Walker, H. M., Schwartz, D. M., O'Hara, D. M., O'Hara, C, & Wehmeyer, M. L. (2011). Lessons learned in scaling up effective practices: Implications for promoting self-determination within developmental disabilities. *Exceptionality*, 19(1), 46–60. https://doi.org/10.1080/09362835.2011.537233

Bahr, M. W., Leduc, J. D., Hild, M. A., Davis, S. E., Summers, J. K., & McNeal, B. (2017). Evidence for the expanding role of consultation in the practice of school psychologists. *Psychology in the Schools*, 65(6), 581–595. https://doi.org/10.1002/pits.22020

Balas, E. A., & Boren, S. A. (2000). Managing clinical knowledge for health care improvement. *Yearbook of Medical Informatics*, 1(1), 65–70. https://pdfs.semanticscholar.org /1bf7/726a95b7dab8f02ebc57493b69ea206c1c70.pdf?_ga=2.98897693.20286212. 1606529680-225638425.1597108317

Bambara, L. M., Nonnemacher, S., & Kern, L. (2009). Sustaining school-based individualized positive behavior support: Perceived barriers and enablers. *Journal of Positive Behavior Interventions*, 11(3), 161–176. https://doi.org/10.1177/1098300708330878

Bauer, M. S., Damschroder, L., Hagedorn, H., Smith, J., & Kilbourne, A. M. (2015). An introduction to implementation science for the non-specialist. *BMC Psychology*, 3(2), 1–12. https://doi.org/10.1186/s40359-015-0089-9

Bauer, M. S., & Kirchner, J. (2020). Implementation science: What is it and why should I care? *Psychiatry Research*, 283, 112376. https://doi.org/10.1016/j.psychres.2019.04.025

Becker, K. D., Darney, D., Domitrovich, C., Keperling, J. P., & Ialongo, N. S. (2013). Supporting universal prevention programs: A two-phased coaching model. *Clinical Child and Family Psychology Review*, 16(2), 213–228. https://doi.org/10.1007/s10567-013-0134-2

Bell, S. T., Brown, S. G., Colaneri, A., & Outland, N. (2018). Team composition and the ABCs of teamwork. *The American Psychologist*, 73(4), 349–362. https://doi.org/10.1037/ amp 0000305

Belser, C. T., Shillingford, M. A., & Joe, J. R. (2016). The ASCA model and a multi-tiered systems of supports: A framework to support students of color with problem behavior. *The Professional School Counselor*, 6(3), 251–262. https://doi.org/10.5330/1096-2409-20.1.159

Berger, E. (2019). Multi-tiered approaches to trauma-informed care in schools: A systemic review. *School Mental Health*, 11(1), 650–664. https://doi.org/10.1007/ s12310-019-09326-0

Bernhardt, V. L. (2017). *Data analysis for continuous school improvement* (5th ed.). Routledge.

Bertram, R. M., Blasé, K. A., & Fixsen, D. L. (2015). Improving programs and outcomes: Implementation frameworks and organization change. *Research on Social Work Practices*, 25(4), 477–487. https://doi.org/10.1177/1049731514537687

Bethell, C. D., Carle, A., Hudziak, J., Gombojav, N., Powers, K., Wade, R., & Braveman, P. (2017). Methods to assess adverse childhood experiences of children and families: Toward approaches to promote child well-being in policy and practice. *Academic Pediatrics*, 17(Suppl 7), S51–S69. https://doi.org/10.1016/j.acap.2017.04.161

Björn, P. M., Aro, M. T., Koponen, T. K., Fuchs, L. S., & Fuchs, D. H. (2016). The many faces of special education within RTI frameworks in the United States and Finland. *Learning Disability Quarterly*, 39(1), 58–66. https://doi.org/10.1177/0731948715594787

Blackborby, J., & Cameto, R. (2004). *Changes in school engagement and academic performance of students with disabilities. In wave 1 wave 2 overview (SEELS)*. SRI International. www.seels.net/designdocs/w1w2/SEELS_W1W2_chap8.pdf

Blueprints for Healthy Youth Development. (2020). *Program search*. www.blueprintsprograms.org/program-search/

Bohanon, H., Gilman, C., Parker, B., Amell, C., & Sortino, G. (2016). Using school improvement and implementation science to integrate multi-tiered systems of support in secondary schools. *Australasian Journal of Special Education, 40*(2), 99–116. https://doi.org/10.1017/jse.2016.8

Bowers, H., Lemberger-Truelove, M. E., & Brigman, G. (2018). A social-emotional leadership framework for school counselors. *Professional School Counseling, 21*(1b), 1–10. https://doi.org/10.1177/2156759X18773004

Bowman-Perrott, L., Burke, M. D., Zaini, S., Zhang, N., & Vannest, K. (2015). Promoting positive behavior using the good behavior game: A meta-analysis of single-case research. *Journal of Positive Behavior Interventions, 18*(3), 180–190. https://doi.org/10.1177/1098300715592355

Bradshaw, C. P., Waasdorp, T. E., & Leaf, P. J. (2012). Effects of school-wide positive behavioral interventions and supports on child behavior problems. *Pediatrics, 130*(5), e1136–e1145. https://doi.org/10.1542/peds.2012-0243

Brännlund, A., Strandh, M., & Nilsson, K. (2017). Mental-health and educational achievement: The link between poor mental-health and upper secondary school completion and grades. *Journal of Mental Health, 26*(4), 318–325. https://doi.org/10.1080/09638237.2017.1294739

Bridgeland, J., Bruce, M., & Hariharan, A. (2013). *The missing piece: A national teacher survey on how social and emotional learning can empower children and transform schools: A report for CASEL*. Civic Enterprises with Peter D. Hart Research Associates. www.casel.org/wp-content/uploads/2016/01/the-missing-piece.pdf

Brown, C. H., Chamberlain, P., Saldana, L., Padgett, C., Wang, W., & Cruden, G. (2014). Evaluation of two implementation strategies in 51 child county public service systems in two states: Results of a cluster randomized head-to-head implementation trial. *Implementation Science, 9*(134). https://doi.org/10.1186/s13012-014-0134-8

Brown, C. H., Maggin, D. M., & Buren, M. (2018). Systematic review of cultural adaptations of school-based social, emotional, and behavioral interventions for students of color. *Education and Treatment of Children, 41*(4), 431–456. https://doi.org/10.1353/etc.2018.0024

Brownell, M. T., Sindelar, P. T., Kiely, M. T., & Danielson, L. C. (2010). Special education teacher quality and preparation: Exposing foundations, constructing a new model. *Exceptional Children, 76*(3), 357–377. https://doi.org/10.1177/001440291007600307

Bruhn, A. L., McDaniel, S. C., Rila, A., & Estrapala, S. (2018). A step-by-step guide to Tier 2 behavioral progress monitoring. *Beyond Behavior, 27*(1), 15–27. https://doi.org/10.1177%2F1074295618756984

Bruhn, A. L., Woods-Groves, S., & Huddle, S. (2014). A preliminary investigation of emotional and behavioral screening practices in K-12 schools. *Education & Treatment of Children, 37*(4), 611–634. https://doi.org/10.1353/etc.2014.0039

Bryan, J. A., Young, A., Griffin, D., & Holcomb-McCoy, C. (2018). Leadership practices linked to involvement in school—family—community partnerships: A national study. *Professional School Counseling, 21*(1), 1–13. https://doi.org/10.1177/2156759X18761897

Bumbarger, B. K. (2015). Readiness assessment to improve program implementation: Shifting the lens to optimizing intervention design. *Prevention Science, 16*(8), 1118–1122. https://doi.org/10.1007/s11121-015-0591-6

Cahill, C. (n.d.). *Basic guide to outcomes-based evaluation for nonprofit organizations with very limited resources.* https://managementhelp.org/evaluation/outcomes-evaluation-guide.htm

Carroll, C., Patterson, M., Wood, S., Booth, A., Rick, J., & Balain, S. (2007). A conceptual framework for implementation fidelity. *Implementation Science, 2*(40), 1–9. https://doi.org/10.1186/1748-5908-2-40

Castro-Olivo, S. M., Cramer, K. & Garcia, N. M. (2016). Manualized school-based social-emotional curricula for ethnic minority populations. In S. L. Graves, Jr. & J. J. Blake (Eds.), *Psychoeducational assessment and nterventions for ethnic minority children: Evidence-based approaches* (pp. 183–196). American Psychological Association. https://doi.org/10.1037/14855-011

Centers for Disease Control and Prevention. (2012, May 11). *Program evaluation for public health programs: A self-study guide.* www.cdc.gov/eval/guide/introduction/index.htm#:~:text=of%20This%20Manual,What%20Is%20Program%20Evaluation%3F,collected%20to%20improve%20the%20program

Centers for Disease Control and Prevention. (2020a). *What are childhood mental disorders?* www.cdc.gov/childrensmentalhealth/basics.html#:~:text=Based%20on %20the%20National%20Research,costs%20to%20individuals%2C%20families%2C%20and

Chalmers, I., & Glasziou, P. (2009). Avoidable waste in the production and reporting of research evidence. *Lancet (London, England), 374*(9683), 86–89. https://doi.org/10.1016/S0140-6736(09)60329-9

Children's Hospital Association. (2018, January 19). *Pediatric workforce shortages persist.* www.childrenshospitals.org/Issues-and-Advocacy/Graduate-Medical-Education/Fact-Sheets/2018/Pediatric-Workforce-Shortages-Persist

Choi, J. H., McCart, A. B., Hicks, T. A., & Sailor, W. (2019). An analysis of mediating effects of school leadership on MTSS implementation. *Journal of Special Education, 53*(1), 15–27. https://doi.org/10.1177/0022466918804815

Christ, T. J., Zopluoglu, C., Monaghen, B. D., & Van Norman, E. R. (2013). Curriculum-based measurement of oral reading: Multi-study evaluation of schedule, duration, and dataset quality on progress monitoring outcomes. *Journal of School Psychology, 51*(1), 19–57. https://doi.org/10.1016/j.jsp.2012.11.001

Coburn, C. E. (2003). Rethinking scale: Moving beyond numbers to deep and lasting change. *Educational Researcher, 32*(6), 3–12. https://doi.org/10.3102/0013189X032006003

Cognitive Behavioral Intervention for Trauma in Schools. (n.d.). https://cbitsprogram.org/

Collaborative for Academic, Social, and Emotional Learning [CASEL]. (2019). *Overview of SEL.* https://casel.org/overview-sel/

Cook, B. G., & Cook, S. C. (2011). Unraveling evidence-based practices in special education. *The Journal of Special Education, 47*(2), 71–82. https://doi.org/10.1177/0022466911420877

Cook, D. A. (2010). Twelve tips for evaluating educational programs. *Medical Teacher, 32*(4), 296–301. https://doi.org/10.3109/01421590903480121

Crean, H. F., & Johnson, D. B. (2013). Promoting alternative thinking strategies (PATHS) and elementary school aged children's aggression: Results from a cluster randomized trial. *American Journal of Community Psychology, 52*(1–2), 56–72. https://doi.org/10.1007/s10464-013-9576-4

Crooks, C. V., Bax, K., Delaney, A., Haesoo, K., & Shokoohi, M. (2020). Impact of MindUP among young children: Improvements in behavioral problems, adaptive skills, and executive functioning. *Mindfulness, 11*(7), 2433–2444. https://doi.org/10.1007/s12671-020-01460-0

Crow, G. M., & Pounder, D. G. (2000). Interdisciplinary teacher teams: Context, design, and process. *Educational Administration Quarterly, 36*(2), 216–254. https://doi.org/10.1177/0013161X00362004

Cuellar, A. (2015). Preventing and treating mental health problems. *The Future of Children, 25*(1), 111–134. https://doi.org/10.1353/foc.2015.0005

Daly, B. P., Nicholls, E., Aggarwal, R., & Sander, M. (2014). Promoting social competence an reducing behavior problems in at-risk students: Implementation and efficacy of universal and selective prevention programs in schools. In M. Weist, N. Lever, C. Bradshow, & J. Owens (Eds.) *Handbook of school mental health issues in clinical child psychology.* Springer. https://doi.org/10.1007/978-1-4614-5_10

Dane, A. V., & Schneider, B. H. (1998). Program integrity in primary and early secondary prevention: Are implementation effects out of control? *Clinical Psychology Review, 18*(1), 23–45. https://doi.org/10.1016/s0272-7358(97)00043-3

Dart, E. H., Arora, P. G., Collins, T. A., & Doll, B. (2019). Progress monitoring measures for internalizing symptoms: A systematic review of the peer-reviewed literature. *School Mental Health: A Multidisciplinary Research and Practice Journal, 11*(2), 265–275. https://doi.org/10.1007/s12310-018-9299-7

de Carvalho, J. S., Pinto, A. M., & Marôco, J. (2017). Results of a mindfulness-based social-emotional learning program on Portuguese elementary students and teachers: A quasi-experimental study. *Mindfulness, 8*(2), 337–350. https://doi.org/10.1007/s12671-016-0603-z

DeRigne L. (2010). What are the parent-reported reasons for unmet mental health needs in children?. *Health & Social work, 35*(1), 7–15. https://doi.org/10.1093/hsw/35.1.7

Deutz, M. H. F., Shi, Q., Vossenm, H. G. M., Huijding, J., Prinzie, P., Dekovic, M., van Baar, A. L., & Woltering, S. (2018). Evaluation of the strengths and differences questionnaire-dysregulation profile (SDQ-DP). *Psychological Assessment, 30*(9), 1174–1185. https://doi.org/10.1037/pas0000564

Dix, K. L., Slee, P. T., Lawson, M. J., & Keeves, J. P. (2012). Implementation quality of whole-school mental health promotion and students' academic performance. *Child and Adolescent Mental Health, 17*(1), 45–51. https://doi.org/10.1111/j.1475-3588.2011.00608.x

Doherty Kurtz, K., Pearrow, M., Snyder Battal, J., Collier-Meek, M. A., Archer Cohen, J., & Walker, W. (2022). Adapting social-emotional learning curricula for an urban context via focus groups: Process and outcomes. *School Psychology Review.* https://doi.org/10.1080/2372966X.2021.2021782

Douglas, N. F., & Burshnic, V. L. (2018). Implementation science: Tackling the research to practice gap in communication sciences and disorders. *Perspectives of the ASHA Special Interest Groups, 4*(1), 3–7. https://doi.org/10.1044/2018_PERS-ST-2018-0000

Drevon, D. D., Hixson, M. D., Wyse, R. D., & Rigney, A. M. (2018). A meta-analytic review of the evidence for check-in check-out. *Psychology in the Schools, 56*(3), 393–412. https://doi.org/10.1002/pits.22195

Drummond, R. (1994). *The student risk screening scale (SRSS).* Josephine County Mental Health Program.

Duda, M. A., & Wilson, B. A. (2015). *Using implementation science to close the policy to practice gap* [White paper]. A Literate Nation. www.wilsonlanguage.com/wp-content/uploads/2016/06/Implementation_Science_White_Paper_for_Literate_Nation.pdf

Duppong Hurley, K., Lambert, M. C., Epstein, M. H., & Stevens, A. (2015). Convergent validity of the strength-based behavioral and emotional rating scale with youth in a residential setting. *The Journal of Behavioral Health Services & Research, 42*(3), 346–354. https://doi.org/10.1007/s11414-013-9389-0

Durlak, J. A. (2016). Programme implementation in social and emotional learning: Basic issues and research findings. *Cambridge Journal of Education, 46*(3), 333–345. https://doi.org/10.1080/0305764X.2016.1142504

Durlak, J. A., Weissberg, R. P., Dymnicki, A. B., Taylor, R. D., & Schellinger, K. B. (2011). The impact of enhancing students' social and emotional learning: A meta-analysis of school-based universal interventions. *Child Development, 82*(1), 405–432. https://doi.org/10.1111/j.1467-8624.2010.01564.x

Dye, H. (2018). The impact and long-term effects of childhood trauma. *The Journal of Human Behavior in the Social Environment, 23*(3), 381–382. https://doi.org/10.1080/10911359.2018.1435328

Eagle, J. W., Dowd-Eagle, S. E., Synder, A., & Holtzman, E. G. (2015). Implementing a multi-tiered system of support (MTSS): Collaboration between school psychologists and administrators to promote systems-level change. *Journal of Educational and Psychological Consultation, 25*(2–3), 160–177. https://doi.org/10.1080/10474412.2014.929960

Eccles, M. P., & Mittman, B. S. (2006). Welcome to implementation science. *Implementation Science, 1*(1), 1–3. https://doi.org/10.1186/1748-5908-1-1

Eklund, K., Kilpatrick, K. D., Kilgus, S. P., & Haider, A. (2018). A systemic review of state-level social-emotional learning standards: Implications for practice and research. *School Psychology Review, 47*(3), 316–326. https://doi.org/10.17105/SPR-2017.0116.V47-3

Elias, M. J. (2015). What if the doors of every schoolhouse opened to social-emotional learning tomorrow: Reflections on how to feasibly scale up high-quality SEL. *Educational Psychologist, 54*(3), 233–245. https://doi.org/10.1080/00461520.2019.1636655

Evans, R., Murphy, S., & Scourfield, J. (2015). Implementation of a school-based social and emotional learning intervention: Understanding diffusion process within complex systems. *Prevention Science, 16*(5), 754–764. https://doi.org/10.1007/s11121-015-0552-0

Fairman, J. C., & Mackenzie, S. V. (2015). How teacher leaders influence others and understand their leadership. *International Journal of Leadership in Education, 18*(1), 61–87. https://doi.org/10.1080/13603124.2014.904002

Farmer, E. M., Burns, B. J., Phillips, S. D., Angold, A., & Costello, E. J. (2003). Pathways into and through mental health services for children and adolescents. *Psychiatric Services, 54*(1), 60–66. https://doi.org/10.1002/pits.20203

Fegert, J. M., Vitiello, B., Plener, P. L., & Clemens, V. (2020). Challenges and burden of the Coronavirus 2019 (COVID-19) pandemic for child and adolescent mental health: A narrative review to highlight clinical land research needs in the acute phase and the long return to normality. *Child and Adolescent Psychiatry and Mental Health, 14*, 20–31. https://doi.org/10.1186/s13034-020-00329-3

Felitti, V. J., Anda, R. F., Nordenberg, D., Williamson, D. F., Spitz, A. M., Edwards, V., Koss, M. P., & Marks, J. S. (1998). Relationship of childhood abuse and household dysfunction to many of the leading causes of death in adults. The adverse childhood experiences

(ACE) study. *American Journal of Preventive Medicine, 14*(4), 245–258. https://doi.org/10.1016/S0749-3797(98)00017-8

Fisher-Borne, M., Montana Cain, J., & Martin, S. L. (2015). From mastery to accountability: Cultural humility as an alternative to cultural competence. *Social Work Education, 34*(2), 165–181. https://doi.org/10.1080/02615479.2014.977244

Fixsen, D. L., & Blase, K. A. (2009). *Implementation tracker.* Active Implementation Research Network. www.activeimplementation.org/resources/implementation-tracker/

Fixsen, D. L., Naoom, S. F., Blase, K. A., & Wallace, F. (2007). Implementation: The missing link between research and practice. *APSAC Advisor, 19*(1 & 2), 4–11.

Fixsen, D. L., & Blase, K. A. (2011). *Stage-based measures of implementation components installation stage assessment.* National Implementation Research Network. www.orspdgdata.net/Downloads/Installation_Stage_Assessment.doc

Fixsen, D. L., Blase, K. A., Naoom, S. F., & Wallace, F. (2009). Core implementation components. *Research on Social Work Practice, 19*(5), 531–540. https://doi.org/10.1177/1049731509335549

Fixsen, D. L., Blase, K. A., Timbers, G. D., & Wolf, M. M. (2001). In search of program implementation: 792 replications of the teaching family model. In G. A. Bernfeld, D. P. Farrington, & A. W. Leschied (Eds.), *Wiley series in forensic clinical psychology. Offender rehabilitation in practice: Implementing and evaluating effective programs* (pp. 149–166). John Wiley & Sons Ltd.

Fixsen, D. L., Blase, K. A., & Van Dyke, M. K. (2019). *Implementation quotient.* Active Implementation Research Network. www.activeimplementation.org/wp-content/uploads/2019/05/ImplementationQuotientforOrganizations.pdf

Fixsen, D. L., Naoom, S. F., Blase, K. A., Friedman, R. M., & Wallace, F. (2005). *Implementation research: A synthesis of the literature.* University of South Florida. http://nirn.fpg.unc.edu/sites/nirn.fpg.unc.edu/files/resources/NIRN-Monograph Full-01-2005.pdf

Forman, S. G., Shapiro, E. S., Codding, R. S., Gonzales, J. E., Reddy, L. A., Rosenfield, S. A., Sanetti, L., & Stoiber, K. C. (2013). Implementation science and school psychology. *School Psychology Quarterly, 28*(2), 77–100. https://doi.org/10.1037/spq0000019

Foley, E. A., Dozier, C. L., & Lessor, A. L. (2019). Comparison of components of the good behavior game in a preschool classroom. *Journal of Applied Behavior Analysis, 52*(1), 84–104. https://doi.org/10.1002/jaba.506

Forman, S. G., Shapiro, E. S., Codding, R. S., Gonzales, J. E., Reddy, L. A., Rosenfield, S. A., Sanetti, L., & Stoiber, K. C. (2013). Implementation science and school psychology. *School Psychology Quarterly, 28*(2), 77–100. https://doi.org/10.1037/spq0000019

Foronda, C., Baptiste, D., Reinholdt, M. M., & Ousman, K. (2016). Cultural humility: A concept analysis. *Journal of Transcultural Nursing, 27*(3), 210–217. https://doi.org/10.1177/1043659615592677

Franco, D. (2018). Trauma without borders: The necessity for school-based interventions in treating unaccompanied refugee minors. *Child and Adolescent Social Work Journal 35*(6), 551–565. https://doi.org/10.1007/s10560-018-0552-6

Franklin, C. G. S., Kim, J. S., Ryan, T. N., Kelly, M. S., & Montgomery, K. L. (2012). Teacher involvement in school mental health interventions: A systematic review. *Children and Youth Services Review, 34*(5), 973–982. https://doi.org/10.1016/j.childyouth.2012.01.027

Fredrick, S. S., Drevon, D. D., & Jervinsky, M. (2019). Measurement invariance of the student risk screening scale across time and gender. *School Psychology, 34*(2), 159–167. https://doi.org/10.1037/spq0000278

Freeman, R., Miller, D., & Newcomer, L. (2015). Integration of academic and behavioral MTSS at the district level using implementation science. *Learning Disabilities: A Contemporary Journal, 13*(1), 59–72.

Frye, A. W., & Hemmer, P. A. (2012). Program evaluation models and related theories: AMEE guide 67. *Medical Teacher, 34*(5), e288–e299. https://doi.org/10.3109/01421 59X.2012.668637

Gerstner, J. J., & Finney, S. J. (2013). Measuring the implementation fidelity of student affairs programs: A critical component of the outcomes assessment cycle. *Research and Practice in Assessment, 8*, 15–28. www.rpajournal.com/dev/wp-content/uploads/2013/11/SF2.pdf

Giancola, S. P. (2014). *Evaluation matters: Getting the information you need from your evaluation.* U. S. Department of Education.

Gilliam, W. S. (2005). *Prekindergarteners left behind: Expulsion rates in state prekindergarten systems.* Foundation for Child Development. https://medicine.yale.edu/childstudy/zigler/publications/National%20Prek%20Study_expulsion%20brief_34775_5379_v1.pdf

Goldstein, H., & Olswang, L. (2017). Is there a science to facilitate implementation of evidence-based practices and programs? *Evidence-Based Communication Assessment and Intervention, 11*(3–4), 55–60. https://doi.org/10.1080/17489539.2017.1416768

González, M. J. (2005). Access to mental health services: The struggle of poverty affected urban children of color. *Child and Adolescent Social Work Journal, 22*(3–4), 245–256. https://doi.org/10.1007/BF02679471

Gopalkrishnan, N. (2018). Cultural diversity and mental health: Considerations for policy and practice. *Frontiers in Public Health, 6*, 1–7. https://doi.org/10.3389/fpubh.2018.00179

Gotay, S. (2013). Enhancing emotional awareness of at-risk youth through game play. *Journal of Creativity in Mental Health, 8*(2), 151–161. https://doi.org/10.1080/15401383.20 13.792221

Gottfredson, D. C., Cook, T. D., Gardner, F. E. M., Gorman-Smith, D., Howe, G., Sandler, I. N., & Zafft, K. M. (2015). Standards of evidence for efficacy, effectiveness, and scale-up research in prevention science: Next generation. *Prevention Science, 16*(7), 893–926. https://doi.org/10.1007/s11121-015-0555-x

Grant, A. M., & Parker, S. K. (2017). Redesigning work design theories: The rise of relational and proactive perspectives. *Academy of Management Annals, 3*(1), 273–331. https://doi.org/10.5465/19416520903047327

Greenberg, M. T., Domitrovich, C. E., Weissberg, R. P., & Durlak, J. A. (2017). Social and emotional learning as a public health approach to education. *Future of Children, 27*(1), 13–32. https://doi.org/10.1353/foc.2017.0001

Gresham, F. M. (2005). Response to intervention: An alternative means of identifying students as emotionally disturbed. *Education and Treatment of Children, 28*(4), 328–344. www.pent.ca.gov/pos/rti/rtialternativemeans_gresham.pdf

Gresham, F. M., Reschly, D., & Shinn, M. R. (2010). RTI as a driving force in educational improvement: Historical legal, research, and practice perspectives. In M. Shinn & H. Walker (Eds.), *Interventions for achievement and behavior problems in a three-tier model, including RTI* (pp. 47–78). National Association of School Psychologists.

Guo, J. J., Wade, T. J., Pan, W., & Keller, K. N. (2010). School-based health centers: Cost-benefit analysis and impact on health care disparities. *American Journal of Public Health, 100*(9), 1617–1623. https://doi.org/10.2105/AJPH.2009.185181

Halle, T., Paulsell, D., Daily, S., Douglass, A., Moodie, S., & Metz, A. (2015). *Implementing parenting interventions in early care and education settings: A guidebook for implementation.* Office of Planning, Research and Evaluation, Administration for Children and Families. www.acf.hhs.gov/sites/default/files/ecd/parenting_implementation_guidebook_109.pdf

Hamza, D., Henry, S., Greenshaw, A., Hamza, S. M., Engles, R. C., & Silverstone, P. H. (2018). "Bouncing-back" and relaxation were the most valued skills acquired by 369 students during a school-based resiliency program. *Journal of Addition Prevention, 6*(1), 1–7. https://doi.org/10.13188/2330-2178.1000043

Harn, B., Basaraba, D., Chard, D., & Fritz, R. (2015). The impact of schoolwide prevention efforts: Lessons learned from implementing independent academic and behavior support systems. *Learning Disabilities: A Contemporary Journal, 13*(1), 3–20. www.morningsideacademy.org/wp-content/uploads/2015/10/LDCJ-3-15-web.pdf#page=10www.morningsideacademy.org/wp-content/uploads/2015/10/

Hasbro. (2017). *Don't break the ice* [Board game]. Hasbro.

Heward, W. L., Alber-Morgan, S. R., & Konrad, M. (2017). *Exceptional children: An introduction to special education* (11th ed.). Pearson.

Higa-McMillan, C. K., Francis, S. E., Rith-Najarian, L., & Chorpita, B. F. (2016). Evidence base update: 50 years of research on treatment for child and adolescent anxiety. *Journal of Clinical Child and Adolescent Psychology, 45*(2), 91–113. https://doi.org/10.1080/1537 4416.2015.1046177

Higgins, M. C., Weiner, J., & Young, L. (2011). Implementation teams: A new level for organizational change. *Journal of Organizational Behavior, 33*(3), 366–388. https://doi.org/10.1002/job.1773

Hollands, F. M., Hanisch-Cerda, B., Levin, H. M., Belfield, C. R., Menon, A., Shand, R., Pan, Y., Bakir, I., & Cheng, H. (2015). *CostOut—the CBCSE cost tool kit* [Computer program]. Center for Benefit-Cost Studies of Education, Teachers College, Columbia University. www.cbcsecosttoolkit.org

Hoover, J. J., & Patton, J. R. (2008). The role of special education in a multitiered instructional system. *Intervention in School and Clinic, 43*(4), 195–202. https://doi.org/10.1177/1053451207310345

Horner, R. H., Carr, E. G., Halle, J., McGee, G., Odom, S., & Wolery, M. (2005). The use of single-subject research to identify evidence-based practice in special education. *Exceptional Children, 71*(2), 165–179. https://doi.org/10.1177/001440290507100203

Hughes, C. A., Morris, J. R., Therrien, W. J., & Benson, S. K. (2017). Explicit instruction: Historical and contemporary contexts. *Learning Disabilities Research and Practice, 32*(3), 140–148. https://doi.org/10.1111/ldrp.12142

Hughes, K., Bellis, M. A., Hardcastle, K. A., Sethi, D., Butchart, A., Mikton, C., Jones, L., & Dunne, M. P. (2017). The effect of multiple adverse childhood experiences on health: A systemic review and meta-analysis. *The Lancet Public Health, 28*(8), e356–e366. https://doi.org/10.1016/S2468-2667(17)30118-4

Humphrey, N., Barlow, A., Wigelsworth, M., Lendrum, A., Pert, K., Joyce, C., Stephens, E., Wo, L., Squires, G., Woods, K., Calam, R., & Turner, A. (2016). A cluster randomized controlled trial of the promoting alternative thinking strategies (PATHS) curriculum. *Journal of School Psychology, 58*, 73–89. https://doi.org/10.1016/j.jsp.2016.07.002

Hunter, K. K., Chenier, J. S., & Gresham, F. M. (2014). Evaluation of check in/check out for students with internalizing problems. *Journal of Emotional and Behavioral Disorders, 22*(3), 135–148. https://doi.org/10.1177/1063426613476091

Hunter, L. J., DiPerna, J. C., Hart, S. C., & Crowley, M. (2018). At what cost? Examining the cost effectiveness of a universal social-emotional learning program. *School Psychology Quarterly, 33*(1), 147–154. https://doi.org/10.1037/spq0000232

The Incredible Years. (2013). *The incredible years.* www.incredibleyears.com/

January, S. A. A., Lambert, M. C., Epstein, M. H., Walrath, C. M., & Gebreselassie, T. (2015). Cross-informant agreement of the behavioral and emotional rating scale for youth in community mental health settings. *Children and Youth Services Review, 53,* 34–38. https://doi.org/10.1016/j.childyouth.2015.03.015

Janz, P., Dawe, S., & Wyllie, M. (2019). Mindfulness-based program embedded within the existing curriculum improves executive functioning and behavior in young children: A waitlist controlled trial. *Frontiers in Psychology, 10,* 1–17. https://doi.org/10.3389/fpsyg.2019.02052

Jenkins, J. R., Hudson, R. F., & Johnson, E. (2007). Screening for at-risk readers in a response to intervention framework. *School Psychology Review, 36*(4), 582–600. https://doi.org/10.1080/02796015.2007.12087919

Jenkins, L. N., Demaray, M. K., Wren, N. S., Secord, S. M., Lyell, K. M., Magers, A. M., Setmeyer, A. J., Rodelo, C., Newcomb-McNeal, E., & Tennant, J. (2014). A critical review of five commonly used social-emotional and behavioral screeners for elementary or secondary schools. *Contemporary School Psychology, 18*(4), 241–254. https://doi.org/10.1007/s40688-014-0026-6

Jimenez, M. E., Martinez Alcaraz, E., Williams, J., & Strom, B. L. (2017). Access to developmental pediatrics evaluations for at-risk children. *Journal of Developmental and Behavioral Pediatrics, 38*(3), 228–232. https://doi.org/10.1097/DBP.0000000000000427

Joyce-Beaulieu, D., & Sulkowski, M. L. (2020). *Cognitive behavior therapy in k-12 school settings: A practitioner's workbook* (2nd ed.). Springer.

Juszczak, L., Melinkovich, P., & Kaplan, D. (2003). Use of health and mental health services by adolescents across multiple delivery sites. *Journal of Adolescent Health, 32*(Suppl. 6), 108–118. https://doi.org/10.1016/s1054-139x(03)00073-9

Kamphaus, R. W., & Reynolds, C. R. (2015). *Behavior assessment system for children—third edition (BASC-3): Behavioral and emotional Screening System (BESS).* Pearson.

Kang-Yi, C. D., Wolk, C. B., Locke, J., Beidas, R. S., Lareef, I., Pisciella, A. E., Lim, S., Evans, A. C., & Mandell, D. S. (2018). Impact of school-based and out-of-school mental health services on reducing school absence and school suspension among children with psychiatric disorders. *Evaluation and Program Planning, 67,* 105–112. https://doi.org/10.1016/j.evalprogplan.2017.12.006

Kansas Technical Assistance Network. (2012, October 12). *Kansas MTSS: Living a culture of engagement* [Conference session]. National Association of State Directors of Special Education Annual Conference, Sacramento, CA, United States. https://ksdetasn.s3.amazonaws.com/uploads/resource/upload/668/NASDSE_2012_Kansas_MTSS.pdf

Kear, N. C. (2017). *Fix it friends: Have no fear!* Imprint.

Kellam, S. G., Mackenzie, A. C., Brown, C. H., Poduska, J. M., Wang, W., Petras, H., & Wilcox, H. C. (2011). The good behavior game and the future of prevention and treatment. *Addiction Science and Clinical Practice, 6*(1), 73–84. www.ncbi.nlm.nih.gov/pmc/articles/PMC3188824/

Kendall, P. C., Crawford, E. A., Kagan, E. R., Furr, J. M., & Podell, J. L. (2018). Child-focused treatment for anxiety. In J. R. Weisz & A. E. Kazdin (Eds.), *Evidence-based psychotherapies References 207 for children and adolescents* (pp. 17–34). The Guilford Press.

Kennedy, K. (2019). Centering equity and caring in leadership for social-emotional learning: Toward a conceptual framework for diverse learners. *Journal of School Leadership, 29*(6), 1–20. https://doi.org/10.1177/1052684619867469

Kerker, B. D., Zhang, J., Nadeem, E., Stein, R. E., Hurlburt, M. S., Heneghan, A., Landsverk, J., & McCue Horwitz, S. (2015). Adverse childhood experiences and mental health, chronic medical conditions, and development in young children. *Academic Pediatrics, 15*(5), 510–517. https://doi.org/10.1016/j.acap.2015.05.005

Kern, L., Mathur, S. R., Albrecht, S. F., Poland, S., Rozalski, M., & Skiba, R. J. (2017). The need for school-based mental health services and recommendations for implementation. *School Mental Health, 9*(3), 205–217. https://doi.org/10.1007/s12310-017-9216-5

Khang, K. H. (2017). A better state-of-mind: Deep breathing reduces state anxiety and enhances test performance through regulating test cognitions in children. *Cognition and Emotion, 31*(7), 1502–1510. https://doi.org/10.1080/02699931.2016.1233095

Kilgus, S. P., Taylor, C. N., & von der Embse, N. P. (2018). Screening for behavioral risk: Identification of high risk cut scores within the social, academic, and emotional behavior risk screener. *School Psychology Quarterly, 33*(1), 155–159. https://doi.org/10.1037/spq0000230

Kilpatrick, K. D., Maras, M. A., Brann, K. L., & Kilgus, S. P. (2018). Universal screening for social, emotional, and behavioral risk in students: DESSA-mini risk stability over time and its implications for screening. *School Psychology Review, 47*(3), 244–257. https://doi.org/10.17105/SPR-2017-0069.V47-3

Kim-Cohen, J., Caspi, A., Moffitt, T. E., Harrington, H., Milne, B. J., & Poulton, R. (2003). Prior juvenile diagnoses in adults with mental disorder: Developmental follow-back of a prospective-longitudinal cohort. *Archives of General Psychiatry, 60*(7), 709–717. https://doi.org/10.1001/archpsyc.60.7.709

King, D., & Coughlin. (2016). Looking beyond RTI standard treatment approach: It's not too late to embrace the problem-solving approach. *Preventing School Failure, 60*(3), 244–251. https://doi.org/10.1080/1045988X.2015.1110110

King-Sears, M. E., Walker, J. D., & Barry, C. (2018). Measuring teachers' intervention fidelity. *Intervention in School and Clinic, 54*(2), 89–96. https://doi.org/10.1177/1053451218765229

Klingbeil, D. A., & Renshaw, T. L. (2018). Mindfulness-based interventions for teachers: A meta-analysis of the emerging evidence base. *School Psychology Quarterly, 33*(4), 501–511. http://dx.doi.org/10.1037/spq0000291

Klinger, J. K., Boardman, A. G., & Mcmaster, K. L. (2013). What does it take to scale up and sustain evidence-based practices? *Exceptional Children, 79*(2), 195–2011. https://doi.org/10.1177/001440291307900205

Kozina, A. (2021). Can FRIENDS for Life social-emotional programme be used for preventing anxiety and aggression in a school environment: 6 months, 1-year and 1-and-a-half-year follow-up. *European Journal of Developmental Psychology, 182*, 214–229. https://doi.org/10.1080/17405629.2020.1776103

Langer, D. A., Wood, J. J., Wood, P. A., Garland, A. F., Landsverk, J., & Hough, R. L. (2015). Mental health service use in schools and non-school-based outpatient settings: Comparing predictors of service use. *School Mental Health, 7*(3), 161–173. https://doi.org/10.1007/s12310-015-9146-z

Lawson, G. M., McKenzie, M. E., Becker, K. D., Selby, L., & Hoover, S. A. (2019). The core components of evidence-based social emotional learning programs. *Prevention Science: The Official Journal of the Society for Prevention Research, 20*(4), 457–467. https://doi.org/10.1007/s11121-018-0953-y

Leko, M. M., Roberts, C., Peyton, D., & Pua, D. (2019). Selecting evidence-based practices: What works for me. *Intervention in School and Clinic, 54*(5), 286–294. https://doi.org/10.1177/1053451218819190

Lenz, A. S. (2015). Meta-analysis of the coping cat program for decreasing severity of anxiety symptoms among children and adolescents. *Journal of Child and Adolescent Counseling, 1*(2), 51–65. https://doi.org/10.1080/23727810.2015.1079116

Lesesne, C. A., Lewis, K., Fisher, D., House, D. L., Mueller, T., Fuller, T. R., Brittain, A., & Wandersman, A. (2016). *Promoting science-based approaches to teen pregnancy prevention using getting to outcomes for teen pregnancy.* www.cdc.gov/teenpregnancy/practitioner-tools-resources/psba-gto-guide/pdf/tools/psba-gto_complete_508tag.pdf

Lessard, S., Bareil, C., Lalonde, L., Duhamel, F., Hudon, E., Goudreau, J., & Lévesque, L. (2016). External facilitators and interprofessional facilitation teams: A qualitative study of their roles in supporting practice change. *Implementation Science, 11*(97), 1–12. https://doi.org/10.1186/s13012-016-0458-7

Lever, N., Castle, M., Cammack, N., Bohnenkamp, J., Stephan, S., Bernstein, L., Chang, P., Lee, P., & Sharma, R. (2014). *Resource mapping in schools and school districts: A resource guide.* University of Maryland School of Medicine. https://dm0gz550769cd.cloudfront.net/shape/78/7836bc25375bed7ed2bc906407be674e.pdf

Lightfoot, E., Simmelink, J., & Lum, T. (2014). Asset mapping as a research tool for community-based participatory research in social work. *Social Work Research, 38*(1), 59–64. https://doi.org/10.1093/swr/svu001

Little, S., Marrs, H., & Bogue, H. (2017). Elementary school psychologists and response to intervention (RTI). *Contemporary School Psychology, 21*(2), 103–114. https://doi.org/10.1007/s40688-016-0104-z

Lizuka, C. A., Barrett, P., Gillies, R., Cook, C., & Marinovic, W. (2015). Preliminary evaluation of the friends for life program on students' and teachers' emotional states for a school in a low socio-economic status area. *Australian Journal of Teacher Education, 40*(3), 1–20. https://files.eric.ed.gov/fulltext/EJ1057927.pdf

Lopez, S. J., Edwards, L. M., Teramotto Pedrotti, J., Ito, A., & Rasmussen, H. N. (2002). Culture count: Examinations of recent applications of the Penn Resiliency Program or, toward a rubric for examining cultural appropriateness of prevention programming. *Prevention & Treatment, 5*(1), https://doi.org/10.1037/1522-3736.5.1.512c

Macklem, G. L. (2011). *Evidence-based school mental health services: Affect education, emotion regulation training, and cognitive behavior therapy.* Springer. https://doi.org/10.1007/978-1-4419-7907-0_1

Maras, M. A., Thompson, A. M., Lewis, C., Thornburg, K., & Hawks, J. (2015). Developing a tiered response model for social-emotional learning through interdisciplinary collaboration. *Journal of Educational and Psychological Consultation, 25*(2–3), 198–223. https://doi.org/10.1080/10474412.2014.929954

March, A. L., Castillo, J. M., Batsche, G. M., & Kincaid, D. (2016). Relationship between systems coaching and problem-solving implementation fidelity in a response-to-intervention model. *Journal of Applied School Psychology, 32*(2), 147–177. https://doi.org/10.10.80/15377903.2016.1165326

Marrs, H., & Little, S. (2014). Perceptions of school psychologists regarding barriers to response to intervention (RTI) implementation. *Contemporary School Psychology, 18*(1), 24–34. https://doi.org/10.1007/s40688-013-0001-7

Martin, S. L., Ashley, O. S., White, L., Axelson, S., Clark, M., & Burrus, B. (2017). Incorporating trauma-informed care into school-based programs. *The Journal of School Health*, *87*(12), 958–967. https://doi.org/10.1111/josh.12568

Mason, D. J., & Cox, K. (2014). Toxic stress in childhood: Why we all should be concerned. *Nursing Outlook*, *62*(6), 382–383. https://doi.org/10.1016/j.outlook.2014.09.001

McCormick, M. P., Cappella, E., O'Connor, E., Hill, J. L., & McClowry, S. (2016). Do effects of social-emotional learning programs vary by level of parent participation? Evidence from the randomized trial of insights. *Journal of Research on Educational Effectiveness*, *9*(3), 364–394. https://doi.org/10.1080/19345747.2015.1105892

McCormick, M. P., Cappella, E., O'Connor, E., & McClowry, S. G. (2013). Parent involvement, emotional support, and behavior problems: An ecological approach. *The Elementary School Journal*, *114*(2), 277–300. https://doi.org/10.1086/673200

McDougal, J. L., Bardos, A. N., & Meier, S. T. (2016). Behavior intervention monitoring system 2 [Measurement instrument]. http://www.edumetrisis.com/products/282- bimas-2

McGoldrick, B., & Tobey, D. (2016). *Needs assessment basics* (2nd ed.). ATD Press.

McGorry, P. D., & Mei, C. (2018). Early intervention in youth mental health: Progress and future directions. *Evidence-Based Mental Health*, *21*(4), 182–184. http://dx.doi.org/10.1136/ebmental-2018-300060

McKay, M. M., Pennington, J., Lynn, C. J., & McCadam, K. (2001). Understanding urban child mental health l service use: Two studies of child, family, and environmental correlates. *The Journal of Behavioral Health Services & Research*, *28*(4), 475–483. https://doi.org/10.1007/BF02287777

McKenna, J. W., & Parenti, M. (2017). Fidelity assessment to improve teacher instruction and school decision-making. *Journal of Applied School Psychology*, *33*(2), 331–346. https://doi.org/10.1080/15377903.2017.1316334

McKevitt, B. C. (2012). School psychologists' knowledge and use of evidence-based, social-emotional learning interventions. *Contemporary School Psychology*, *16*(1), 33–45. https://doi.org/10.1007/BF03340974

McNamara, C.. (n.d.). *Basic guide to outcomes-based evaluation for nonprofit organizations with very limited resources*. https://managementhelp.org/evaluation/outcomes-evaluation-guide.htm

Menold, N. (2020). Double barreled questions: An analysis of the similarity of elements and effects on measurement quality. *Journal of Official Statistics*, *36*(4), 855–886. https://doi.org/10.2478/jos-2020-0041

Mesman, J., Bongers, I. L., & Koot, H. M. (2001). Preschool developmental pathways to preadolescent internalizing and externalizing problems. *Journal of Child Psychology and Psychiatry*, *42*(5), 679–689. https://doi.org/10.1111/1469-7610.00763

Metz, A., & Bartley, L. (2012). Active Implementation Frameworks for Program Success: How to Use Implementation Science to Improve Outcomes for Children. *Zero to Three Journal*, *34*(4), 11–18.

Metz, A., Naoom, S. F., Halle, T., & Bartley, L. (2015). *An integrated stage-based framework for implementation of early childhood programs and systems* (OPRE Research Brief OPRE 2015–48). Office of Planning, Research, and Evaluation, Administration for Children and Families, U. S. Department of Health and Human Services. www.acf.hhs.gov/sites/default/files/opre/es_cceepra_stage_based_framework_brief_508.pdf

Meyers, D. C., Durlak, J. A., & Wandersman, A. (2012). The quality implementation framework: A synthesis of critical steps in the implementation process. *American Journal of Community Psychology, 50*(3–4), 462–480. https://doi.org/10.1007/s10464-012-9522-x

Mian, N. D., Wainwright, L., Briggs-Gowan, M. J., & Carter, A. S. (2011). An ecological risk model for early childhood anxiety: The importance of early child symptoms and temperament. *Journal of Abnormal Child Psychology, 39*(4), 501–512. https://doi.org/10.1007/s10802-010-9476-0

Miller, C. J., Smith, S. N., & Pugatch, M. (2020). Experimental and quasi-experimental designs in implementation research. *Psychiatry Research, 283*, 112452. https://doi.org/10.1016/j.psychres.2019.06.027

Miller, D. N. (2014). Levels of responsibility in school-based suicide prevention: Legal requirements, ethical duties, and best practices. *International Journal of Behavioral Consultation and Therapy, 9*(3), 15–18. https://doi.org/10.1037/h0101635

Moir, T. (2018). Why is implementation science important for intervention design and evaluation within educational settings? *Frontiers in Education, 3*(61), 1–9. https://doi.org/10.3389/feduc.2018.00061

Morris, Z. S., Wooding, S., & Grant, J. (2011). The answer is 17 years, what is the question: Understanding time lags in translational research. *Journal of the Royal Society of Medicine, 104*(12), 510–520. https://doi.org/10.1258/jrsm.2011.110180

Morrison, J. Q., & Harms, A. L. (2018). *Advancing evidence-based practice through program evaluation: A practical guide for school-based professionals.* Oxford University Press.

Mosher, D. K., Hook, J. N., Captari, L. E., Davis, D. E., Deblaere, C., & Owen, J. (2017). Cultural humility: A therapeutic framework for engaging diverse clients. *Practice Innovations, 2*(4), 221–233. https://doi.org/10.1037/pri0000055

Moy, G. E., & Hazen, A. (2018). A systematic review of the second step program. *Journal of School Psychology, 71*, 18–41. https://doi.org/10.1016/j.jsp.2018.10.006

Murphy, J. M., Guzmán, J., McCarthy, A. E., Squicciarini, A. M., George, M., Canenguez, K. M., Dunn, E. C., Baer, L., Simonsohn, A., Smoller, J. W., & Jellinek, M. S. (2015). Mental health predicts better academic outcomes: A longitudinal study of elementary school students in Chile. *Child Psychiatry and Human Development, 46*(2), 245–256. https://doi.org/10.1007/s10578-014-0464-4

Nancarrow, S. A., Booth, A., Ariss, S., Smith, T., Enderby, P., & Roots, A. (2013). Ten principles of good interdisciplinary team work. *Human Resources for Health, 11*(19), 1–11. https://doi.org/10.1186/1478-4491-11-19

National Association of School Psychologists [NASP]. (2015). *School psychologists: Qualified health professionals child and adolescent mental and behavioral health services* [White paper]. www.nasponline.org/x32089.xml

National Association of School Psychologists [NASP]. (2016). *Leveraging essential school practices, ESSA, MTSS, and the NASP practice model: A crosswalk to help every school and student succeed.* www.nasponline.org/research-and-policy/current-law-and-policy-priorities/policy-priorities/the-every-student-succeeds-act/essa-crosswalk

National Association of School Psychologists (2020). *The professional standards of the National Association of School Psychologists.* Bethesda, MD: Author.

National Center for School Mental Health [NCSMH]. (2020a). *School mental health quality guide: Impact.* NCSMH, University of Maryland School of Medicine.

National Center for School Mental Health [NCSMH]. (2020b). *School mental health quality guide: Mental health promotion services & supports (Tier 1)*. NCSMH, University of Maryland School of Medicine.

National Implementation Research Network. (n.d.). *Active implementation hub*. https://nirn.fpg.unc.edu/module-1/usable-innovations

National Institute of Mental Health. (2019). *Child and adolescent mental health*. www.nimh.nih.gov/health/topics/child-and-adolescent-mental-health/index.shtml

New York State Office of Professions. (2021/2022, April 19). *License statistics*. New York State Office of Professions. www.op.nysed.gov/prof/psych/psychcounts.htmwww.op.nysed.gov/prof/psych/psychcounts.htm

Nickerson, A. B., & Fishman, C. E. (2013). Promoting mental health and resilience through strength-based assessment in US schools. *Educational and Child Psychology, 30*(4), 7–17. www.researchgate.net/publication/280137713_Promoting_mental_health_and_resilience_through_strength-based_assessment_in_US_schools/link/5a55793caca272bb69623dfa/download

Nickerson, A. B., & Sulkowski, M. L. (2021). The COVID-19 pandemic as a long-term school crisis: Impact, risk, resilience, and crisis management. *School Psychology, 36*(5), 271–276. https://doi.org/10.1037/spq0000470

Nielsen, K., Randall, R., & Christensen, K. B. (2017). Do different training conditions facilitate team implementation? A quasi-experimental mixed methods study. *Journal of Mixed Methods Research, 11*(2), 223–247. https://doi.org/10.1177/1558689815589050

Norris, L. A., & Philip, K. P. (2020). A close look into coping cat: Strategies within an empirically supported treatment for anxiety in youth. *Journal of Cognitive Psychotherapy, 34*(1), 4–20. https://doi.org/10.1007/s12310-015-9146-z

Oakes, W. P., Lane, K. L., & Ennis, R. P. (2016). Systematic screening at the elementary level: Considerations for exploring and installing universal behavior screening. *Journal of Applied School Psychology, 32*(3), 214–233. https://doi.org/10.1080/15377903.2016.1165325

O'Connell, M. E., Boat, T., & Warner, K. E. (Eds.). (2009). *Preventing mental, emotional, and behavioral disorders among young people: Progress and possibilities*. The National Academies Press.

Oral, R., Ramirez, M., Coohey, C., Nakada, S., Walz, A., Kuntz, A., Benoit, J., & Peek-Asa, C. (2016). Adverse childhood experiences and trauma informed care: The future of health care. *Pediatric Research, 79*(1–2), 227–233. https://doi.org/10.1038/pr.2015.197

Owens, J. S., Lyon, A. R., Brandt, N. E., Warner, C. M., Nadeem, E., Spiel, C., & Wagner, M. (2014). Implementation science in school mental health: Key constructs in a developing research agenda. *School Mental Health, 6*(2), 99–111. https://doi.org/10.1007/s12310-013-9115-3

Owens, J. S., Lyon, A. R., Warner, C. M., Nadeem, E., Spiel, C., & Wagner, M. (2014). Implementation science in school metal health: Key constructs in a developing research area. *School Mental Health, 6*(2), 99–111. https://doi.org/10.1007/s12310-013-9115-3

Parris, D., St. John, V., & Bartlett, J. D. (2020). *Resources to support children's emotional well-being amid anti-Black racism, racial violence, and trauma*. www.childtrends.org/publications/resources-to-support-childrens-emotional-well-being-amid-anti-black-racism-racial-violence-and-trauma

Perfect, M. M., Turley, M. R., Carlson, J. S., Yohanna, J., & Saint Gilles, M. P. (2016). School-related outcomes of traumatic event exposure and traumatic stress symptoms in students: A systematic review of research from 1990 to 2015. *School Mental Health: A Multidisciplinary Research and Practice Journal, 8*(1), 7–43. https://doi.org/10.1007/s12310-016-9175-2

Pinkelman, S. E., McIntosh, K., Rasplica, C. K., Berg, T., & Strickland-Cohen, M. K. (2015). Perceived enablers and barriers related to sustainability of school-wide positive behavioral intervention and supports. *Behavioral Disorders, 40*(3), 171–183. https://doi.org/10.17988/0198-7429-40.3.171

Prenger, R., & Schildkamp, K. (2018). Data-based decision making for teacher and student learning: A psychological perspective on the role of the teacher. *Educational Psychology, 38*(6), 734–752. https://doi.org/10.1080/01443410.2018.1426834

Puga, F., Stevens, K. R., & Patel, D. I. (2013). Adopting best practices from team science in a healthcare improvement research network: The impact on dissemination and implementation. *Nursing Research and Practice, 2013*(1), 1–7. https://doi.org/10.1155/2013/814360

Pullen, P. C., van Dijk, W., Gonsalves, V. E., Lane, H. B., & Ashworth, K. E. (2018). Response to intervention and multi-tiered systems of support: How do they differ and how are they the same, if at all? In P. C. Pullen & M. J. Kennedy (Eds.), *Handbook of response to intervention and multi-tiered systems of support* (pp. 5–10). Routledge.

Raffaele Mendez, L. M. (2017). *Cognitive behavioral therapy in schools: A tiered approach to youth mental health services*. Routledge.

Ranjbar, N., & Erb, M. (2019). Adverse childhood experiences and trauma-informed care in rehabilitation clinical practice. *Archives of Rehabilitation Research and Clinical Translation, 1*(1–2), 1–8. https://doi.org/10.1016/j.arrct.2019.100003

Reinke, W. M., Smith, T. E., & Herman, K. C. (2019). Family-school engagement across child and adolescent development. *School Psychology, 34*(4), 346–349. https://doi.org/10.1037/spq0000322

Richerme, L. K. (2020). Every student succeeds act and social emotional learning: Opportunities and considerations for P-12 arts educators. *Arts Education Policy Review*. https://doi.org/10.1080/10632913.2020.1787284

Rossen, E. (Ed.). (2020). *Supporting and educating traumatized students: A guide for professionals* (2nd ed.). Oxford University Press. https://doi.org/10.1093/med-psych/9780190052737.001.0001

Royse, D., Thyer, B. A., & Padgett, D. K. (2016). *Program evaluation: An introduction to an evidence-based approach* (6th ed.). Cengage Learning.

Sanetti, L. M. H., & Collier-Meek, M. A. (2019a). Increasing implementation science literacy to address the research-to-practice gap in school psychology. *Journal of School Psychology, 76*, 33–47. https://doi.org/10.1016/j.jsp.2019.07.008

Sanetti, L. M. H., & Collier-Meek, M. C. (2019b). *Supporting successful interventions in schools: Tools to plan, evaluate, and sustain effective implementation*. Guilford Press.

Sanetti, L.M.H., Kratochwill, T.R., Collier-Meek, M.A., & Long, A.C.J. (2014). *PRIME: Planning realistic implementation and maintenance by educators*. University of Connecticut. https://implementationscience.uconn.edu/wpcontent/uploads/sites/1115/2014/12/PRIME_guide1.pdf

Sanetti, L. M. H., Kratochwill, T. R., Volpiansky, P., & Ring, M. (2011). *Enacting the EOCA vision for school success: Resource mapping: A toolkit for education communities*. Wisconsin Department of Public Instruction. www.coursehero.com/file/45199161/EOCA-Wisconsinpdf/

Sapthiang, S., Van Gordon, W., & Shonin, E. (2019). Mindfulness in schools: A health promotion approach to improving adolescent mental health. *International Journal of Mental Health, 17*(1), 112–119. https://doi.org/10.1007/s11469-018-0001-y

Saunders, R. P., Evans, M. H., & Joshi, P. (2005). Developing a process-evaluation plan for assessing health promotion program implementation: A how-to guide. *Health Promotion Practice, 6*(2), 134–147. https://doi.org/10.1177/1524839904273387

Schaffer, G. E. (2017). *Nuts and bolts: Multi-tiered systems of support: A basic guide to implementing preventative practice in our schools and community.* Bookbaby.

Schaffer, G. E. (2023). *Multi-tiered systems of support: A practical guide to preventative practice.* SAGE Publications, Inc.

Schildkamp, K. (2019). Data-based decision making for school improvement: Research insights and gaps. *Educational Research, 61*(3), 257–273. https://doi.org/10.1080/0013 1881.2019.1625716

Schildkamp, K., Poortman, C., Luyten, H., & Ebbler, J. (2017). Factors promoting and hindering data-based decision making in schools. *School Effectiveness and School Improvement, 28*(2), 242–258. https://doi.org/10.1080/09243453.2016.1256901

Schonert-Reichl, K. A. (2017). Social and emotional learning and teachers. *Future of Children, 27*(1), 137–155. www.doi.org/10.1353/foc.2017.0007

Schonert-Reichl, K. A., Oberle, E., Lawlor, M. S., Abbott, D., Thomson, K., Oberlander, T. F., & Diamond, A. (2015). Enhancing cognitive and social—emotional development through a simple-to-administer mindfulness-based school program for elementary school children: A randomized controlled trial. *Developmental Psychology, 51*(1), 52–66. https://doi.org/10.1037/a0038454

Schultz, D., Barnes-Proby, D., Chandra, A., Jaycox, L. H., Maher, E., & Pecora, P. (2012). Toolkit for adapting cognitive behavioral intervention for trauma in schools (CBITS) or supporting students exposed to trauma (SSET) for implementation with youth in foster Care. *Rand Health Quarterly, 2*(1), 1–45. www.rand.org/pubs/technical_reports/TR772.html

Shanklin, N. (2008). At the crossroads: A classroom teacher's key role in RTI. *Voices in the Middle, 16*(2), 62–63. https://library.ncte.org/journals/VM/issues/v16-2/6860

Shapiro, E. S. (2013). Commentary on progress monitoring with CBM-R and decision making: Problems found and looking for solutions. *Journal of School Psychology, 51*(1), 59–66. https://doi.org/10.1016/j.jsp.2012.11.003

Shapiro, E. S., DuPaul, G. J., Barnabas, E., Benson, J. L., & Slay, P. M. (2010). Facilitating school, family, and community partnerships: Enhancing student mental health: An overview of the special series. *School Mental Health: A Multidisciplinary Research and Practice Journal, 2*(2), 45–51. https://doi.org/10.1007/s12310-010-9033-6

Shaw, S. R. (2021). Implementation evidence-based practices in school psychology: Excavation by de-implementing the disproved. *Canadian Journal of School Psychology, 36*(2), 91–92. https://doi.org/10.1177/08295735211000513

Shernoff, D. J., Ruzek, E. A., & Sinha, S. (2017). The influence of the high school classroom environment on learning as mediated by student engagement. *School Psychology International, 38*(2), 201–218. https://doi.org/10.1177/0143034316666413

Shinn, M. R., & Walker, H. M. (2010). *Interventions for achievement and behavior problems in a three-tier model including RTI.* National Association of School Psychologists.

Simonsen, B., Shaw, S. F., Faggella-Luby, M., Sugae, G., Coyne, M. D., Rhein, B., Madaus, J. W., & Alfano, M. (2010). A schoolwide model for service delivery: Redefining educators and interventionists. *Remedial and Special Education, 31*(1), 17–23. https://doi.org/10.1177/0741932508324396

Sink, C. A. (2016). Incorporating a multi-tiered systems of supports into school counselor preparation. *The Professional Counselor, 6*(3), 203–219. https://doi.org/10.15241/cs.6.3.203

Skalski, A. K., Minke, K., Rossen, E., Cowan, K. C., Kelly, J., Armistead, R., & Smith, A. (2015). *NASP practice model implementation guide.* National Association of School Psychologists.

Slade, M., & Longden, E. (2015). Empirical evidence about recovery and mental health. *BMC Psychiatry, 15*(1), 1–14. https://doi.org/10.1186/s12888-015-0678-4

Slavin, R. (2002). Evidence-based education policies: Transforming educational practice and research. *Educational Researcher, 31*(7), 15–21. https://doi.org/10.3102/0013189X031007015

Smith, T. E., Holmes, S. R., Sheridan, S. M., Cooper, J. M., Bloomfield, B. S., & Preast, J. L. (2020). The effects of consultation-based family-school engagement on student and parent outcomes: A meta-analysis. *Journal of Educational and Psychological Consultation.* https://doi.org/10.1080/10474412.2020.1749062

Spaulding, S., Horner, R., May, S., & Vincent, C. G. (2008). *Implementation of school-wide PBIS across the United States* (Evaluation brief). Center on Positive Behavior Intervention and Supports. www.pbis.org/resource/implementation-of-school-wide-pbis-across-the-united-states

Splett, J. W., Fowler, J., Weist, M. D., & McDaniel, H. (2013). The critical role of school psychology in the school mental health movement. *Psychology in the Schools, 50*(3), 245–257. https://doi.org/10.1002/pits.21677

Steinman, K. J., Shoben, A. B., Dembe, A. E., & Kelleher, K. J. (2015). How long do adolescents wait for psychiatry appointments? *Community Mental Health Journal, 51*(7), 782–789. https://doi.org/10.1007/s10597-015-9897-x

Stewert, R. M., Benner, G. J., Martella, R. C., & Marchand-Martella, N. E. (2007). Three-tier models of reading and behavior: A research review. *Journal of Positive Interventions, 9*(4), 239–252. https://doi.org/10.1177/10983007070090040601

Stirman, S. W., Baumann, A. A., & Miller, C. J. (2019). The FRAME: An expanded framework for reporting adaptations and modifications to evidence-based interventions. *Implementation Science, 14*, 58–68. https://doi.org/10.1186/s13012-019-0898-y

Sue, D. W., & Sue, D. (2016). *Counseling the culturally diverse: Theory and practice* (7th ed.). Wiley.

Sugai, G., & Horner, R. H. (2008). What we know and need to know about preventing problem behavior in schools. *Exceptionality, 16*(2), 67–77. https://doi.org/10.1080/09362830801981138

Sugai, G., & Horner, R. H. (2020). Sustaining and scaling positive behavioral interventions and supports: Implementation drivers, outcomes, and considerations. *Exceptional Children, 86*(2), 120–136. https://doi.org/10.1177/0014402919855331

Support Student Exposed to Trauma. (n.d.). https://ssetprogram.org/

Swick, D., & Powers, J. D. (2018). Increasing access to care by delivering mental health services in schools: The school-based support program. *School Community Journal, 28*(1), 129–144. https://scholarworks.boisestate.edu/cgi/viewcontent.cgi?article=1065&context=socialwork_facpubs

Taylor, C. N., Kilgus, S. P., & Huang, F. (2018). Treatment utility of universal screening for behavioral risk: A manipulated assessment study. *Journal of Applied School Psychology, 34*(3), 242–258. https://doi.org/10.1080/15377903.2017.1394949

Taylor, R. D., Oberle, E., Durlak, J. A., & Weissberg, R. P. (2017). Promoting positive youth development through school-based social and emotional learning interventions: A meta-analysis of follow-up effects. *Child Development*, 88(4), 1156–1171. https://doi.org/10.1111/cdev.12864

Teague, G. M., & Anfara, V. A. (2012). Professional learning communities create sustainable change through collaboration. *Middle School Journal*, 44(2), 58–64. https://doi.org/10.1080/00940771.2012.11461848

Teo, A., Carlson, E., Mathieu, P. J., Egeland, B., & Sroufe, L. A. (1996). A prospective longitudinal study of psychosocial predictors of achievement. *Journal of School Psychology*, 34(3), 285–306. https://doi.org/10.1016/0022-4405(96)00016-7

Thompson, A. M., Herman, K. C., Stormont, M. A., Reinke, W. M., & Webster-Stratton, C. (2017). Impact of incredible years on teacher perceptions of parental involvement: A latent transition analysis. *Journal of School Psychology*, 62, 51–65. https://doi.org/10.1016/j.jsp.2017.03.003

Tibbets, T. J. (2013). *Identifying and assessing students with emotional disturbance*. Brookes Publishing.

Tout, K., Metz, A., & Bartley, L. (2013). Considering statewide professional development systems. In T. Halle, A. Metz, & I. Martinez-Beck (Eds.), *Applying implementation science in early childhood programs and systems* (pp. 269–294). Brookes Publishing.

Tusing, M. E., & Breikjern, N. A. (2017). Using curriculum-based measurements for program evaluation: Expanding roles for school psychologists. *Journal of Applied Psychology*, 33(1), 43–66. https://doi.org/10.1080/15377903.2016.1229707

Vaillancourt, K., & Amador, A. (2014). School-community alliances enhance mental health services: Resource-stretched schools can ensure comprehensive mental health care for students by creating partnerships with community-based service providers. *Phi Delta Kappan*, 96(4), 57–62. https://doi.org/10.1177/0031721714561448

van Geel, M., Keuning, T., Visscher, A. J., & Fox, J.-P. (2016). Assessing the effects of a school-wide data-based decision-making intervention on student achievement growth in primary schools. *American Educational Research Journal*, 53(2), 360–394. https://doi.org/10.3102/0002831216637346

Vannest, K. J., Ura, S. K., Lavadia, C., & Zolkoski, S. (2019). Self-report measures of resilience in children and youth. *Contemporary School Psychology*. https://doi.org/10.1007/s40688-019-00252-1

Vekaria, H. (2017). Ask the administrators: Interviews provide guidance for MTSS implementation. *Perspectives on Language and Literacy*, 43(4), 37–39. https://mydigitalpublication.com/publication/?i=445106&article_id=2908449&view=articleBrowser&ver=html5

Vernez, G., Karam, R., Mariano, L. T., & DeMartini, C. (2006). *Evaluating comprehensive school reform models at scale: Focus on implementation*. RAND Corporation. www.rand.org/pubs/monographs/MG546.html

Walker, H. M., Severson, H. H., & Feil, E. G. (2014). *Systemic screening for behavior disorders (SSBD): Administrator's guide* (2nd ed.). Pacific Northwest Publishing.

Wang, M. T., Hill, N. E., & Hofkens, T. (2014). Parental involvement and African American and European American adolescents' academic, behavioral, and emotional development in secondary school. *Child Development*, 85(6), 2151–2168. https://doi.org/10.1111/cdev.12284

Webster-Stratton, C. (2001). The incredible years: Parents, teachers, and children training series. *Residential Treatment for Children & Youth*, 18(3), 31–45. https://doi.org/10.1300/J007v18n03_04

Webster-Stratton, C., Reid, J. M., & Stoolmiller, M. (2008). Preventing conduct problems and improving school readiness: Evaluation of the incredible years teacher and child training programs in high-risk schools. *Journal of Child Psychology and Psychiatry, and Allied Disciplines, 49*(5), 471–488. https://doi.org/10.1111/j.1469-7610.2007.01861.x

Webster-Stratton, C., & Reid, M. J. (2017). The Incredible Years Parents, Teachers, and Children Training Series: A multifaceted treatment approach for youth children with conduct problems. In J. Weisz & A. Kazdin (Eds.), *Evidence-based psychotherapies for children and adolescents* (3rd ed.). Guilford Publications.

Wenzel, A. (2018). Cognitive reappraisal. In S. C. Hayes & S. G. Hofmann (Eds.), *Process-based CBT: Science and core clinical competencies of cognitive behavioral therapy* (pp. 325–338). Context Press.

Werts, M. G., & Carpenter, E. S. (2013). Implementation of tasks in RTI: Perceptions of special education teachers. *Teacher Education and Special Education, 36*(3), 247–257. https://doi.org/10.1177/0888406413495420

Wexler, D. (2018). School-based multi-tiered systems of support (MTSS): An introduction to MTSS for neuropsychologists. *Applied Neuropsychology: Child, 7*(4), 306–316. https://doi.org/10.1080/21622965.2017.1331848

What Works Clearinghouse. (n.d.). *Welcome to what works clearinghouse.* https://ies.ed.gov/ncee/wwc/

Wixson, K. K., & Valencia, S. W. (2011). Assessment in RTI: What teachers and specialists need to know, 64(6), 466–469. https://doi.org/10.1598/RT.64.6.13

Wlodarczyk, O., Pawils, S., Metzner, F., Kriston, L., Klasen, F., Ravens-Sieberer, U., & BELLA Study Group. (2017). Risk and protective factors for mental health problems in preschool-aged children: Cross-sectional results of the BELLA preschool study. *Child and Adolescent Psychiatry and Mental Health, 11*(12), 1–12. https://doi.org/10.1186/s13034-017-0149-4

Yates, R. L., Treyvaud, K., Doyle, L. W., Ure, A., Cheong, J. L. Y., Lee, K. J., Inder, T. E., Spencer-Smith, M., & Anderson, P. J. (2020). Rates and stability of mental health disorders in children born very preterm at 7 and 13 years. *Pediatrics, 145*(5), Article e20192699. https://doi.org/10.1542/peds.2019-2699

Yoon, S. Y. (2016). Principals' data-driven practice and its influence on teacher buy-in and student achievement in comprehensive school reform models. *Leadership and Policy in Schools, 15*(4), 500–523. https://doi.org/10.1080/15700763.2016.1181187

Youth.gov. (n.d.). *Mental health.* https://youth.gov/youth-topics/youth-mental-health

Zeng, S., Corr, C. P., O'Grady, C., & Guan, Y. (2019). Adverse childhood experiences and preschool suspension expulsion: A population study. *Child Abuse and Neglect: The International Journal, 97*(1), 1–9. https://doi.org/10.1016/j.chiabu.2019.104149

Ziomek-Daigle, J., & Heckman, B. D. (2019). Integrating behavioral and social/emotional supports within the response to intervention (RtI) Model. *Journal of Professional Counseling: Practice, Theory, & Research, 46*(1–2), 27–38. https://doi.org/10.1080/15566382.2019.1671741

Zyromski, B., Dimmitt, C., Mariani, M., & Griffith, C. (2018). Evidence-based school counseling: Models for integrated practice and school counselor education. *Professional School Counseling, 21*(1), 1–12. https://doi.org/10.1177/2156759X18801847

Index

Note: Page numbers in *italics* indicate a figure on the corresponding page.

For Product Safety Concerns and Information please contact our EU
representative GPSR@taylorandfrancis.com
Taylor & Francis Verlag GmbH, Kaufingerstraße 24, 80331 München, Germany